VI   MULTILINGUAL SPEAKERS (ESL)   97

29   **American Style in Writing**   99
30   **Verbs**   100
31   **Nouns   (Count and Non-count)**   103
32   **Articles**   104
33   **Prepositions**   105
34   **Omitted/Repeated Words**   106
35   **Idioms**   108

VII   RESEARCH PAPERS   109

36   **Doing Print and Online Research**   112
37   **Evaluating Print and Internet Sources**   129
38   **Integrating Sources**   137
39   **Document Design**   144

VIII   DOCUMENTATION   149

40   **MLA Style**   152
41   **APA Style**   185
42   **Chicago Manual of Style**   203
43   **CSE (Council of Science Editors)**   212
44   **COS and Style Manuals for Various Fields**   217

GLOSSARY OF USAGE   229
GLOSSARY OF GRAMMATICAL TERMS   238
INDEX   256
CORRECTION SYMBOLS   263
USER'S GUIDE   264

THE WRITER'S FAQS
A POCKET HANDBOOK

SECOND EDITION

MURIEL HARRIS
Purdue University

PEARSON

Prentice
Hall

**Upper Saddle River
New Jersey 07458**

Harris, Muriel
   The writer's FAQs: a pocket handbook / Muriel Harris. -2nd ed.
      p. cm.
      Includes index.
      ISBN 0-13-183125-9
      1. English language–Rhetoric–Handbooks, manuals, etc.
2. English language–Grammar–Handbooks manuals, etc.
3. Report writing–Handbooks, manuals, etc. I Title. Writer's
frequently asked questions. II. Title.
PE1408.H3458 2004
808'.042–dc21   2003049855

Editor in Chief: Leah Jewell
Senior Acquisitions Editor: Stacy Best Ruel
Editorial Assistant: Steve Kyritz
AVP/Director of Production
   and Manufacturing: Barbara Kittle
Production Editor: Terry Routley, Carlisle Communications, Inc.
Manufacturing Manager: Nick Sklitsis
Asst. Manufacturing Manager: Mary Ann Gloriande
Director of Marketing: Beth Mejia
Executive Marketing Manager: Brandy Dawson
Marketing Assistant: Allison Peck
Creative Design Director: Leslie Osher
Interior and Cover Designer: Wanda España/wee design group
Cover Art: Eyewire.com

To Sam, David, Bekki, Dan, Hannah, and Eitan
As Always and Ever

This book was set in 8/11 Serifa by Carlisle Communications Inc.,
and was printed and bound by R.R. Donnelley & Sons Company.
The cover was printed by The Lehigh Press, Inc.

© 2004, 2000 by Pearson Education, Inc.
Upper Saddle River, New Jersey 07458

Printed in the United States of America
10   9   8   7   6   5   4   3   2   1

ISBN 0-13-183125-9

Pearson Education LTD., London
Pearson Education Australia PTY, Limited, Sydney
Pearson Education Singapore, Pte. Ltd
Pearson Education North Asia Ltd, Hong Kong
Pearson Education Canada, Ltd., Toronto
Pearson Educación de Mexico, S.A. de C.V.
Pearson Education--Japan, Tokyo
Pearson Education Malaysia, Pte. Ltd
Pearson Education, Upper Saddle River, New Jersey

How to Use This Book

Keep this book nearby to help you find answers to your writing questions in the quickest, easiest manner possible.

- **Before you start**

Read the "Writing" part for reminders, advice, and writing tips.

- **As you write a draft of your paper**

For sentence structure:
Check "Sentence Choices" for suggestions for general sentence construction, clarity, word choice, and smooth flow.

For research papers and finding information:
The "Research" section offers advice on choosing a topic, finding information, using the library, evaluating and integrating sources into your paper, and avoiding plagiarism. This section will also help you use search engines efficiently, locate useful resources, find Web addresses to lead you to useful starting places, and follow guidelines for document design.

- **As you write a bibliography or reference list**

For your list of sources, you'll find explanations for MLA, APA, *Chicago Manual of Style,* Council of Science Editors (CSE), and Columbia Online Style (COS) in the "Documentation" section.

- **As an ESL student looking for information on using English**

If you are a multilingual speaker (ESL=English as a Second Language), the whole book is useful as a guide for all writers. But questions that don't come up for native speakers are in the "Multilingual Speakers (ESL)" part and in **ESL HINTS** boxes.

- **As you finish up and are editing and polishing a draft**

When you are ready to check a point of grammar and mechanics, use "Sentence Grammar," "Punctuation," and "Mechanics" for the frequently used rules of grammar, spelling, capitalization, and other matters that indicate to readers that you're a literate user of the English language and that your ideas have merit. But what do you do if, like many writers, you can tell when something *isn't* right, but aren't sure what *is* right or where in this pocket guide you need to go to find the answer? Read on because this book is designed to help.

How do you find what you're looking for?

- **If you know the term (or want to check on a term)**
  1. Go to the **Index** at the back of the book.
  2. Go to the **Glossary of Usage** and **Glossary of Grammatical Terms** near the end of the book.

- **If you know the general topic (such as using commas)**
  1. Find the topic in the **Brief Contents** inside the front cover.
  2. Read the descriptions listed and then do one or more of the following:
     a. Browse in the **Brief Contents.**
     b. Turn to the **User's Guide,** a list of questions inside the back cover.
     c. Look at the **Questions to Ask Yourself** at the beginning of that part of the book. Each of these parts of the book are listed here.

Writing

Suggestions on writing concerns, linking sentences and paragraphs, writing introductions and conclusions, and so on.

Sentence Choices

Information on writing clear, effective sentences that don't overuse the passive and are varied, concise, and nonsexist in word choices.

Sentence Grammar

Grammar rules to help you avoid errors such as fragments, comma splices, and so on.

Punctuation

Guidelines for punctuation marks as well as a useful diagram indicating the punctuation patterns for sentences.

Mechanics

Guidelines for capitalization, use of italics, numbers, abbreviations, and spelling.

Multilingual Speakers

Help with questions about English ESL students are likely to have.

Research Papers

Advice and guidelines for moving through the research paper process and help with using the library and going online to find, evaluate, and document information.

Documentation

Guidelines for documentation formats.

Glossary of Usage

Questions about word choices (Do I use "accept" or "except"?) and whether a certain word is acceptable in standard English (Can I write "and etc."?).

Glossary of Grammatical Terms

Definitions of grammatical terms (such as "linking verb" or "reflexive pronoun") and charts to illustrate terms such as "personal pronouns" and "sentence diagram."

- **If you have a question**
  1. If it's about one of those sticky word choices (for ex-ample: Is it "affect" or "effect"? Should I write "it's" or "its"?), go to the **Glossary of Usage** near the end of the book.
  2. If the question is one that writers frequently have (the kind where you don't quite know the terminol-ogy to use), go to the inside back cover of the book and see if your question is like the one in the **User's Guide.** If so, you'll find the section you need to go to in order to answer the question.

You'll also find **HINT** and **ESL HINT** boxes throughout the book offering advice to avoid various problems writers en-counter. Other user-friendly aids are lists and diagrams to help explain and clarify. As the term "user-friendly" implies, I hope this book is easy to use and becomes a writing friend that you keep nearby as you write.

Muriel Harris

I Writing

Contents of this section

1 Checklist for Effective Papers

1a HOCs (Higher Order Concerns)   **3**
- Purpose   3
- Audience   3
- Thesis statement   3
- Organization   4
- Development   5
- Paragraph length   5
- Transitions between sentences and paragraphs   5
- Introductions and conclusions   5

1b LOCs (Later Order Concerns)   **6**

1c Strategies for checking on HOCs and LOCs   **6**

1d Strategies for using computers   **8**

Questions to ask yourself

The sections in this part of the book offer help with general writing processes and answer the following questions:

	SECTION	PAGE
• When I start planning or when I'm drafting my paper, what questions should I ask myself?	1a	3
• What are HOCs (Higher Order Concerns), and why are they important?	1a	3
• Why is thinking about the purpose and audience for an assignment important?	1a	3
• What's a thesis statement, and how can I tell when I've phrased it appropriately?	1a	3

- How can I make my paper flow?   1a   5

- What should I put in the introduction and conclusion?   1a   5

- When the paper is close to being done, what should I check for?   1b   6

- What are LOCs (Later Order Concerns), and why are they important?   1b   6

- How do I proofread the paper before I hand it in?   1c   6

- What are some techniques for proofreading?   1c   6

- How do I proofread for spelling?   1c   7

- Should I depend on the spell checker on my computer?   1c   7

- If I plan and write my paper on a computer, are there some strategies that I can use on a computer to help?   1d   8

1

CHECKLIST FOR EFFECTIVE PAPERS

1a   HOCs (Higher Order Concerns)

Listed here are the Higher Order Concerns (HOCs) that help to make your writing effective:

Purpose

Be sure your purpose fits the assignment. If you are asked to persuade your readers, that is different than writing to explain or summarize. If you are asked to describe, your purpose is to help your readers envision your subject. Read the assignment carefully, and note the verbs carefully. Are you asked to **compare** two or more things? **Analyze? Describe? Explain? Persuade? State** your opinion?

You can clarify your purpose by answering the questions, "Why am I writing this? What am I trying to accomplish?" For example, do you want your readers to take some action? Accept your view? Understand something they didn't know before? Share some experience of yours?

Audience

Think about your readers. Check to see that they are the appropriate audience for your assignment and purpose. Think about what they already know and what they most likely want to know or don't need to know. Should you add any information or background summary to help them understand your topic?

If you are arguing or persuading, are you writing to those who are likely to disagree? If so, how can you convince them? Is there some common ground, some aspects of the argument you share with them, that will help in getting those who disagree to consider what you are writing?

Thesis statement

Your thesis is the main idea or subject of the paper. You should be able to summarize the thesis briefly in a sentence or two, and your paper should state it clearly. Think of the thesis as a promise that you will discuss this topic—a contract that you will fulfill. When you read over your draft, check to see that you have kept all parts of your promise.

It's best to start with a working thesis that may change or become clearer as you write. Having a working thesis as you start will help you focus your thinking and research, keep you on track as you find and develop the content of your essay, and assist in determining the audience, purpose, and type of support you will need. Later, you can revise the thesis.

There are two parts to an effective thesis statement, a topic that states the subject and a comment that makes an important point about the topic:

<u>Genetically modified foods</u>   <u>have not been shown to</u>
     (topic)   (comment)
   <u>cause health problems in people who eat them.</u>

An effective thesis statement should have a topic of potential interest to your readers, be as specific as possible, and be limited enough to make it manageable. For example, for a short paper on citizens' right to privacy (maybe limited to several pages), you can't include discussions of the many ways privacy can be invaded (phone taps, e-mail, videotaping in the workplace, etc.). Similarly, for a paper of maybe fifteen to twenty pages, you aren't likely to find enough material to write about if you want to argue that Harry Potter books appeal to children's imaginations.

Consider this thesis statement. Is it well formulated?

The beetle is a very interesting insect.

The topic of beetles isn't likely to interest a broad range of readers, the comment isn't specific because we don't know what the writer means by "interesting," and we don't know what kind of support the writer will offer. Thus, this is not an effective thesis statement.

Organization

As you look over your draft, note the central idea of each paragraph (the topic sentence) and ask yourself if each paragraph contributes to the larger thesis in some way and if each paragraph leads logically to the next one. You want to avoid gaps or jumps in the development of your thesis that might confuse the reader. One way to check this is to look at the topic sentences of your paper as an outline. Do those sentences, once collected, make a smooth, coherent outline?

Development

Be sure you have enough details, examples, specifics, supporting evidence, and information to support your thesis. You may need to delete material that is not relevant or add material that will strengthen your thesis and help you achieve your purpose. Try to read the paper as an uninformed reader would and ask yourself what else you'd need to know.

Paragraph length

Paragraphs are the large building blocks of the paper. As you look over your draft, check to see that the paragraphs are of the same approximate length on the page. If you have a paragraph that takes most of a page, followed by a paragraph that has only two sentences, you probably need to make the paragraphs more equal in length. Check to see that a long paragraph doesn't cover too much content or that a short paragraph needs more specifics.

Transitions between sentences and paragraphs

Transitions connect or knit sentences and paragraphs together into a smooth whole. Like road signals, they indicate where the writing is heading and keep your reader following along easily. Check to see that you've supplied the needed connectors to indicate how your writing is moving forward. (See section 9.)

Introductions and conclusions

The introduction brings the reader into your world, builds interest in your subject, and announces the thesis or topic of the paper. Sometimes, writers write the introduction after revising the rest of the paper and clarifying their topic through their writing and revising.

The conclusion of the paper signals the end is approaching and helps the reader to put the whole paper in perspective. You can look backward and offer a conclusion that summarizes the content or refers to something in the

introduction. Or you can look forward and offer advice, suggestions, or actions the reader can take, based on what you
have presented.

1b LOCs (Later Order Concerns)

> ## *hint*
>
> **LOCs (Proofreading Checklist)**
>
> After your draft is well on the way to being completed,
> check for the Later Order Concerns (LOCs) that should
> be considered as you edit and proofread.

When you have finished your major revisions and checked
the HOCs (section 1a), look more closely at words, sentences, and punctuation for problem areas that detract from
your credibility as a writer. As you make your own list of
problems to check for, consider whether you need to check
for these common problems:

fragments	(see section 11, page 30)
subject-verb agreement	(see section 13a, page 33)
verb endings	(see section 13b, page 37)
verb tenses	(see section 13b, page 37)
comma splices and run-on sentences	
	(see section 12, page 32)
misplaced or omitted apostrophes	
	(see section 21, page 69)
pronoun reference	(see section 14c, page 48)
omitted words	(see section 34, page 106)
omitted commas	(see section 19, page 62)
unnecessary commas	(see section 19, page 66)
spelling errors	(see section 28, page 92)

1c Strategies for checking on HOCs and LOCs

Find writing strategies that are effective for you, such as the
following:

- Have someone (such as a tutor in your writing center
  who will help with this) read your paper aloud as you lis-
  ten and look at it, or read the paper aloud yourself. You'll

see problems that won't be as evident when you read silently.

- Put the draft away for a while so that when you read, the paper is not as fresh in your mind. To revise effectively, you need to have some distance from the paper so that you can more easily identify readers' concerns.

- Try to put yourself in the place of your intended readers and think about what they would want to know, what they might object to in your arguments, what counter-arguments they would make, what questions they would have. Ask yourself if your paper responds adequately to these considerations.

- For proofreading you need to help your eyes slow down and see each word. (Readers tend to see whole groups of words at once.) Try sliding a card down the page as you read because that permits your eyes and ears to work to-gether.

- Proofread for spelling by reading backwards, either from the end of the paper to the beginning or from the right side of the line to the left. Then you are not focusing on the meaning of the sentences and can notice smaller matters such as word choice, punctuation, and spelling. Computer spellcheckers will catch some, but not all, spelling errors.

- Don't depend on computerized grammar checkers. They may help slightly, but they cannot analyze language well enough to check completely for grammar problems, and the options suggested are sometimes not appropriate.

- Draw up a personal list of problem areas and keep those in mind as you reread your draft.

Make a personal checklist here.

Areas I should check for:

1d Strategies for using computers

Word processing on a computer can help as you write and as you check your paper. Try the following strategies to see which are helpful for you:

- Copy the topic sentences from each paragraph and put them in an outline onscreen. If you have any questions about the organization, cut and paste and see if there are other arrangements you think are more effective.

- Be sure to use a spell checker because it is especially useful in catching typos. But remember that spell checkers can't find all spelling problems. They cannot, for example, distinguish between "it's" and "its" or "here" and "hear" to see if you have used the right form of these sound-alike words.

- As you write, highlight in some way (such as boldface) problem areas or phrases you have questions about. Then you can find them later on and consider them then.

- If you think it might be better to delete a chunk of text, cut and paste it to a new file or the end of the paper while you see if the paper is better without it. By putting it in a separate file, you can save it for later use or retrieve it if you decide you need it.

- If a fresh idea pops into your mind as you're writing but probably belongs elsewhere in the paper, write that in a separate file. (Some word processing programs will permit you to make notes to yourself as you write that are not visible in the main text.)

- Many writers need to print out a hard copy of the paper as it develops to get a better sense of the whole paper.

- To check on paragraph length, switch to page or print view so that you can see a whole page on the monitor. See if the paragraphs look about the same length.

- Working with a copy of your file, hit the return key after each period so that each sentence looks like a separate paragraph. If all the sentences are approximately the same length, you may need to consider varying your sentences more (see section 4). If most of the sentences begin the same way (with the subject of the main clause), you need to think about using different sentence patterns.

II Sentence Choices

Contents of this section

2 **Clarity**   12

  2a **Positive instead of negatives**   **12**

  2b **Double negatives**   **12**

  2c **Known information to new or unknown
information**   **13**

  2d **Verbs instead of nouns**   **13**

  2e **Intended subject as sentence subject**   **14**

3 **Conciseness**   14

4 **Variety**   16

5 **Voice (Formal and Informal)**   17

6 **Mixed Constructions**   18

7 **Active and Passive Verbs**   19

8 **Parallelism**   20

9 **Transitions**   22

10 **Nonsexist Language**   24

Questions to ask yourself

The sections in this part of the book discuss choices you make as you write. In most cases, there is no right or wrong answer, but you want to choose carefully so your writing is clear, concise, and smooth.

	SECTION	PAGE
• Why shouldn't I use negatives such as "no" and "not" in my writing?	2a	12
• Why is "don't want no paper" wrong?	2b	12
• What are some other negatives I should watch out for?	2	12

- What's the best order for including information in a sentence? Why?   2c   13

- Should I write "the consideration of" or "they consider" or "the preparation of" or "they prepare"? Which is better and why?   2d   13

- I sometimes start sentences with "It is . . ." or "There is the problem that. . . ." How can I make such sentences more effective?   2e   14

- What are some ways to eliminate wordiness in my writing?   3   14

- Sometimes my writing sounds choppy. I write short sentences. How can I make the writing smoother or add variety to the sentences I write?   4   16

- When should writing be formal? Is it OK to use slang or jargon?   5   17

- When I write, sometimes parts of the sentence don't fit smoothly together. What's the problem, and how can I fix it?   6   18

- What's the active voice? What is passive voice?   7   19

- When should I use active verbs? Are there occasions when passive verbs are appropriate?   7   19

- What's parallel structure?   8   20

- What's wrong with combining two phrases that have different verb forms such as "to start the car" and "feeding it gas"?   8   20

- When I have lists or topics in an outline, how do I know if the verbs are phrased in the same way?   8   20

- When I connect two items with "both . . . and" or "either . . . or," what do I need to check to be sure I'm phrasing them the same way?   8   20

- What are transitions? Why do I need them in my writing?   9   22

- What are some ways to connect my sentences together and connect paragraphs so that my paper flows? 9 22

- What are some of the connectors (like "however" and "in addition") I can use? 9 22

- Can I start sentences with "But" and "And"? 9 22

- What is sexist language? 10 24

- What's wrong with using words like "policeman" and "mailman"? 10 24

- How can I avoid the ordinary male pronouns that are commonly used? 10 24

- Is it OK to write "everyone raised his hand"? 10 24

2

CLARITY

2a Positive instead of negative

Put information in the positive because negative statements
are harder to understand than positive ones.

Unclear negative: Less attention is paid to commercials
that lack human interest stories.

Revised: People pay more attention to
commercials with human interest stories.

Negatives can also make the writer seem evasive or unsure.

Evasive negative: Congresswoman Petros is not often
heard to favor raising the minimum
wage.

Revised: Congresswoman Petros prefers
keeping the minimum wage at its
present level.

2b Double negatives

Use only one negative at a time in your sentences. Double
negatives are grammatically incorrect and may be difficult
to understand.

Double negative: They don't want no phone calls.
Revised: They don't want any phone calls.

---

hint

Avoiding Negative Words

Watch out for negative words such as the following:

hardly	no place	nothing
neither	nobody	nowhere
no one	none	scarcely

They hardly had ~~no~~ popcorn left.
^ *any*

12

2c   Known information to new or unknown information

Start your sentences with information that is known or generally familiar to your reader before you introduce new or unknown material.

Familiar ⟶ Unfamiliar

Familiar to new: When I visit my grandmother, she often has an old book from her childhood days to show me.

(This sentence should be easy to understand.)

New to familiar: An old book from her childhood days is something my grandmother often shows me when I visit.

(This sentence takes longer to understand and is less clear.)

2d   Verbs instead of nouns

Actions expressed as verbs are more easily understood and usually more concise than actions named as nouns.

Unnecessary noun forms: Pay raises are a motivation improvement.
Revised: Pay raises improve motivation.

---

hint

Using Verbs Instead of Nouns

Try rereading your sentences to see which nouns could be changed to verbs.

Some noun forms	Verbs to use instead
The determination of	They determine
The approval of	They approve
The preparation of	They prepare
The utilization of	They use
The analysis of	They analyze

2e Intended subject as sentence subject

The real subject or doer of the action in the verb should be the grammatical subject of the sentence. Sometimes the real subject can get buried in prepositional phrases or other less noticeable places.

Buried subject: It was the preference of the instructor to begin each lecture with a quiz.

(The grammatical subject here is "it." Who begins each lecture? The instructor.)

Revised: The instructor preferred to begin each lecture with a quiz.

3

CONCISENESS

To be concise, eliminate the following:

- what your readers do not need to know
- what your readers already know
- whatever doesn't further the purpose of your paper

Sometimes writers are wordy when they are tempted to include everything they know about a subject, add a description of how they found their information (to impress readers with how hard they've worked to get the information), or add words they think will make their writing sound more formal or academic.

Strategies to eliminate unnecessary words:

- **Avoid repetition.** Some phrases, such as the following, say the same thing twice:

first beginning	9 a.m. in the morning
circular in shape	true facts
return again	really and truly
green in color	each and every

- **Avoid fillers.** Some phrases, such as the following, add little or nothing to your meaning:

  in view of the fact that   due to the fact that
  I am going to discuss   there are (or) is
  the topic that I will explain here

             T
  ~~I am going to discuss~~ the cloning of human beings, ~~which~~
               ^

  is a subject with many difficult ethical questions.

- **Combine sentences.** When the same nouns appear in two sentences, combine the sentences.

              and
  Global warming is a critically important topic ~~. Global~~
                ^

  ~~warming~~ has been the subject of recent TV specials, government regulations, and conferences.

- **Eliminate** *who, which,* **and** *that.*
  The marking pen ~~that was~~ on my desk is gone.

- **Turn phrases and clauses into adjectives and adverbs.**
  The football player who was graceful = the graceful football player
  The building built out of cement = the cement building

  The entrance to the station = the station entrance

- **Remove excess nouns and change to verbs whenever possible.**

             agreed
  He ~~made the statement that he was in agreement with the~~
            ^

  ~~concept~~ that inflation could be controlled.

- **Use active rather than passive.** (See section 7, page 19.)

  research department   *the figures.*
  The ~~figures were~~ checked ~~by the research department~~.
     ^   ^

4

VARIETY

A series of short sentences or sentences with the same subject-verb word order can be monotonous and sound choppy. Try these strategies for adding variety.

- **Combine short, choppy sentences.**

  Connect two sentences into one longer sentence with one subject and two verbs, or a comma and coordinating conjunction (see section 12, page 32), or a semicolon, (see section 18, page 61).

  The school band performed at the local Apple

  Festival. ~~They~~ were a great success.

, and they

  Tuck a phrase, clause, or sentence inside a related sentence.

  The school band performed at the local Apple

, who

  Festival. ~~They~~ were a great success.

,

- **Rearrange sentence order.**

  Often, a series of sentences that sound choppy all have a subject-verb-object order. You can make one sentence depend on another or add or change phrases and clauses to break up the monotonous sound.

Choppy: The reporter asked each candidate the same question. He wanted to compare their campaign promises. They all evaded his questions. He wrote a story about their lack of answers.

Revised: Because the reporter wanted to compare the candidates' campaign promises, he asked each one the same question. Hearing them evade his questions, he wrote a story about their lack of answers.

5

VOICE (FORMAL AND INFORMAL)

In writing, an appropriate voice is one that fits the level of formality of your paper and your subject. Just as you don't wear a suit or dress when you go on a picnic or jeans to a formal dinner, you should match your word choices to the type of paper you are writing.

Formal documents such as research papers, reports, and applications avoid slang but may include some technical language, or jargon, appropriate to the field and the intended readers. Such documents are normally written in the third person, using "he" and "they."

Informal documents such as e-mail and letters to friends, informal essays, and some memos may include more informal word choices (for example, "kids" instead of "children") and frequent contractions, and they are normally written in the first person, using "I."

Compare these recommendations:

Informal: Be sure to see *Titanic.* I saw it last week, and it's great!

Formal: The laminate is the recommended choice for this product because test results show that it holds up well under stress and heat.

Slang

Slang words may be shared by a small group or may be generally known. Some slang enters the general vocabulary, such as "cab" or "yuppie," and some eventually disappears or becomes outdated, such as "far out" or "BMOC" (Big Man on Campus). It is usually too informal for most written work.

Jargon

Jargon words are specialized terms used by those in the same field or profession to refer quickly to complex concepts. For someone who is knowledgeable about computers, the terms "gigabytes" and "bit maps" are useful technical terms when writing to someone else in that field. Such shorthand vocabulary should only be used when you are sure your readers will be familiar with the words.

The term "jargon" is also applied to pompous language that is inflated and unnecessarily formal. The result is wordy prose that is hard to read and makes the writer sound pretentious.

Pompous: She was inordinately predisposed to render her perspective on all matters of national and international import.

Revised: She frequently offered her opinion on world affairs.

6

MIXED CONSTRUCTIONS

Mixed constructions are caused by mismatches when fitting parts of a sentence together. A writer can start off in one direction and then switch to another, causing grammar or logic problems in the sentence.

Mixed: For groups who want to reduce violence on television, students carrying knives to school are acting out what they see on the television screen.

Revised: Groups who want to reduce violence on television claim that students carrying knives to school are acting out what they see on the television screen.

Dangling modifiers

Some mixed constructions are caused by dangling modifiers—phrases or clauses that should modify the subject but don't.

Dangling: After finishing her degree, the search for a job began.

(This sentence says that the search, the subject of the sentence, finished her degree.)

Revised: After finishing her degree, she began the search for a job.

Mismatched subjects and predicates

Sometimes the subject and predicate don't match or fit together.

Mismatched: <u>Driver education</u> in high schools <u>assumes</u> that parents can pay the costs involved.

(<u>Driver education</u>, the subject, can't make assumptions about anything.)

Revised: High school administrators assume that parents can pay the costs involved for driver education programs.

7

ACTIVE AND PASSIVE VERBS

An active verb expresses the action completed by the subject. A passive verb expresses action done to the subject.

The active voice is usually more direct, clearer, and more concise than passive. However, sometimes the passive is a better choice.

Active: Paul **drove** the car.

(The verb is drove, and <u>Paul</u>, the subject, did the driving.)

Passive: The car <u>was driven</u> by Paul.

(The verb is <u>was driven</u>, and <u>the car</u>, the subject, was acted upon.)

Active verbs are clearer than passive because they indicate who is doing the action and add a better sense of immediateness and vigor. In a sentence with a passive verb, the "by the" phrase where the doer of the action is indicated may be left out or put far from the verb. Compare these sentences:

Passive: The photographs showing the tornado were snapped in a hurry by me.

Active: I hurriedly snapped the photographs of the tornado.

Because active verbs add directness and force, they are often a better choice for sentences containing action that begin with "there is" or "there are."

Original:	**Revised:**
There were six victims of the crime whose accounts of what happened agreed.	Six of the crime victims gave the same accounts of the crime.

However, there are occasions to use the passive:

- When the doer of the action is not known or not important:
  The water temperature was recorded.

- When you want to focus on the receiver of the action:
  Historical fiction is not widely read.

- When you want to focus on the action, not the doer:
  The records have been destroyed.

- When you want to avoid blaming or giving credit:
  The candidate concedes that the election is lost.

- When you want a tone of objectivity or wish to exclude yourself:
  The complete report was drafted and on the president's desk yesterday.

8

PARALLELISM

Parallel structure exists when the same grammatical form or structure is used for equal ideas in a list or in a comparison. That similar form helps your reader locate the similar or compared ideas. Often, the equal elements repeat words or sounds.

Parallel: The computer manual explained <u>how to boot</u>
                                                                          (1)

<u>up the hard drive</u> and <u>how to install the software.</u>
                                                (2)

(Phrases (1) and (2) are parallel because both start with how to.)

Parallel: <u>Watching Walt fumble with his headgear</u> was

_(1)_

as funny as <u>seeing him try to skate</u>.

_(2)_

(Phrases (1) and (2) are parallel because both start with -ing verb forms.)

Parallel: Three keys to marketing success include the following:

<u>To listen</u> to the customer's wishes

_(1)_

<u>To offer</u> several alternatives

_(2)_

<u>To motivate</u> the customer to buy

_(3)_

(Phrases (1), (2), and (3) are parallel items in a list because all begin with <u>to</u> + verb.)

Parallel is also needed when you link items using the following:

both . . . as	_either . . . or_
not only . . . but	_neither . . . nor_

coordinating conjunctions: _and, but, for, or, nor, so, yet_
comparisons using _than_ or _as_

Parallel: Job opportunities are not only <u>increasing</u> in

_(1)_

the health fields but <u>expanding</u> in many areas

_(2)_

of manufacturing as well.

(1) and (2) are parallel items using <u>-ing</u> verbs linked with but.

Faulty parallelism is not only grammatically incorrect but can also lead to possible lack of clarity.

Dr. Willo explained that either <u>starting</u>

_(1)_

the treatment or ~~to avoid~~ avoiding surgery was impossible.

_(2)_ ^

> ## hint
>
> **Parallel Structure**
>
> As you proofread, do the following:
>
> * Listen to the sound when you are linking equal ideas or comparing two or more elements. (Parallelism can add emphasis to your writing and public speaking by that repetition of sound.)
>
> * Visualize similar elements in a list and check to see if they are in the same grammatical structure.

Tara wondered whether it was better <u>to tell</u> her mother
(1)

that she had wrecked the car or maybe <u>fixing</u> it herself.
to fix
^ (2)

9

TRANSITIONS

Transitions are words and phrases that build bridges to connect sentences, parts of sentences, and paragraphs together. These bridges show relationships and add smoothness (or "flow") to your writing.

There are several types of transitions you can use:

* Repetition of a key term or phrase
  Delegates at the conference could not agree on the degree of danger from <u>global warming</u>. But no one disputed the existence of <u>global warming</u>.

* Synonyms
  The <u>movie industry</u> is expanding to produce a variety of forms of entertainment, such as television films and music videos. But <u>Hollywood</u> will always have movies as its main focus.

* Pronouns
  <u>College tuition</u> has been increasing rapidly for several years. But <u>it</u> still does not finance needed improvements on many campuses.

- Transition words and phrases
  The investigators looking into the cause of the pollution
  pinpointed one farm. <u>Therefore</u>, the owner was forced to
  reduce his use of the fertilizers that were washing into
  the stream. <u>In the meantime</u>, the local chemical plant
  continued its dumping practices.

TRANSITIONS	
Adding:	and, besides, in addition, also, too, furthermore, third
Comparing:	similarly, likewise, in the same way, at the same time
Contrasting:	but, yet, on the other hand, instead, whereas, although
Emphasizing:	indeed, in fact, above all, and also, obviously, clearly
Ending:	after all, finally, in sum
Giving examples:	for example, for instance, namely, specifically, that is
Showing cause and effect:	thus, therefore, consequently, as a result, accordingly, so
Showing place or direction:	over, above, next to, beneath, to the left, in the distance
Showing time:	meanwhile, later, afterward, now, finally, in the meantime
Summarizing:	in brief, on the whole, in conclusion, in other words

hint

Words That Start Sentences

Although some instructors prefer that you don't use or
overuse the transitions "But" or "And" as sentence starters,
it is not wrong to use them. Any word can start a sentence.

10

NONSEXIST LANGUAGE

Language that favors the male noun or pronoun or excludes females is sexist. To avoid such language, do the following:

- Use alternatives to <u>man</u>:

man	alternative
man	person
mankind	people, human beings
man-made	machine-made, synthetic
to man	to operate

- Use alternatives for job titles:

man	alternative
chairman	chair, chairperson
mailman	letter carrier, postal worker
policeman	police officer
fireman	firefighter

- Use the plural instead.

Sexist: Give the customer <u>his</u> receipt immediately.
Revised: Give customers <u>their</u> receipts immediately.

- Reword and eliminate the male pronoun.

Sexist: Give the customer <u>his</u> receipt.
Revised: Give the customer <u>the</u> receipt.

- Replace the male pronoun with <u>one</u>, <u>you</u>, <u>he or she</u>, and so on.

Sexist: The student can select <u>his</u> preferred residence hall.
Revised: The student can select <u>his or her</u> preferred residence hall.

- Address the reader directly.

Sexist: The applicant should mail two copies of <u>his</u> form by Monday.
Revised: Mail two copies of <u>your</u> form by Monday.

hint

Using "Everyone . . . His"

For indefinite pronouns such as "everyone" and "any-body," the traditional practice is to use the masculine singular to refer back to that pronoun:

Traditional: Everyone brought his own pen and paper.

To avoid the male pronoun, which is seen by many people as sexist, you can use the strategies listed. Others, however, such as the National Council of Teachers of English, accept the plural as a way to avoid sexist language:

Everyone brought their own pen and paper.

III Sentence Grammar

Contents of this section

11 Fragments   30

12 Comma Splices and Fused Sentences   32

13 Subjects and Verbs   33

13a **Subject-verb agreement**   33

13b **Verbs**   37

14 Pronouns   43

14a **Pronoun case**   43

14b **Pronoun antecedents**   47

14c **Pronoun reference**   48

15 Adjectives and Adverbs   50

16 Modifiers   53

16a **Dangling modifiers**   53

16b **Misplaced modifiers**   54

16c **Split infinitives**   54

17 Shifts   55

Questions to ask yourself

The sections in this part offer help with grammatical rules for the most common problems writers have. If you are not familiar with the grammatical terms, such as "fragment," "comma splice," "subject-verb agreement," "pronoun reference," etc. and want to look up the rules for these, you can check the glossary of terms at the back of the book, use the index to find the term you are looking for, or use the question section here.

	SECTION	PAGE
• What is a sentence fragment, and how do I recognize one?	11	30
• Is "Because she wanted to pass the course" a sentence or a fragment?	11	30

- Is "Such as the way he explained the joke" a sentence or a fragment?   11   30

- How can I proofread for fragments?   11   30

- What are comma splices, fused sentences, and run-on sentences?   12   32

- When do I use a comma, and when do I use a semicolon to join two clauses that could be sentences by themselves?   12   32

- What are the sentence patterns I can use to avoid comma splices, fused sentences, and run-on sentences?   12   32

- What is subject-verb agreement?   13a   33

- Is it correct to write "Nearly every one of the other students in my classes are complaining about the test"?   13a   33

- How can I check for subject-verb agreement? And what are some of the different subject-verb complications?   13a   33

- When I have two subject terms such as "Talesha" and "her friends," is the verb "is" or "are"?   13a   33

- Do I use singular or plural verbs with collective nouns such as "family" and "group"? (The family is/are moving.")   13a   33

- Do I use singular or plural verbs with plural subjects such as "mathematics" or "jeans" and names like General Foods?   13a   33

- Do I use singular or plural verbs with phrases and clauses that start with "who" or "which" in the middle of sentences (such as "He is the person on those committees who want/wants to change the rules.")?   13a   33

- What are the regular verb endings?   13b   37

- What is the past tense for irregular verbs such as "swim," "lie/lay," or "forbid"?   13b   37

- Are the following verb forms correct?
  -may have <u>like</u> to come along
  -could <u>of</u>
  -<u>suppose</u> to   13b   37

- What are active and passive verbs, and
  when should they be used?   13b   37

- Should I use an apostrophe with pronouns
  such as "his" or "theirs"?   14a   43

- Is the phrase "<u>them</u> boxes" wrong?   14a   43

- Which is correct?
  -The coach liked <u>his/him</u> pitching to the right.   14a   43

- Which is correct?
  -The musicians and <u>myself/I</u> took a short
  break.
  -She gave <u>myself/me</u> and Tim some good
  advice.   14a   43

- Should I write "between you and I" or
  "between you and me"?   14a   43

- When do I use "who," and when do I use
  "whom"?   14a   43

- What is "vague pronoun reference," and
  how can I avoid it?   14b   47

- Is there a problem with using "this" or
  "they" (or "it") in sentences such as
  "Caitlin lost her umbrella, and <u>this</u> problem
  she has really bothers me" or "<u>They</u> say
  it's going to be a very cold winter"?   14b   47

- What's wrong with the phrase "real bad"?   15   50

- When do I use "good," and when do I use "well"?   15   50

- How should I correct the following sentence?
  "After eating dinner, the doorbell rang."   16a   53

- When I use modifying words such as
  "only," "even," or "nearly," where
  should I place them in the sentence?   16b   54

- How should I correct the following
  sentence? "For most <u>people</u>, the career
  <u>you</u> decide on isn't always the major
  <u>they</u> had in college."   17   55

11

FRAGMENTS

A sentence fragment is an incomplete sentence. To recognize a fragment consider the basic requirements of a sentence:

- A sentence is a group of words with at least one independent clause.
- An independent clause has a subject and complete verb plus an object or a complement if needed.
- An independent clause can stand alone as a thought, even though it may need other sentences before and after it to clarify the thoughts being expressed.

Independent clause: Jeremy's picture was in the newspaper.

Independent clause: He scored six three-point baskets during the game.

(We don't know who "he" is in this sentence, but a pronoun can be a subject, and we don't know which game is being referred to. But those bits of information, if needed, would be explained in accompanying sentences. The clause has a subject ["he"], a verb ["scored"], and an object ["baskets"].)

Not an independent clause: Because he scored six three-point baskets during the game.

(Say that clause out loud, and you will hear that it's not a complete sentence. The problem is that we don't know the result of the "because" clause.)

Not an independent clause: Luis who was one of my closest friends in third and fourth grade and is now moving with his family to another city.

(This is not a complete sentence because it has a subject, "Luis," but no main verb that tells us what Luis did. The verbs "was" and "is moving" belong to another subject [the pronoun "who"] and tell us what "who" did.)

Some fragments are unintended:

Unintended fragment: There were some complications with her phone bill. <u>Such as two calls she did not make and a long distance charge for a local call.</u>

(The second sentence is an unintended fragment because it has no subject and verb. It is a phrase that got disconnected from the independent clause that came before it.)

30

Unintended fragment: The doctor's recommendation
that I get more sleep because I
was becoming very stressed out
while taking too many classes
which I need for my major.

*(The subject is "recommendation" but there is no main
verb to complete that thought.)*

Some fragments are intentional when they are used to add an
effect such as emphasis or sudden change in tempo. However,
intended fragments should be used only when the writing
clearly indicates that the writer chose to include a fragment.

Intended fragment: Never had there been such a decisive
victory in the school's history of partici-
pating in the tournament, and no one
stayed at home that night when the
team's bus pulled into town. <u>No one.</u>

(The fragment, "No one," is used here to add emphasis.)

---

hint

Avoiding Fragments

HINT 1

To proofread for fragments caused by misplaced periods, read your paper backward, from the last sentence
to the first. You will notice a fragment more easily when
you hear it without the sentence to which it belongs.
Most, but not all, fragments occur after the main clause.

HINT 2

Some fragments are caused by a marker word typically
found at the beginning of the clause that requires a second clause to finish the thought. Consider a marker word
such as "if" and how it affects the clause:

If A happens ⟶ ?

When you hear that, you want to know what B is, that is,
what the result is if A happens.
Watch for other, similar marker words such as the following:

after	before	since
although	even though	unless
because	if	when

12

COMMA SPLICES AND FUSED SENTENCES

A comma splice and a fused sentence (also called a run-on sentence) are punctuation problems in compound sentences. (A compound sentence is one that joins two or more independent clauses—clauses that could have been sentences by themselves.)

To avoid comma splices and fused sentences, note the three patterns for commas and semicolons in compound sentences:

1. Join an independent clause with a comma and one of the seven joining words listed here:

Independent clause, and independent clause.

> but
> for
> or
> nor
> so
> yet

No one was home, but the door was open.

2. Join two independent clauses with a semicolon and no joining words:

Independent clause; independent clause.

No one was home; the door was open.

3. Join two independent clauses with a semicolon and any connecting word other than one of the seven joining words for commas listed above: "and," "but," "for," "or," "nor," "so," or "yet."

Independent clause; however, independent
clause.

> therefore,
> consequently,
> thus,

No one was home; however, the door was open.

If you don't use one of these three patterns for compound sentences, the sentence will have a comma splice:

Comma splice: No one was home, the door was open.

---

hint

Using Commas in Compound Sentences

HINT 1

When punctuating compound sentences, think of the comma as only half of the needed connection to tie two independent clauses together. The other half is the connecting word. You need both the comma and the connecting word.

HINT 2

Don't put commas before every "and" or "but" in your sentences. "And" and "but" have other uses in sentences in addition to joining two independent clauses.

13
SUBJECTS AND VERBS

13a Subject-verb agreement

Subjects and verbs should agree in number and person.

- To agree in number, the verb used with a plural subject should have a plural ending, and a verb used with a singular subject should have a singular ending.

The customer	orders
(singular subject)	*(singular verb)*

The customers	order
(plural subject)	*(plural verb)*

- To agree in person, the verb should be in the same person (first person= I/we; second person = you; third person = he/they) as the subject.

  I know   you know   she knows   they know

(For verb tense endings, see page 41.)

- Some subjects are hard to find because they are buried among many other words. In that case, disregard the prepositional phrases, modifiers, and other surrounding words.

Almost every <u>one</u> of the applicants for the job who
(subject) ➘

came for interviews <u>is</u> highly qualified.
(verb)

---

hint

Subject-Verb Agreement

HINT 1

The letter –s is used both for subject endings (plural) and for verb endings (singular). Because a plural subject can't have a singular verb, and a singular verb can't have a plural subject, the letter –s should not normally be the ending for both subject and verb.

chime(s) ring the chime ring(s)

HINT 2

When you check subject-verb endings, start by finding the verb. The main verb is the word that changes when you change the time of the sentence, from past to present or present to past. Then, ask yourself "who" or "what" is doing that action, and you will find the subject.

HINT 3

To find a subject buried among other words and phrases, start by eliminating phrases starting with prepositions; "who," "that," or "which" clauses; or words such as the following:

including	along with	together with
accompanied by	in addition to	as well as
except	with	no less than

Compound subjects

Subjects joined by "and" take a plural verb (X and Y = more than one).

The (stereo) and the (speaker) are sold as a unit.

Sometimes, words joined by "and" act together as a unit and are thought of as one thing. If so, use a singular verb.

(Peanut butter and jelly) is his favorite sandwich spread.

Either/or subjects

When the subject words are joined by "either . . . or," "neither . . . nor," or ""not only . . . but also," the verb agrees with the closest subject word.

Either (Maylene) or her (children) are going to bed early.

Indefinites as subjects

Indefinite words with singular meanings such as "each," "every," and "any" take a singular subject when (1) they are the subject word or (2) they precede the subject word.

Each (book) on the shelves is marked with a barcode.

However, when indefinite words such as "none," "some," "most," or "all" are the subject, the number of the verb depends on the meaning of the subject.

(Some) of the movie is difficult to understand.

(Some) of those movies are difficult to understand.

Collective nouns and amounts as subjects

Nouns that refer to groups or a collection (such as "family," "committee," or "group") are collective nouns. When the collective noun refers to the group acting as a whole or single unit, the verb is singular.

Our (family) needs a new car.

Occasionally, a collective noun refers to a member of a group acting individually, not as a unit. In that case, the verb is plural.

The (committee) are happy with each other's decisions.

Plural words as subjects

Some words that have an *-s* ending, such as "news" or "mathematics" are thought of as a single unit and take a singular verb.

Physics is. . . . Economics is. . . . Measles is. . . .

Some words, such as those in the following examples, are treated as plural and take a plural verb, even though they refer to one thing. (In many cases, though, there are two parts to these things.)

Jeans are. . . . Pants are. . . . Scissors are. . . .

Titles, company names, and terms as subjects

For titles of written works, names of companies, and words used as terms, use singular verbs.

All the King's Men is the book assigned for this week.

General Foods is hiring people for its new plant.

"Cheers" is a word he often uses when leaving.

Linking verbs

Linking verbs agree with the subject rather than the word that follows (the complement).

Those poems are my favorites.

The poem is their favorite.

There is/there are/it

When a sentence begins with "there is," "there are," or "it," the verb depends on the complement that follows it.

There is a surprise ending to that story.

There are surprise endings in many of her stories.

Who, which, that and one of . . . who/which/that as subjects

When "who," "which," and "that" are used as subjects, the verb agrees with the previous word it refers to (the antecedent).

They are the students who want to change the parking rules.

He is the student who wants to change the parking rules.

In the phrase "one of those who," it is necessary to decide whether the "who," "which," or "that" refers only to the one or to the whole group. Only then can you decide whether the verb is singular or plural.

Mr. Liu is one of the (salespersons) who <u>know</u> the product.

(In this case, Mr. Liu is part of a large group, those salespersons who know the product.)

Mr. Liu is the only (one) of the salespersons who <u>knows</u> the product.

13b Verbs

Regular and irregular verb forms

Verbs that add *–ed* for the past tense and the past participle are regular verbs.

I <u>talk</u>   I <u>talked</u>   I have <u>talked</u>
(present)   *(past)*   *(past participle)*

The past participle is the form that has a helping verb such as "has" or "had."

VERB FORMS (REGULAR)			
	PRESENT	**PAST**	**FUTURE**
Simple	I walk	I walked	I will walk
Progressive	I am walking	I was walking	I will be walking
Perfect	I have walked	I had walked	I will have walked
Perfect Progressive	I have been walking	I had been walking	I will have been walking

VERB FORMS (IRREGULAR)

Verb	PRESENT		PAST	
	singular	plural	singular	plural
to be	I am you are he, she, it is	we are you are they are	I was you were he, she, it was	we were you were they were
to have	I have you have he, she, it has	we have you have they have	I had you had he, she, it had	we had you had they had
to do	I do you do he, she, it does	we do you do they do	I did you did he, she, it did	we did you did they did

Some of the frequently used irregular verb forms include the following:

IRREGULAR VERBS

BASE (PRESENT)	PAST	PAST PARTICIPLE
awake	awoke	awoken
be	was, were	been
beat	beat	beaten
become	became	become
begin	began	begun
bet	bet	bet
bite	bit	bitten (or) bit
bleed	bled	bled
blow	blew	blown
break	broke	broken
bring	brought	brought
build	built	built
burst	burst	burst
buy	bought	bought
catch	caught	caught

BASE (PRESENT)	PAST	PAST PARTICIPLE
choose	chose	chosen
come	came	come
cost	cost	cost
cut	cut	cut
dig	dug	dug
do	did	done
draw	drew	drawn
drink	drank	drunk
drive	drove	driven
eat	ate	eaten
fall	fell	fallen
feed	fed	fed
feel	felt	felt
fight	fought	fought
find	found	found
fling	flung	flung
fly	flew	flown
forbid	forbade	forbidden
forget	forgot	forgotten
freeze	froze	frozen
get	got	gotten
give	gave	given
go	went	gone
grow	grew	grown
hang	hung	hung
have	had	had
hear	heard	heard
hit	hit	hit
hold	held	held
hurt	hurt	hurt
keep	kept	kept
know	knew	known
lay	laid	laid
lie	lay	lain
make	made	made
mean	meant	meant
meet	met	met
mistake	mistook	mistaken
pay	paid	paid
prove	proved	proved (or) proven
put	put	put
read	read	read
ride	rode	ridden

BASE (PRESENT)	PAST	PAST PARTICIPLE
ring	rang	rung
rise	rose	risen
run	ran	run
say	said	said
see	saw	seen
sell	sold	sold
send	sent	sent
set	set	set
shake	shook	shaken
shine	shone	shone
shoot	shot	shot
shrink	shrank	shrunk
shut	shut	shut
sing	sang	sung
sit	sat	sit
sleep	slept	slept
slide	slid	slid
speak	spoke	spoken
spend	spent	spent
spin	spun	spun
split	split	split
spread	spread	spread
spring	sprang	sprung
stand	stood	stood
steal	stole	stolen
stick	stuck	stuck
stink	stank	stunk
strike	struck	struck
swear	swore	sworn
sweep	swept	swept
swim	swam	swum
swing	swung	swung
take	took	taken
teach	taught	taught
tear	tore	torn
tell	told	told
understand	understood	understood
wear	wore	worn
weep	wept	wept
win	won	won
wind	wound	wound
write	wrote	written

Lie/lay, sit/set, rise/raise

Three sets of verbs that cause problems are "lie/lay," "sit/set," and "rise/raise." Because they are related in meaning and sound, they are sometimes confused with each other. In each case, one of the set takes an object and the other doesn't, and each member of the set has a somewhat different meaning:

Lie (recline)   She <u>lies</u> in bed all day. (present)

She <u>lay</u> in bed all last week. (past)

Lay (put)   He <u>lays</u> his dishes on the table. (present)

He <u>laid</u> his dishes on the table. (past)

Sit (be seated)   Please <u>sit</u> here by the window. (present)

He <u>sat</u> by the window in class. (past)

Set (put)   Please <u>set</u> the flowers on the table. (present)

He <u>set</u> the flowers on the chair before he left. **(past)**

Rise (get up)   They all <u>rise</u> early in the morning. (present)

They all <u>rose</u> early yesterday too. (past)

Raise (lift up)   Can you <u>raise</u> that weight above your head? **(present)**

He <u>raised</u> the curtain for the play. (past)

Verb tense

The four verb tenses for present, past, and future are as follows:

- Simple:
  I see   I saw   I will see

- Progressive: "be" + *–ing* form of the verb
  I am seeing   I was seeing   I will be seeing

- Perfect: "have," "had," or "shall" + the *–ed* form of the verb
  I have walked   I had walked   I will have walked

- Perfect progressive: "have" or "had" + "been" +*–ing* form of the verb

I have been singing	I had been singing	I will have been singing

(For a guide to using the tenses, see section 30a.)

---

hint

Verb Endings

Avoid the verb ending problem that omits the final "d" or uses "of" instead of "have" in such forms as the following:

might have <u>like</u> to (should be: might have <u>liked</u> to)

could <u>of</u> (should be: could <u>have</u>)

<u>suppose</u> to (should be: <u>supposed</u> to)

Verb voice

Verb voice tells whether the verb is in the active or passive voice. In the active voice, the subject performs the action of the verb. In the passive voice, the subject receives the action. The doer of the action in the passive voice may be omitted or may appear in a "by the . . . " phrase.

Active: The child sang the song.

Passive: The song was sung by the child.

Verb mood

The mood of a verb tells whether it expresses a fact or opinion (**indicative** mood); expresses a command, request, or advice (**imperative** mood); or expresses a doubt, wish, recommendation, or something contrary to fact (**subjunctive** mood).

Indicative: The new software <u>runs</u> well on this computer.

Imperative: <u>Watch</u> for falling rock.

Subjunctive: In the subjunctive, present tense verbs stay in the simple base form and do not indicate the number and person of the subject. Use the subjunctive mood in "that" clauses following verbs such as "ask," "insist," and "request."

In the past tense, the same form as simple past is used; however, for the verb "be," "were" is used for all persons and numbers.

It is important that he <u>join</u> the committee.

He insisted that she <u>be</u> one of the leaders of the group.

If I <u>were</u> you, I wouldn't ask that question.

14
PRONOUNS

14a   14a Pronoun case

Pronouns, the words that substitute for nouns, change case according to their use in a sentence.

Subject: <u>He</u> bought some film. It is <u>he</u>.
Object: Cherise gave <u>him</u> the film.
Possessive: No one used <u>his</u> film.

PRONOUN CASE						
	SUBJECT		**OBJECT**		**POSSESSIVE**	
	sing.	pl.	sing.	pl.	sing.	pl.
1st person	I	we	me	us	my, mine	our, ours
2nd person	you	you	you	you	your, yours	your, yours
3rd person	he	they	him	them	his	their, theirs
	she	they	her	them	her, hers	their, theirs
	it	they	it	them	it, its	their, theirs

hint

Common Problems with Pronouns:

HINT 1

Remember that "between," "except," and "with" are prepositions, and they take pronouns in the object case:

between you and me   (*not:* between you and I)

except Amit and her   (*not:* except Amit and she)

HINT 2

Possessive case pronouns never take apostrophes:

his shoes   (*not:* his' shoes)

its eye   (*not:* it's eye)

HINT 3

Don't use "them" as a pointing pronoun in place of "those" or "these." Use "them" only as the object by itself.

those pages   (*not:* them pages)

HINT 4

Use possessive case before *–ing* verb forms.

They applauded his scoring a goal. (*not:* him scoring)

HINT 5

Reflexive pronouns are those that end in "*–self*" or "*–selves*" and are used to intensify the nouns they refer back to:

I soaked myself in suntan oil.

Please help yourself.

Don't use the reflexive pronoun in other cases because it sounds as if it might be more correct. (It isn't.)

$$I$$
Joseph and ~~myself~~ went to pick up the tickets.
^

$$Me$$
They included ~~myself~~ in the group.
^

Pronoun case in compound constructions

To find the right case when your sentence has two pronouns
or a noun and a pronoun, temporarily eliminate the noun or
one of the pronouns as you read the sentence to yourself.
You will hear the case that is needed.

Which is correct?   Nathan and him ordered a pizza.

(or)

Nathan and he ordered a pizza.

Test: Would you say "Him ordered a pizza"?
The correct pronoun here is "he."

Which is correct?   I gave those tickets to Mikki and she.

(or)

I gave those tickets to Mikki and her.

Test: Would you say, "I gave those tickets to
she"? When in doubt, some writers
mistakenly choose the subject case,
thinking it sounds more formal. But the
correct pronoun here is "her," the
object case, because it is the object of
the preposition "to."

Who/whom

In informal speech, some writers do not distinguish between
"who" and "whom." But for formal writing, the cases are as
follows:

Subject	Object	Possessive
who	whom	whose
whoever	whomever	

Subject: <u>Who</u> is going to drive that van?
Object: To <u>whom</u> should I give this booklet?
Possessive: Everyone wondered <u>whose</u> coat that was.

hint

Using "Who" and "Whom"

If you aren't sure whether to use "who" or "whom," turn a question into a statement or rearrange the order of the phrase:

Question:	(Who, Whom) are you looking for?
Statement:	You are looking for whom.
Sentence:	She is someone (who,whom) I have already met.
Rearranged order:	I have already met whom.

Pronoun case after "than" or "as"

In comparisons using "than" or "as," choose the correct pronoun case by recalling the words that are omitted:

He is taller than (I, me). (The omitted words are "am tall.")
He is taller than <u>I</u> (am tall).

My sister likes her cat more than (I, me). (The omitted words here are "she likes.")
My sister likes her cat more than (she likes) <u>me</u>.

"We" or "us" before nouns

When combining "we" or "us" with a noun, such as "we players," use the case that is appropriate for the noun. You can hear that by omitting the noun and seeing which sounds correct.

(We, Us) players chose to pay for our own equipment.

Test: Would you say "Us chose to pay for our own equipment"? The correct pronoun here is "We."

hint

"We" or "Us"

Remember the famous opening words of the U.S. Declaration of Independence: "<u>We</u> the people. . . ."

Pronoun case with infinitives ("to" + verb)

When using pronouns after infinitives, verb forms with "to" + verb, use the object case. (You can also hear this by omitting a noun that may precede the pronoun.)

> She offered to drive Orin and (I, me) to the meeting.

> *Test:* Would you say, "She offered to drive I to the meeting? The correct pronoun here is "me."

Pronoun case before gerunds (*–ing* verb forms)

If a pronoun is used to modify a gerund, an *–ing* word, use the possessive case.

> She was proud of (us, our) walking in the fund-raising marathon.

> The correct form here is the possessive, "our."

14b   Pronoun antecedents

Pronouns substitute for nouns. In the sentence "Emilio washed his car," the pronoun "his" is a substitute for the noun Emilio (to avoid unnecessary repetition) and refers back to Emilio. The noun that a pronoun refers back to is its antecedent. For clarity, then, pronouns should agree in number and gender with their antecedents. (In the sentences "Emilio washed their car" or "Emilio washed her car," you would assume there is a different car being referred to.)

Singular: The <u>student</u> turned in <u>her</u> lab report.

Plural: The <u>students</u> turned in <u>their</u> lab reports.

Indefinite pronouns

Indefinite pronouns are those pronouns that don't refer to any specific person or thing such as "anyone," "no one," "someone," "something," "everybody," "none," and "each." Some of them may seem to have a plural meaning, but in formal writing, treat them as singular. Others, such as "many," are always plural, and some can be singular or plural depending on the meaning of the sentence.

When using indefinite pronouns that are normally treated as singular, some writers prefer to use the plural to avoid sexist language (section 10). But as an alternative, you can use "his or her" (which can be wordy) or switch to plural.

Everyone in the class took out his notebook.

Everyone in the class took out his or her notebook.

The students took out their notebooks.

Collective nouns

When you use collective nouns such as "committee," "family," "group," and "audience," treat them as singular because they are acting as a group.

The jury handed in its verdict.

Generic or general nouns

When you use generic nouns to indicate members of a group, such as "voter," "student," and "doctor," treat them as singular. To avoid sexist language, switch to plural.

A truck driver should keep his road maps close at hand.

Truck drivers should keep their road maps close at hand.

14c   Pronoun reference

To avoid reader confusion, be sure that your pronouns have a clear reference to their antecedents. There are several possible problems to avoid:

Ambiguous pronoun reference

When a pronoun does not clearly indicate which of two or more possible antecedents it refers to, the reference is ambiguous. Rewrite the sentence to make sure the reference is clear.

Unclear reference: Marina told Michelle that she took her bike to the library.

her = Marina?   her = Michelle?

(Did Marina take Michelle's bike to the library, or did Marina take her own bike to the library?)

Clear reference: When Marina took Michelle's bike to the library, she told Michelle she was borrowing it.

Vague pronoun reference ("this," "that," and "which")

When you use "this," "that," and "which" to refer to something, be sure that the word refers to a specific antecedent that has been named.

Vague pronoun reference: Ray worked in a national forest last summer, and <u>this</u> may be his career choice.

this = ?

(What does "this" refer to? Because no word or phrase in the first part of the sentence refers to the pronoun, the sentence needs to be revised so that the antecedent is stated.)

Clear pronoun reference: Ray worked in a national forest last summer, and <u>working as a forest ranger</u> may be his career choice.

Indefinite use of "you," "it," and "they"

Avoid the use of "you," "it," and "they" when they don't refer to any specific group.

Vague pronoun reference: Everyone knows <u>you</u> should use sunscreen lotion when out in bright summer sun.

you = ?

Clear pronoun reference: It is well known that <u>people</u> should use sunscreen lotion when out in bright summer sun.

Vague pronoun reference: In Hollywood <u>they</u> don't know what type of movies the American public wants to see.

they = ?

Clear pronoun reference: In Hollywood, <u>screenwriters and producers</u> don't know what type of movies the American public wants to see.

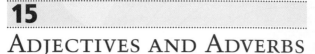

15

ADJECTIVES AND ADVERBS

Adjectives and adverbs are modifiers, but they modify different kinds of words:

Adjectives
- modify nouns and pronouns
- answer the questions "which?" "how many?" and "what kind?"

<u>six</u> packages (how many? <u>six</u>)
<u>cheerful</u> smile (what kind? <u>cheerful</u>)

It is <u>cold.</u>

(An adjective after a linking verb modifies the subject and is called a "subject complement." Here, "cold" is an adjective modifying the subject pronoun "it."

The water tastes <u>salty</u>. water = salty

(Some verbs, such as "taste," "feel," "appear," and "smell," can be linking verbs.)

Adverbs
- modify verbs, verb forms, adjectives, and other adverbs
- answer the questions "how?" "when?" "where?" and "to what extent?"
- Most (but not all) adverbs end in –ly

danced <u>gracefully</u> (how? <u>gracefully</u>)

<u>very</u> long string (how long? <u>very</u> long)

He ran ~~quick~~. *quickly* (How did he run? <u>quickly</u>)

They sing ~~real~~ loud. *really* (How loud? <u>really</u>)

Adjectives	Adverbs
sure	surely
real	really
good	well
bad	badly

"Good," "bad," "badly," and "well"

The modifiers "good," "bad," "badly," and "well" can cause problems because they are occasionally misused in speech. In addition, "well" can function as an adjective or an adverb.

> well (adjective) = healthy   well (adverb) = done
> satisfactorily

He played <u>well</u>. (*not:* good)

Despite the surgery, I feel <u>well</u>. (*not:* good)

The linebacker played <u>badly</u> today. (*not:* bad)

She feels <u>bad</u> about missing that meeting. (*not:* badly)

He looked <u>good</u> in that suit. (*not:* well)

---

hint

Completing Comparisons

When you use adverbs such as "so," "such," and "too," be sure to complete the phrase or clause.

that she laughed out loud

She is so happy.
^

to ask for help

Tran's problem is that he is too proud.
^

Comparatives and superlatives

Adjectives and adverbs are often used to show comparison, and the degree of comparison is indicated in their forms. Adjectives and adverbs with one or two syllables add –er and –est as endings, and longer adjectives and adverbs combine with the words "more" and "most" or "less" and "least."

- Positive (when no comparison is made):
  a <u>large</u> box   a <u>cheerful</u> smile

- Comparative (when two things are compared):
  the <u>larger</u> of the two boxes   a <u>more cheerful</u> smile

- Superlative (when three or more things are compared):

  the <u>largest</u> box   the <u>most cheerful</u> smile

REGULAR FORMS OF COMPARISON		
POSITIVE	**COMPARATIVE**	**SUPERLATIVE**
(*for one*)	(*for two*)	(*for three or more*)
tall	taller	tallest
pretty	prettier	prettiest
selfish	more selfish	most selfish
unusual	more unusual	most unusual

IRREGULAR FORMS OF COMPARISON		
POSITIVE	**COMPARATIVE**	**SUPERLATIVE**
(*for one*)	(*for two*)	(*for three or more*)
good	better	best
well	better	best
little	less	least
some	more	most
much	more	most
many	more	most
bad, badly	worse	worst

Absolute adjectives and adverbs

Some adjectives and adverbs such as "unique," "perfect," and "final" cannot logically be compared because there can't be degrees of being final or unique or perfect.

Terri has a ~~most~~ unique smile.

16

Modifiers

16a 16a Dangling modifiers

A dangling modifier is a word or group of words that refers to (or modifies) a word or phrase that has not been clearly stated in the sentence. When an introductory phrase does not name the doer of the action, the phrase is assumed to refer to the subject of the independent clause that follows.

Having finished the assignment, Jeremy turned on the TV.

("Jeremy," the subject of the independent clause, is the doer of the action in the introductory phrase.)

However, when the intended subject (or doer of the action) of the introductory phrase is not stated, the result is a dangling modifier.

Having finished the assignment, the TV was turned on.

(This sentence is not logical because it implies that the TV finished the homework.)

Dangling modifiers most frequently occur at the beginning of the sentence but can also appear at the end. They often have an *–ing* verb or a "to" + verb phrase near the start of the phrase. To repair a dangling modifier, name the subject in the dangling phrase or as the subject of the sentence.

Dangling: After completing a degree in education, more experience in the classroom is also needed to prepare a good teacher.

Revised: After completing a degree in education, good teachers also need to gain more experience in the classroom.

Dangling: To work as a lifeguard, practice in CPR is required.

Revised: To work as a lifeguard, applicants are required to have practice in CPR.

16b 16b Misplaced modifiers

Misplaced modifiers are words or groups of words placed so far away from what is being referred to that the reader may be confused.

Misplaced modifier: The assembly line workers were told that they had been fired <u>by the personnel director</u>.

(Were the workers told by the personnel director that they had been fired? Or were they told by someone else that the personnel director had fired them?)

Revised: The assembly line workers were told by the personnel director that they had been fired.

Misplaced modifiers are often the source of comedians' humor, as in the classic often used by Groucho Marx and others:

The other day I shot an elephant in my pajamas. How he got in my pajamas I'll never know.

Single-word modifiers such as "only," "even," and "hardly" should be placed immediately before the words they modify or as close to that word as possible. Note the difference in meaning in these two sentences:

I earned nearly $50. (The amount was almost $50, but not quite.)

I nearly earned $50. (I almost had the opportunity to earn $50, but it didn't work out.)

---

hint

Placing Modifiers Correctly

Some one-word modifiers that may get misplaced:

almost	hardly	merely	only
even	just	nearly	simply

16c Split infinitives

Split infinitives occur when modifiers are inserted between "to" and the verb. Some people object to split infinitives, but others consider them grammatically acceptable when other phrasing would be less natural.

to _easily_ reach

(Here "easily" fits naturally between the "to" and the verb "reach.")

Some split infinitives such as "to more than double" are almost impossible to rephrase so that there is no modifier between "to" and the verb.

17

SHIFTS

To maintain consistency in writing, use the same perspective throughout a paper by maintaining the same person: first person ("I"), second person ("you"), and third person ("he," "she," "it," "one," or "they"). Maintain consistency in number, tense, and tone also.

Unnecessary shift in person:	In a _person's_ life, the most important (3rd person) thing _you_ do is to decide on a career. (2nd person)
Revised:	In a _person's_ life, the most important thing _he_ or _she_ does is to decide on a career.
Unnecessary shift in number:	The working _woman_ faces many (singular) challenges to advancement. When _they_ (plural) marry and have children, _they_ may need to take a leave of absence.
Revised:	Working _women_ face many challenges to advancement. When _they_ marry and have children, _they_ may need to take a leave of absence.

Keep writing with verbs in the same time (past, present, or future) in your verbs unless the logic of what you are writing about requires a switch.

Unnecessary shift in tense:	While we <u>were watching</u> the last
	(past)
	game of the World Series, the picture suddenly <u>gets</u> fuzzy.
	(present)
Revised:	While we <u>were watching</u> the last game of the World Series, the picture suddenly <u>got</u> fuzzy.

Once you choose a formal or informal tone for a paper, keep that tone consistent in your word choices. A sudden intrusion of a very formal word or phrase in an informal narrative or the use of slang or informal words in a formal report or essay indicates the writer's loss of control over tone.

| **Unnecessary shift in tone:** | The job of the welfare worker is to assist in a family's struggle to obtain funds for the <u>kids'</u> clothing and food. |

("Kids" is a very informal word choice here for a sentence that is somewhat formal in tone.)

| **Revised:** | The job of the welfare worker is to assist in a family's struggle to obtain funds for the <u>children's</u> clothing and food. |

IV Punctuation

Contents of this section

18 Sentence Punctuation Patterns   61

19 Commas   62

  19a Commas between independent clauses   62

  19b Commas after introductory word groups   63

  19c Commas before and after nonessential elements   63

  19d Commas in series and lists   63

  19e Commas with adjectives   64

  19f Commas with interrupting words or phrases   65

  19g Commas with dates, addresses, geographical names, and numbers   65

  19h Commas with quotations   66

  19i Unnecessary commas   66

20 Apostrophes   67

  20a Apostrophes with possessives   67

  20b Apostrophes with contractions   67

  20c Apostrophes with plurals   68

  20d Unnecessary apostrophes   68

21 Semicolons   69

  21a Semicolons to separate independent clauses   69

  21b Semicolons in a series   70

  21c Semicolons with quotation marks   70

  21d Unnecessary semicolons   70

22 Quotation Marks   70

  22a Quotation marks with direct quotations of prose, poetry, and dialogue   70

  22b Quotation marks for minor titles and parts of wholes   72

  22c Quotation marks for words   72

  22d Use of other punctuation with quotation marks   72

  22e Unnecessary quotation marks   73

23 Other Punctuation ... 73

23a **Hyphens** ... 73
23b **Colons** ... 75
23c **End punctuation** ... 76
23d **Dashes** ... 77
23e **Slashes** ... 77
23f **Parentheses** ... 78
23g **Brackets** ... 78
23h **Omitted words/ellipsis** ... 78

QUESTIONS TO ASK YOURSELF

This section includes the rules you'll need to use punctuation correctly.

	SECTION	PAGE
• Are there some general patterns for punctuating sentences?	18	61
• When do I use commas to join parts of a sentence?	19a	62
• If I connect two sentences with "and" or "but," do I need a comma or semicolon?	19a	62
• When I write a sentence with introductory words such as "However," "Because it was late," or "On the other hand," do I need a comma after those words?	19b	63
• Does this kind of sentence, with some words in the middle, need any commas? "My sister who works for a computer software company lives in Silicon Valley."	19c	63
• When I write a list of items (such as "long-haired terriers, cocker spaniels, and dachshunds") do I need a comma before that last "and"?	19d	63
• Should I put a comma between two verbs, as in the following sentence? "The movie reviewer praised the director for clever special effects, and complained about the unnecessary violence."	19d	64

- When I put some descriptive words in front of a noun (such as "big white dog"), do I need a comma?   19e   64

- Where should I put commas in dates in a sentence (such as "That bill is due on March 1 1999 and should be paid by check") or in an address in a sentence (such as "Send the check to 130 Grandview St. Chicago IL 60600 along with your signed order")?   19g   65

- Where do I put the comma when I include a quotation such as the following sentence?

  He announced "I will not resign."   19h   66

- Are these uses of a comma correct?
  -Jennifer noticed yesterday, that she had not mailed the letter to her parents.

  -I wanted to share that joke, because it was so funny.
  -There are several different majors in engineering, such as electrical, civil, and mechanical.   19i   66

- Where does the apostrophe belong?
  -two houses' windows (or) two house's windows
  -one box's lid (or) one boxs' lid
  -Maia and Tulio's house (or) Maia's and Tulio's house?
  -son's-in-law's (or) son-in-law's   20a   67

- When do I write "its" and when should I use "it's"?   20b   67

- Should I write "1900s" or "1900's"?   20c   68

- Are these apostrophes correct?
  -his' new car
  -The printers' were delivered   20d   68

- When should I use the semicolon?   21   69

- Is this use of the semicolon correct?

  -The research study included many tables for comparison ; especially the ones on population growth.   21d   70

- When do I use quotation marks for
  quoting poetry, prose, and dialogue?   22a   70

- Are these uses of quotation marks correct?
  -"Take Me Out to the Ballgame"
  - T.S. Eliot's "Wasteland"   22b   72

- Do I put commas inside or outside
  quotation marks?   22d   72

- When do I join words with hyphens such
  as in the following?
  -one half
  -three and four page papers
  -up to date statistics
  -self centered   23a   73

- When I have a list, do I use a colon such as
  in the following?
  -There are three parts in that watch that
  are guaranteed: the battery, the spring,
  and the crystal.   23b   75

- Which abbreviations don't need a period? 23c   76

- Where does the question mark go in this
  sentence?
  -Did she say, "I don't have the answer"? 23c   76

- When is it acceptable to use dashes?   23d   77

- How do I indicate left-out words in a
  quotation?   23h   78

18

SENTENCE PUNCTUATION PATTERNS (FOR COMMAS, SEMICOLONS, AND COLONS)

- (Independent clause).
  Everyone agreed with her suggestion.

- (Independent clause), and (independent clause).
  > but
  > for
  > or
  > nor
  > so
  > yet

  (the coordinating conjunctions)
  It took four years for the tree to produce a crop, but the fruit was abundant.

- (Independent clause); (independent clause).

  They arrived late; they offered no excuse.

- (Independent clause); thus, (independent clause).
  > however,
  > nevertheless,

  (or other independent clause markers)

  They arrived late; however, they offered no excuse.

- (Independent clause): (example, list of items, or explanation).
  They needed three items: a contract, her signature, and payment.

  He had only one fault: stupidity.

- (Independent clause): (independent clause).
  The candidate promised fewer taxes: he campaigned on a platform of eliminating property taxes.

- If (dependent clause), (independent clause).
  After
  Because
  Since
  When
  (or other dependent clause markers)
  If he studies more, his grades will improve.

- Independent clause) *if* (dependent clause).

  > *because*
  > *since*
  > *when*
  > *after*

  His grades will improve *if* he studies more.

- Subject, (nonessential dependent clause), verb/predicate.

  Mako, who is my cousin, is going to major in economics.

- Subject (essential dependent clause) verb/predicate.

  The movie that I rented last night was a box office failure.

19
COMMAS

19a   Commas between independent clauses

To use commas in independent clauses, you need to know the following:

Independent clause: a clause that can stand alone as a sentence
Compound sentence: a sentence with two or more independent clauses

When you join two or more independent clauses to make a compound sentence, use a comma and any of the seven joining words (coordinating conjunctions) listed below. Place a comma before the joining word. A compound sentence that does not have both the comma and the joining word is called a "comma splice" or "run on." (See section 12.)

The seven joining words

F or
A nd
N or   Vanilla is my favorite ice cream, but chocolate is
B ut   a close second.
O r
Y et
S o

(Some writers remember this list as "FAN BOYS," spelled out by the first letters of each word.)

Alternative: If the two independent clauses are very short, some writers leave out the comma.

It started raining but the game continued.

Alternative: If one of the independent clauses has a comma in it, use a semicolon instead as part of the joining pair.

Jillian, not Alesha, is captain of the team; **but** Alesha assists the coach during practices.

19b Commas after introductory word groups

If you include introductory words, phrases, or clauses before the main part of your sentence, place a comma after the introductory part to indicate the break.

Word: However, the farmer switched his crop to hay.
Phrase: Having lived in Korea, he enjoyed eating kim chee.
Clause: While I was working on my car, it started to rain.

Alternative: If the introductory element is short (no more than four or five words) and not likely to cause confusion, some writers leave out the comma. In the second example below, some readers might, at first, misread the sentence as stating that Matt was eating the cat, so a comma is needed there.

In most cases the statistics were reliable.

While Matt ate, the cat watched intently.

19c Commas before and after nonessential elements

When you include words, phrases, or clauses that are not essential to the meaning of the sentence and could be included in another sentence instead, place commas before and after the nonessential element.

Dr. Gupta, who is a cardiac surgeon, retired after fifty years of practice.

19d Commas in series and lists

Use commas when you have three or more items in a series or list.

The painting was done in blues, greens, and reds.

Wherever Mr. Chaugh went in the town, whatever he saw, and whomever he met, he was reminded of his childhood days there.

hint

Essential and Nonessential Clauses

You can decide if an element is essential by reading the sentence without it. If the meaning changes, that element is essential.

ESSENTIAL:

Apples *that are green* are usually very tart.

If you remove the clause "that are green," the statement changes to indicate that all apples are usually very tart.

NONESSENTIAL:

Apples, *which are Bryna's favorite fruit,* are on sale this week at the market.

Whether or not apples are Bryna's favorite fruit, they are still on sale this week at the market. Thus *which are Bryna's favorite fruit* is a nonessential element.

hint

Commas with Lists

Remember that there must be at least three items in a list in order to use commas. Some writers mistakenly put a comma between two items (often verbs) in a sentence.

No one had ever been able to locate the source of the river, and follow all its tributaries.

Alternative: Although most writers prefer to use the comma before "and" in a list of three of more items, some writers omit it.

The menu included omelets, pastas and salads.

19e Commas with adjectives

When you include two or more adjectives that describe a noun equally, separate the adjectives by commas. But not all adjectives describe a noun equally. A quick test to see if the adjectives are equal is to switch the order. If that still sounds correct to your ear, they're equal. Another test is to insert "and" between the adjectives.

happy, healthy child

(You can switch this to "healthy, happy child." You can also write "happy and healthy child.")

six large dogs

(You can not switch this to "large six dogs" or "six and large dogs.")

19f Commas with interrupting words or phrases

Use commas to set off words and phrases that interrupt the sentence.

Louisa Marcos, a math teacher, won the award.

The committee was, however, unable to agree.

The weather prediction, much to our surprise, was accurate.

19g Commas with dates, addresses, geographical names, and numbers

- With dates
  In a heading or list:
  February 25, 2003 (or) 25 February, 2003

  (No commas are needed to separate the day and month if the day is placed before the month.)

  In a sentence:

  The order was shipped on March 9, 2001, and not received until January 18, 2002.

- With addresses
  In a letter heading or on an envelope:

  Michael Cavanaugh, Jr.
  1404 Danton Drive
  Mineola, New Mexico 43723

  In a sentence:

  If you need more information, write to General Investment, 132 Maple Avenue, Martinsville, IL 60122.

- With geographical names
  Put a comma after each item in a place name.
  The conference next year will be in Chicago, Illinois, and
  in New Orleans, Louisiana, the year after that.

- With numbers
  8,190,434   27,000   1,300 (or) 1300
  The herd included 9,200 head of cattle.

19h Commas with quotations

Use a comma after expressions such as "he said."

Everyone was relieved when the chairperson said, "I
will table this motion until the next meeting."

19i Unnecessary commas

- Don't separate a subject from its verb.
Unnecessary: Increasing numbers of eighteen-year-olds
who vote are calling for stricter laws.

- Don't put a comma between two verbs.
Unnecessary: We offered to lend her our notes and
help her with the homework.

- Don't put a comma before every "and" or "but."
Unnecessary: The automobile industry now designs
fuel-efficient cars and is finding a large
market for them.

- Don't put a comma before a direct object, especially a
clause that starts with "that."
Unnecessary: Shaundra explained to me that she was
interested in hearing my view.

- Don't put a comma before a dependent clause when it comes
after an independent clause, except for extreme contrast.
Unnecessary: Deer populations are exploding because
their natural enemies are disappearing.
But: He was delighted with the news, although he needed some time to absorb it.

- Don't put a comma after "such as" or "especially."
Unnecessary: The take-out shop sold various soups , such
as minestrone, bean, and chicken noodle.

20

APOSTROPHES

20a Apostrophes with possessives

The apostrophe indicates a form of ownership, but this is not
always obvious. To test for possession, turn the two words
around into an "of the" phrase.

Manuel's skates   day's pay

the skates of Manuel   the pay of the day

- For singular nouns, use 's:

  book's cover   river's edge

- For singular nouns ending in –s, the –s after the apostrophe
  is optional if adding that –s makes the pronunciation difficult.

  James's coat   (or)   James' coat
  Mr. Mendoses' coat   grass's color

- For plural nouns ending in –s, add an apostrophe.

  books' covers   rivers' edges

- For plural nouns that do not end in –s, use 's.

  children's toys   oxen's tails

- For possession with two or more nouns:

When jointly owned: Jim and Sabrina's house

  (The house belongs jointly to both Jim and Sabrina.)

When individually owned: Jim's and Sabrina's plans

  (Jim and Sabrina each have their own plans.)

- For compound nouns:

  sister-in-law's car   secretary of state's office

- For indefinite pronouns (someone, everybody, etc.), use 's.

  no one's fault   somebody's hat

20b Apostrophes with contractions

Use the apostrophe to mark the omitted letter or letters in
contractions.

  it's = it is   don't = do not   they're = they are
  o'clock = of the clock   '89 = 1989

hint

Using Apostrophes

When you aren't sure where the apostrophe goes, follow this order. Notice that everything to the left of the apostrophe is the word and its plural. Everything after the plural is the possessive marker.

1. First write the word.
2. Then put in the plural if needed.
3. Then put in the apostrophe for possession.

	Word	Plural	Possessive marker
girl's glove:	girl		's
girls' gloves	girl	s	'
men's gloves	men		's

20c Apostrophes with plurals

Use the apostrophe to form the plurals of letters, abbreviations with periods, numbers, and words used as words.

She got all A's last semester.

They all have Ph.D.'s.

He picked all 5's in the lottery.

Melissa's "maybe's" were irritating.

Alternative: For some writers, the apostrophe is optional if the plural is clear.

| 9s | (or) | 9's |
| 1960s | (or) | 1960's |

But the apostrophe is needed here:

a's   A's

(Without the apostrophe, these might be the word "as.")

20d Unnecessary apostrophes

- Don't use an apostrophe with possessive pronouns (his, hers, its, yours, whose, etc.).

| **Not correct:** | his' arm | it's edge | yours' |
| **Revised:** | his arm | its edge | yours |

- Don't use an apostrophe with regular forms of plurals that do not show possession.

Not correct: The apple's were ripe. They reduced the prices!

Revised: The apples were ripe. They reduced the prices.

21

SEMICOLONS

The semicolon is a stronger mark of punctuation than the comma, and it is used with two kinds of closely related elements:

1. between independent clauses
2. between items in a series

It is almost like a period but does not come at the end of the sentence.

21a Semicolons to separate independent clauses

Use a semicolon when joining two independent clauses not joined by the seven connectors that require a comma: *and, but, for, or, nor, so,* and *yet.*

Two patterns for using semicolons:

1. independent clause **+ semicolon** + independent clause

The television shots showed extensive flood damage; houses were drifting downriver.

2. independent clause **+ semicolon + joining word + comma** + independent clause

There was no warning before the flood **; however,** no lives were lost.

Some frequently used joining words:

also,	finally,	instead,
besides,	for example,	on the contrary,
consequently,	however,	still,
even so,	in addition,	therefore,

Alternative: You can use a semicolon between two independent clauses joined with a coordinating conjunction (section 19a) when one of those clauses has its own comma. The semicolon makes the break between the two clauses clearer.

The police officer, who was the first person on the scene, wrote down the information; and the newspaper relied on his account of the accident.

21b Semicolons in a series

Normally, commas are used between three or more items in a series (page 63), but when each item has its own comma, a semicolon can be used between items for clarity.

Luanne, Mina, and Karla

(or)

Luane, my first cousin; Mina, my best friend; and Karla, my neighbor

21c Semicolons with quotation marks

If a semicolon is needed, put it after the quotation marks.

Her answer to every question was, "I'll think about that"; she wasn't ready to make a decision.

21d Unnecessary semicolons

- Don't use a semicolon between a clause and a phrase.
  Mexico is my favorite vacation place; especially the
  (should be a comma)
  beaches in Cancun.

- Don't use a semicolon in place of a dash, comma, or colon.
  She spent the funds on a necessary piece of equipment for her home office; a computer.
  (should be a colon)

22

QUOTATION MARKS

22a Quotation marks with direct quotations of prose, poetry, and dialogue

When you are writing the exact words you've seen in print or heard, use quotation marks when the quotation is less than four lines. For quotations that are four lines or longer, indent with no quotation marks.

> Mrs. Alphonse said, "The test scores show improved reading ability."

> In his poem, "Mending Wall," Robert Frost says: "Something there is that doesn't love a wall, / That sends the frozen-ground-swell under it."

> *(Notice the use of the slash to separate the two lines of poetry here.)*

> In his poem, "Mending Wall," Robert Frost questions the building of barriers and walls:

> Something there is that doesn't love a wall,

> That sends the frozen-ground-swell under it,

> And spills the upper boulders in the sun;

> And makes gaps even two can pass abreast.

- If you have a quotation within a quotation, use single quotation marks (') to set off the quotation enclosed inside the longer quotation.

> The newspaper reporter explained: "When I interviewed the lawyer, he said, 'No comment.'"

- If you leave words out of a quotation, use an ellipsis mark (three periods, see page 78) to indicate the missing words.

> The lawyer stated that he "would not ... under any circumstances violate the client's desire for privacy."

- If you add material within a quotation, use brackets [ ] (see section 23g).

> No one, explained the scientist, "could duplicate [Mayhiew's] experiment without having his notes."

- If you quote dialogue, write each person's speech as a separate paragraph. Closely related bits of narrative can be included with a paragraph with dialogue. If one person's speech goes on for several paragraphs, use quotation marks at the beginning of each paragraph, but not at the end of all paragraphs before the last one. To signal the end of the person's speech, put quotation marks at the end of the last paragraph.

22b Quotation marks for minor titles and parts of wholes

Use quotation marks for titles of parts of larger works (titles of book chapters, magazine articles, and episodes of television and radio series) and for short minor works (songs, short stories, essays, short poems, one-act plays). Do not use quotation marks when referring to the Bible or legal documents. For larger, more complete works, use italics (see section 25a).

"The Star Spangled Banner"   Exodus 2:1
"Think Warm Thoughts" (an episode on *ER*)

22c Quotation marks for words

Use quotation marks (or italics) for words that are used as words rather than for their meaning.

It was tiresome to hear her always inserting "cool" or "like" in each sentence she spoke.

22d Use of other punctuation with quotation marks

- Place commas and periods inside quotation marks. However, in MLA format, when you include a page reference, put the period after the page reference.

  . . . was an advantage," she said.

  . . . until tomorrow."

  . . . when the eclipse occurs" (9).

- Place colons and semicolons outside the quotation marks.

  . . . until tomorrow":   Moreover, this is done"; . . .

- Place the dash, exclamation mark, and question mark before the end set of quotation marks when the punctuation mark applies to the quotation. When the punctuation mark does not apply to the quotation, put the punctuation after the end set of quotation marks.

  He asked, "Should I return the book to her?"

  "Should I return the book to her?" he asked.

  Did Professor Sandifur really say, "No class tomorrow"?

22e Unnecessary quotation marks

Don't use quotation marks around titles of your essays, common nicknames, bits of humor, technical terms, and trite or well-known expressions.

~~"~~Bubba~~"~~ wanted the fastest ~~"~~modem~~"~~ available.

23
OTHER PUNCTUATION

23a Hyphens

Hyphens have a variety of uses:

- For compound words:
  Some compound words are one word:

  weekend   mastermind   granddaughter   homepage

  Some compound words are two words:

  high school   executive director   turn off

  Some compound words are joined by hyphens:

  father-in-law   president-elect   clear-cut

  Fractions and numbers from twenty-one to ninety-nine that are spelled out have hyphens.

  one-half   thirty-six   nine-tenths

  Particularly for new words or compounds that you are forming, check your dictionary. You may find an answer there, but not all hyphenated words appear there yet, especially new ones. Also, you will find that usage varies between dictionaries for some compounds.

  e-mail (or) email   witch-hunt (or) witch hunt

  wave-length (or) wavelength (or) wave length

  For hyphenated words in a series, use hyphens as follows:

  four-, five-, and six-page essays

- For two-word units:
Use a hyphen when two or more words placed before a noun work together as a single unit to describe the noun. When these words come after the noun, they are usually not

hyphenated. But don't use hyphens with adverbs such as *–ly* modifiers.

He needed up-to-date statistics. (or) He needed statistics that were up to date.

They repaired the six-inch pipe. (or) They repaired the pipe that was six inches long.

(but not with adverbs such as those ending in *–ly*) That was a widely known fact.

● For prefixes, suffixes, and letters joined to a word:
Use hyphens between words and prefixes *self-*, *all-*, and *ex-*.

self-contained   all-American   ex-president

For other prefixes, such as *anti-*, *pro-*, and *co-*, use the dictionary as a guide.

co-author   antibacterial   pro-choice

Use a hyphen when joining a prefix to a capitalized word or to figures and numbers.

anti-American   non-Catholic   pre-1998

Use a hyphen when you add the suffix *-elect*.

president-elect

Use a hyphen to avoid doubling vowels and tripling consonants and to avoid ambiguity.

anti-intellectual   bell-like   re-cover   re-creation

● To divide words between syllables when the last part of the word appears on the next line.

Every spring the nation's capitol is flooded with tourists snapping pictures of the cherry blossoms.

When dividing words at the end of a line:

● Don't divide one-syllable words.
● Don't leave one or two letters at the end of a line.
● Don't put fewer than three letters on the next line.
● Don't divide the last word in a paragraph or the last word on a page.
● Divide compound words so that the hyphen for the compound comes at the end of the line. Or put the whole compound word on the next line.

23b Colons

Use colons as follows:

● To announce elements at the end of the sentence

The company sold only electronics they could service: computers, stereos, CD players, and television sets.

● To separate independent clauses
Use a colon instead of a semicolon to separate two independent clauses when the second restates or amplifies the first.

The town council voted not to pave the gravel roads outside of town: they did not have the funds for road improvement.

● To announce long quotations
Use a colon to announce a long quotation (more than one sentence) or a quotation not introduced by words such as "said," "remarked," or "stated."

The candidate for office offered only one reason to vote for her: "I will not raise parking meter rates."

● In salutations and between elements

Dear Dr. Philippa:	6:12 a.m.
Genesis 1:8	scale of 1:3
Maryland: My Home	Chicago: Howe Books

● With quotation marks
If a colon is needed, put it after the closing quotation mark.

"One sign of intelligence is not arguing with your boss": that was her motto for office harmony.

● Unnecessary colons
Do not use a colon after a verb or phrases like "such as" or "consisted of."

Not correct:	The two most valuable players were: Timon Lasmon and Maynor Field.
Revised:	The two most valuable players were Timon Lasmon and Maynor Field.
Not correct:	The camping equipment consisted of: tents, bug spray, lanterns, matches, and dehydrated food.
Revised:	The camping equipment consisted of tents, bug spray, lanterns, matches, and dehydrated food.

23c End punctuation

Periods

Use a period at the end of a sentence that is a statement, mild command, indirect question, or polite question where an answer isn't expected.

> Electric cars are growing in popularity. (statement)

> Do not use your calculator during the test. (mild command)

> Would you please let me know when you're done. (polite question)

Use a period with abbreviations, but don't use a second period if the abbreviation is at the end of the sentence.

> R.S.V.P.　　U.S.A.　　Dr.　　Mr.　　8 a.m.

A period is not needed after agencies, common abbreviations, names of well-known companies, and state abbreviations used by the U.S. Postal Service.

> NATO　　NBA　　CIA　　YMCA　　IBM　　DNA　　TX

Put periods that follow quotations inside the quotation mark. But if there is a reference to a source, put the period after the reference.

> She said, "I'm going to Alaska next week."

> Neman notes "the claim is unfounded" (6).

Question marks

Use a question mark after a direct question but not after an indirect one.

> Did anyone see my laptop computer? (direct question)

> Jules wonders if he should buy a new stereo. (indirect question)

Place a question mark inside the quotation marks if the quotation is a question. Place the question mark outside the quotation marks if the whole sentence is a question.

> Drora asked, "Is she on time?"

> Did Eli really say, "I'm in love"?

Question marks may be used between parts of a series.

> Would you like to see a movie? go shopping? eat at a restaurant?

Use a question mark to indicate doubt about the correctness of the preceding date, number, or other piece of information. But do not use it to indicate sarcasm.

> The ship landed in Greenland about 1521(?) but did not keep a record of where it was.

Not correct: Matti's sense of humor (?) evaded me.
Revised: Matti's sense of humor evaded me.

Exclamation marks

● Use the exclamation mark after a strong command or a statement said with great emphasis or with strong feeling. But do not overuse the exclamation mark.

> I'm absolutely delighted!

> **Unnecessary:**   Wow! What a great party! I enjoyed every minute of it!

Enclose the exclamation mark within the quotation marks only if it belongs to the quotation.

> He threw open the door and exclaimed, "I've won the lottery!"

23d   Dashes

The dash is somewhat informal but can be used to add emphasis or clarity, to mark an interruption or shift in tone, or to introduce a list. Use two hyphens to indicate the dash when you are typing, and do not leave a space before or after the hyphen.

> To be a millionaire, the owner of a yacht, and a race car driver—this was his goal.

> The cat looked at me so sweetly—with a dead rat in its mouth.

23e   Slashes

Use the slash to mark the end of a line of poetry and to indicate acceptable alternatives. For poetry, leave a space before and after the slash. For alternatives, leave no space. The slash is also used in World Wide Web addresses.

> pass/fail   and/or

> He reiterated Milton's great lines: "The mind is its own place, and in itself / Can make a Heaven of Hell, a Hell of Heaven."

> **http://www.whitehouse.gov**

23f   Parentheses

Use parentheses to enclose supplementary or less important material added as further explanation or example or to enclose figures or letters that enumerate a list.

> The newest officers of the club (those elected in May) were installed at the ceremony.

> They had three items on the agenda: (1) a revised budget, (2) the parking permits, and (3) a new election procedure.

23g   Brackets

Use brackets to add your comments or additional explanation within a quotation and to replace parentheses within parentheses. The Latin word *sic* in brackets means that you copied the original quotation exactly as it appeared, but you think there's an error there.

> We all agreed with Fellner's claim that "this great team [the Chicago Bears] is destined to go to the Super Bowl next year."

> The lawyer explained, "We discussed the matter in a fiendly [*sic*] manner."

> For the use of brackets around ellipsis points in MLA format, see 23h.

23h   Omitted words/ellipsis

Use an ellipsis (a series of three periods, with one space between each period) to indicate that you are omitting words or part of a sentence from the source you are quoting. If you omit a whole sentence or paragraph, add a fourth period with no space after the last word preceding the ellipsis.

"modern methods . . . with no damage."

"the National Forest System . . . " (Smith 9).

"federal lands. . . . They were designated for preservation."

If you omit words immediately after a punctuation mark in the original, include that mark in your sentence.

"because of this use of the forest, . . . "

V Mechanics

Contents of this section

24 Capitalization   83

  24a Proper nouns vs. common nouns   83

  24b Capitals in sentences, quotations, and lists   85

25 Italics   86

  25a Titles   86

  25b Other uses of italics/underlining   87

26 Numbers   87

27 Abbreviations   89

  27a Abbreviating titles   89

  27b Abbreviating places   89

  27c Abbreviating numbers   90

  27d Abbreviating measurements   90

  27e Abbreviating dates   90

  27f Abbreviating names of familiar organizations and other entities   91

  27g Abbreviating Latin expressions and documentation terms   91

28 Spelling   92

  28a Some spelling guidelines   93

  28b Sound-alike words (homonyms)   96

Questions to ask yourself

In this section are the rules for matters of mechanics, including capitalization, italics, numbers, abbreviations, and spelling.

	SECTION	PAGE
• Should I capitalize words such as "spring," "kleenex," "sister," and "history"?	24a	83
• When I have a quotation, when do I capitalize the first word of the quotation?	24b	85

- Should I capitalize the first word in each item in a list?   24b   85

- Are book titles underlined, or should I use italics?   25   86

- When do I use italics instead of quotation marks with various kinds of titles and names?   25a   86

- Should I write out "six" or use the numeral "6"?   26   87

- When do I write "May fifth," and when do I write "May 5"?   26   88

- Which titles of people can be abbreviated?   27a   89

- Do I write "U.S." or "United States"?   27b   89

- Do I write "six million" or "6,000,000"?   27c   90

- Should I write CIA or C.I.A.?   27f   91

- There are some Latin abbreviations such as "cf." and "e.g." What do they mean?   27g   91

- Should I use "e.g." or the English phrase for it?   27g   91

- How useful is a spell checker?   28   92

- What are some strategies for checking spelling?   28   92

- What's the "ie/ei" rule that tells me whether to write "receive" or "recieve"?   28a   93

- How can I remember whether to write words such as "beginning" (with two "n's") or "begining (with one "n")?   28a   94

- What's the rule for the "-e" in words such as "truly" or "likely"?   28a   94

- Are words such as "data" and "media" singular or plural?   28a   94

- Is it correct to include an apostrophe for plurals such as the following:

  three crayons' in the box   28a   94

- What's the difference in meaning and spelling for words such as these sound-alike words?
  -accept and except
  -affect and effect
  -its and it's
  -your and you're   28b   96

24

CAPITALIZATION

24a Proper nouns vs. common nouns

Capitalize proper nouns, words that name one particular thing, most often a person or place rather than a general type or group of things.

Listed here are categories of words that should be capitalized. If you are not sure about a particular word, check your dictionary.

Proper noun	Common noun
James Joyce	man
Thanksgiving	holiday
University of Maine	state university
Macintosh	personal computer
May	spring

---

hint

Capitalizing Academic Subjects

Remember that general names of academic subjects, such as "history" or "economics," are not capitalized. However, the name of a specific department will be capitalized: The History Department. (This proper noun describes a particular department. Another history department might be called The Department of Historical Studies.)

- *Persons*

    Caitlin Baglia   Hannah Kaplan   Masuto Tatami
- *Places, including geographical regions*

    Indianapolis   Ontario   Midwest
- *Peoples and their languages*

    Spanish   Dutch   English
- *Religions and their followers*

    Buddhist   Judaism   Christianity

- *Members of national, political, racial, social, civic, and athletic groups*

Democrat	African American	Chicago Bears
Friends of the Library	Danes	Olympics Committee

- *Institutions and organizations*

Supreme Court	Legal Aid Society	Lions Club

- *Historical documents*

Magna Carta	The Declaration of Independence

- *Periods and events (but not century numbers)*

Middle Ages	Boston Tea Party	eighteenth century

- *Days, months, and holidays (but not seasons)*

Monday	Thanksgiving	winter

- *Trademarks*

Coca-Cola	Kodak	Ford

- *Holy books and words denoting the Supreme Being (including pronouns)*

Talmud	wonders of His creation	the Bible

- *Words and abbreviations derived from specific names (but not the names of things that have lost the specific association and now refer to the general type)*

Stalinism	NATO	CBS
french fry	pasteurize	italics

- *Place words ("City" or "Mountain") that are part of specific names*

New York City	Zion National Park	Wall Street

- *Titles that precede people's names (but not titles that follow names)*

Aunt Sylvia	President Taft	Governor Sam Parma
Sylvia, my aunt		Sam Parma, governor

- *Words that indicate family relationships when used as a substitute for a specific name*

  Here is a gift for Mother.   She sent a gift to her mother.

- *Titles of books, magazines, essays, movies, and other works, but not articles ("a," "an," "the"), short prepositions ("to," "by," "on"), or short joining words ("and," "or") unless they are the first or last word. With hyphenated words, capital-ize the first and other important words. (For APA style, which has different rules, see section 41.)*

The Taming of the Shrew   "The Sino-Soviet Conflict"

A Dialogue Between Body and Soul   "My Brother-in-Law"

- *The pronoun "I" and the interjection "O" (but not the word "oh")*

  "Sail on, sail on, O ship of state," I said as the canoe sank.

- Words placed after a prefix that are normally capitalized

  un-American   anti-Semitic   ex-wife

24b   Capitals in sentences, quotations, and lists

- Capitalize the first word in a sentence.
- Capitalize the first word of a sentence in parentheses but not when the parenthetical sentence is inserted within another sentence.
- Do not capitalize the first word in a series of questions in which the questions are not full sentences.

  What did the settlers want from the natives? food? horses?

- Capitalize the first word of directly quoted speech, but not for the second portion of interrupted direct quota-tions or quoted phrases or clauses integrated into the sentence.

  She answered, "No one will understand."

  "No one," she answered, "will understand."

  When Hemmings declined the nomination, he said that "this is not a gesture of support for the other candidate."

- The first word in a list after a colon if each item in the list is a complete sentence.

  The rule books were very clear: (1) No player could con-tinue to play after committing two fouls. (2) Substitute players would be permitted only with the consent of the other team. (3) Every eligible player had to be desig-nated before the game.

(or)

The rule books were very clear:

1. No player could continue to play after committing two fouls.
2. Substitute players would be permitted only with the consent of the other team.
3. Every eligible player had to be designated before the game.

25

ITALICS

When you are typing or writing by hand, use underlining (a printer's mark to indicate words to be set in italic type font) for the kinds of titles and names indicated in this section. If your computer has an italic font, use that instead of underlining.

italics type font = *italics*
underlining = <u>underlining</u>

25a Titles

Use italics for titles and names of long or complete works, including the following:

Books:	*Catcher in the Rye*
Magazines:	*Time*
Newspapers:	*New York Times*
Works of art (visual and performance):	*Swan Lake*
Pamphlets:	*Coping with Diabetes*
Television and radio series (not titles of individual episodes):	*Sixty Minutes*
Films and videos:	*Titanic*
Long plays:	*Macbeth*
Long musical works:	*Symphony in B Minor*
Long poems:	*Paradise Lost*
Software:	*PageMaker*
Recordings:	*Yellow Submarine*

- Do not italicize or use quotation marks for the Bible and other major religious works or for legal documents.

  Bible, Torah, Koran   The Constitution

- For shorter works or parts of whole works, use quotation marks (see section 22b).

25b Other uses of italics/underlining

- Names of ships, airplanes, and trains

    Queen Mary   *Concorde*   *Orient Express*

- Foreign words and scientific names of plants and animals:

    in vino veritas   *Canis lupis*

- Words used as words or letters, numbers, and symbols used as examples or terms:

    Some words, such as *Kleenex,* are brand names.
    The letters *ph* and *f* often have the same sound.

- Words being emphasized

    It *never* snows here in April.

    (Use italics or underlining for emphasis only sparingly.)

    Do not use italics or underlining for the following:

- Words of foreign origin that are now part of English:

    alumni   karate   hacienda

- Titles of your own papers

26

NUMBERS

Style manuals for different fields and companies vary. The suggestions for writing numbers offered here are generally useful as a guide for academic writing.

- Spell out numbers that can be expressed in one or two words and use figures for other numbers.

Words	Figures
two pounds	126 days
six million dollars	$31.95
thirty-one years	6.381 bushels
eighty-three people	4.6 liters

- When you write several numbers, be consistent in choosing words or figures.

    He didn't know whether to buy ~~nine~~ ⁹ gallons of milk or 125 separate small containers.

1. Use figures for the following:

- **Days and years**
  December 12, 1921   (or)   12 December 1921
  A. D. 1066
  in 1971–72   (or)   in 1971–1972
  the 1990's   (or)   the 1990s

- **Time of day**
  8 p.m. (or) P.M.   (or)   eight o'clock in the evening
  2:30 a.m. (or) A.M.   (or)   half past two in the morning

- **Addresses**
  15 Tenth Avenue
  350 West 114 Street   (or)   350 West 114th Street
  Prescott, AZ 86301

- **Identification numbers**
  Room 8   Channel 18
  Interstate 65   Henry VIII

- **Page and division of books and plays**
  page 30   chapter 6
  act 3, scene 3   (or) Act III, Scene iii

- **Decimals and percentages**
  2.7 average   12 and 1/2 percent
  0.036 metric ton

- **Numbers in series and statistics**
  two apples, six oranges, and three bananas
  115 feet by 90 feet

  (Be consistent whichever form you choose.)

- **Large round numbers**
  four billion dollars   (or) $4 billion
  16,500,000   (or)   16.5 million

- **Repeated numbers (in legal or commercial writing)**
  The bill will not exceed one hundred (100) dollars.

2. Do not use figures for the following:

- **Numbers that can be expressed in one or two words**
  the eighties   the twentieth century

- **Dates when the year is omitted**
  June sixth   May fourteenth

- **Numbers beginning a sentence**
  Ten percent of the year's crop was harvested.

27

ABBREVIATIONS

In government, business, and the fields of social science, science, and engineering, abbreviations are used frequently. But in academic writing in the humanities, only a limited number of abbreviations are generally used.

27a Abbreviating titles

- *Mr.*, *Mrs.*, and *Ms.* are abbreviated when used as titles before the name.

  Mr. Tanato   Mrs. Whitman   Ms. Ojebwa

- *Dr.* and *St.* ("Saint") are abbreviated only when they immediately precede a name; they are written out when they appear after the name.

  Dr. Martin Klein   (but)   Martin Klein, doctor
                                                        of pediatrics

- *Prof.*, *Sen.*, *Gen.*, *Capt.*, and similar abbreviated titles can be used when they appear in front of a name or before initials and a last name. But they are not abbreviated when they appear with the last name only.

  Gen. R.G. Fuller   (but) General Fuller

- *Sr.*, *Jr.*, *Ph.D.*, *M.F.A.*, *C.P.A.*, and other abbreviated academic titles and professional degrees can be used after the name.

  Lisle Millen, Ph.D.   Charleen Dyer, C.P.A.

- *Bros.*, *Co.*, and similar abbreviations are used only if they are part of the exact name.

  Marshall Field & Co.   Brown Bros.

27b Abbreviating places

In general, spell out names of states, countries, continents, streets, rivers, and so on. But there are several exceptions:

- Use the abbreviation *D.C.* in Washington, D.C.
- Use *U.S.* only as an adjective, not as a noun.

  U.S. training bases training   bases in the United States

- If you include a full address in a sentence, citing the street, city, and state, you can use the postal abbreviation for the state.

  For further information, write to the company at 100 Peachtree Street, Atlanta, GA 30300 for a copy of their catalogue.

  (but)

  The company's headquarters in Atlanta, Georgia, will soon be moved.

27c Abbreviating numbers

- Write out numbers that can be expressed in one or two words.

  nine   twenty-seven   135

- The dollar sign abbreviation is generally acceptable when the whole phrase will be more than three words.

  $36 million   one million dollars

- For temperatures, use words if only a few temperatures are cited, but use figures if temperatures are cited frequently in a paper.

  ten degrees below zero, Fahrenheit   − 10° F

27d Abbreviating measurements

Spell out units of measurement, such as acre, meter, foot, and percent, but use abbreviations in tables, graphs, and figures.

27e Abbreviating dates

Spell out months and days of the week. With dates and times, the following are acceptable:

57 A.D. (or) 57 B.C.E. (Before the Common Era)

A.D. 329 (The abbreviation A.D. is placed before the date.)

a.m., p.m. (or) A.M., P.M.

EST (or) E.S.T., est

27f Abbreviating names of familiar organizations and other entities

Use abbreviations for names of organizations, agencies, countries, and things usually referred to by their capitalized initials.

NASA	IBM	VCR	AFL-CIO
UNICEF	USSR	CNN	YMCA

If an abbreviation may not be familiar to your readers, spell out the term the first time you use it, with the abbreviation in parentheses. From then on, you can use the abbreviation.

> The Myer-Briggs Type Inventory (MBTI) is offered in the dean's Career Counseling Office. Students who take the MBTI can then speak to a career counselor about the results.

27g Abbreviating Latin expressions and documentation terms

Some Latin expressions always appear as abbreviations:

Abbreviation	Meaning
cf.	compare
e.g.	for example
et al.	and others
etc.	and so forth
vs. (or) v.	versus
N.B.	note well

These abbreviations are appropriate for bibliographies and footnotes, as well as in informal writing, but for formal writing, use the English phrase instead.

Because the format for abbreviations in documentation may vary from one style manual to another, use the abbreviations listed in the particular style manual you are following. (See, for example, the suggestions for MLA and APA in sections 40–41.)

Abbreviation	Meaning
abr.	abridged
anon.	anonymous
ed., eds.	editor, editors
p., pp.	page, pages
vol., vols.	volume, volumes

28

SPELLING

English spelling is difficult because it contains so many words from other languages that have different spelling conventions. In addition, unlike some other languages that have only one spelling for a sound, English has several ways to spell some sounds. But it's important to spell correctly, to be sure that your reader understands your writing. Also, misspelled words can signal to the reader that the writer is careless and not very knowledgeable.

Because no writer wants to lose credibility, correct spelling is necessary. These suggestions should help to ensure that your papers are spelled correctly:

- *Learn some spelling rules.*

See the following pages for some useful rules.

- *Learn your own misspelling patterns and troublesome words.*

When you identify a word that tends to cause you problems, write it down in a list and, if possible, make up your own memory aid. For example, if you can't remember whether "dessert" is that barren sandy place like the Mohave (or Sahara) or the sweet treat you eat after a meal, try making up some rule or statement that will stick in your mind. For "dessert" and "desert," you might try a reminder such as the fact that the word for the sweet treat has two *s*'s, and you like seconds on desserts.

- *Use a spell checker.*

Spell checkers are helpful tools, but they can't catch all spelling errors. Although different spell checking programs have different capabilities, they are not foolproof, and they do make mistakes. Most spell checkers do not catch the following types of errors:

1. **Omitted words**
2. **Sound-alike words (homonyms)**
   Some words sound alike but are spelled differently. For example, the spell checker cannot distinguish between "there" and "their."
3. **Substitution of one word for another**
   If you meant to write "one" and typed "own" instead, the spell checker will not flag that.

4. **Proper nouns**

   Some well-known proper nouns, such as
   "Washington," may be in the spell checker, but many
   will not be.

5. **Misspelled words**

   If you have misspelled a word, the spell checker may
   be able to suggest the correct spelling. But for other
   misspellings, the spell checker will not be able to
   offer the correct spelling. You will need to know how
   to use a dictionary to look it up.

● **Learn how to proofread.**

Proofreading requires slow and careful reading to catch misspellings and typographical errors. This is hard to do because we are used to reading quickly and seeing a group of
words together. Some useful proofreading strategies are the
following:

1. **Slow down.**

   For best results, slow down your reading rate so you
   actually see each word.

2. **Focus on each word.**

   One way to slow down is to point a pencil or pen at
   each word as you say it aloud or to yourself. Note
   with a check in the margin any word that doesn't
   look quite right, and come back to it later.

3. **Read backward.**

   Don't read right to left, as you usually do, or you will
   soon slip back into a more rapid reading rate. Instead,
   move backward through each line from right to left.
   In this way, you won't be listening for meaning or
   checking for grammatical errors

4. **Cover up distractions.**

   To focus on each word, hold a sheet of paper or a
   notecard under the line being read. That way you
   won't be distracted by other words on the page.

28a   Some spelling guidelines

1. **ie/ei**

   > Write *i* before *e*
   > Except after *c*
   > Or when sounded like "ay"
   > As in "neighbor" or "weigh."

This rhyme reminds you to write *ie*, except under two conditions:

- When the two letters follow a *c*
- When the two letters sound like "ay" (as in "day")

Some *ie* words		**Some *ei* words**	
believe	niece	ceiling	eight
chief	relief	conceit	receive
field	yield	deceive	vein

Some exceptions to this rule

conscience	foreign	neither	species
counterfeit	height	science	sufficient
either	leisure	seize	weird

2. **Doubling consonants**

- **One-syllable words**

   If the word ends in a single short vowel and then a consonant, double the last consonant when you add a suffix beginning with a vowel.

drag	dragged	dragging
star	starred	starring
tap	tapped	tapping
wet	wetted	wetting

- **Two-syllable words**

   If the word has two or more syllables and then a single vowel and a consonant, double the consonant when (1) you are adding a suffix that begins with a vowel, and (2) the last syllable of the base word is accented.

begin		beginning
occur	occurred	occurring
omit	omitted	omitting
prefer	preferred	preferring
refer	referred	referring

3. **Final silent *–e***

   Drop the final silent *–e* when you add a suffix beginning with a vowel. But keep the final *–e* when the suffix begins with a consonant.

line	lining	care	careful
smile	smiling	like	likely

Words such as "true/truly" and "argue/argument" are exceptions to this.

hint

Avoiding Wrong Apostrophes

Some writers mistakenly add an apostrophe for plurals.

one book   *not correct:* two books'   *revised:* two books

a monkey   *not correct:* six monkeys'   *revised:* six monkeys

4. **Plurals**

   Generally, most words add –*s* for plurals. But add –*es*
   when the word ends in –*s*, -*sh*, -*ch*, -*x*, or in -*z* because
   another syllable is needed.

   one apple   two apples
   one box   two boxes
   a brush   some brushes

   With phrases and hyphenated words, pluralize the last
   word unless another word is more important.

   one videocassette recorder   two videocassette recorders
   one sister-in-law   two sisters-in-law

   For words ending in a consonant plus –*y*, change the –*y*
   to –*i* and add –*es*. For proper nouns, keep the –*y*.

   one boy   two boys
   one company   two companies
   Mr. Henry   the Henrys

   For some words, the plural is formed by changing the
   base word. Some other words have the same form for
   singular and plural. And other words, taken from other
   languages, form the plural in the same way as the
   original language.

   one child   two children
   one woman   two women
   one deer   two deer
   one datum   much data
   one medium   many media
   a phenomenon   some phenomena

28b Sound-alike words (homonyms)

accept:	to agree/receive	accept a gift
except:	other than	all except her
affect:	to influence	Insomnia affects me.
effect:	a result	What was the effect?
hear:	(verb)	Did you hear that?
here:	indicates a place	Come here.
its:	shows possession	Its leg is broken.
it's:	= it is	It's raining out.
quiet:	no noise	Be quiet!
quite:	very	That's quite nice.
quit:	give up	He quit his job.
than:	used to compare	taller than I
then:	time word	Then he went home.
to:	preposition	to the house
too:	also (or) very	She is too tired to work.
were:	verb	were singing
we're:	= we are	We're going on vacation.
where:	in what place	Where is he?
who's:	= who is	Who's going to the movies?
whose:	shows possession	Whose book is this?
your:	shows possession	What is your name?
you're:	= you are	You're right!

VI MULTILINGUAL SPEAKERS (ESL)

CONTENTS OF THIS SECTION

29 American Style in Writing   99

30 Verbs   100

    30a Verb tenses   100

    30b Helping verbs with main verbs   102

    30c Two-word (phrasal) verbs   102

    30d Verbs with "–Ing" and with "to" + verb form   102

31 Nouns (Count and Noncount)   103

32 Articles ("A", "An", and "The")   104

33 Prepositions   105

34 Omitted/Repeated Words   106

    34a Omitted words   106

    34b Repeated words   107

35 Idioms   108

QUESTIONS TO ASK YOURSELF

This section includes topics that are especially useful for students whose first language is not English.

	SECTION	PAGE
• What are some of the characteristics of American style in writing?	29	99
• Are conciseness and a clearly announced topic important in American writing?	29	99
• How important is it in American writing to cite sources? Why?	29	99
• What are the verb tenses in English and how are they used?	30a	100

- How do the helping verbs ("be," "do," "have") and the modal verbs (such as "may" and "could") combine with the main verb?   30b   102

- Is there a difference in meaning when different second (or third) words are combined with the main verb (such as "turn on" and "turn out")?   30c   102

- Which is correct?
  -She enjoys to go/going swimming.
  -Mi Lan wants to ask/asking you for a favor.   30d   102

- Is it correct to say "two furnitures" and "six chairs"?   31   103

- When do I use "the," and when do I use "a/an"?   32   104

- Which is the correct preposition?
  -<u>in/on/at</u> Friday   <u>on/at/in</u> the bottle
  -<u>in/on/at</u> 2 p.m.   <u>six of/for</u> the books
  -<u>on/at/in</u> home   a gift <u>of/for</u> her   33   105

- Why are the following sentences not correct?

  - Is going to be a test tomorrow.   34a   106

  - My teacher very good speaker.   34b   107

- Some phrases in English do not mean exactly what the words seem to mean (such as "dead as a doornail"). How do I learn what these mean?   35   108

29

AMERICAN STYLE IN WRITING

If your first language is not English, you may have some writing style preferences and some questions about English grammar and usage. Some of these matters will be addressed in this section. If you have individual questions and are a student at an institution with a writing center, talk with a tutor in the writing center.

Your style preferences and customs will depend on what language(s) you are more familiar with, but in general, consider the following differences between the language(s) you know and academic style in American English. Academic style in American English is characterized by the following:

Conciseness

In some languages, writers strive for a type of eloquence marked by a profusion of words and phrases that elaborate on the same topic. Effective academic and public writing in American English, however, is concise, eliminating extra or unnecessary words.

Clearly announced topic at the beginning of the paper

In some languages, the topic is delayed or not immediately announced. Instead, there are suggestions that will lead readers to formulate the main ideas for themselves. In American English, there is a decided preference for announcing the topic in the opening paragraph or somewhere near the beginning of the paper.

Tight organization

Although digressions into side topics or related matters can be interesting and are expected in the writing in some languages, American academic writing stays on topic and does not wander off into other topics.

Clearly cited sources

In some languages, there is less attention to citing sources of information, ideas, or the exact words used by others. In American academic writing, however, writers are expected to cite all sources other than what is generally known by most people. Otherwise, the writer is in danger of being viewed as plagiarizing.

When you are considering matters of grammar and usage, the following are topics that may cause difficulty as you write in English.

30

VERBS

Unlike some other languages, verbs are required in English sentences because they indicate time and person (see section 13b).

30a Verb tenses

Progressive tenses: use a form of "be" plus "*–ing*" form of the verb such as "going" or "running".

She is going to the concert tonight.

Perfect tenses: use a form of "have" plus the past participle, such as "walked" or "gone".

1. **Present tense**

● Simple present

presents action or condition

> They <u>ride</u> their bikes.

general or literary truth

> States <u>defend</u> their rights.

> Shakespeare <u>uses</u> humor effectively.

habitual action

> I <u>like</u> orange juice for breakfast.

future time

> The plane <u>arrives</u> at 10 p.m. tonight.

● Present progressive

activity in progress, not finished, or continued

> I <u>am majoring</u> in engineering.

- Present perfect

  action that began in the past and leads up to and continues into the present

  > He <u>has worked</u> here since May.

- Present perfect progressive

  action begun in the past, continues to the present, and may continue into the future

  > I <u>have been thinking</u> about buying a car.

2. **Past tense**

- Simple past

  completed action or condition

  > She <u>walked</u> to class.

- Past progressive

  past action over a period of time or interrupted by another action

  > The engine <u>was running</u> while he waited.

- Past perfect

  action or event completed before another event in the past

  > He <u>had</u> already <u>left</u> when I arrived.

- Past perfect progressive

  ongoing condition in the past that has ended

  > She had <u>been speaking</u> to that group.

3. **Future tense**

- Simple

  actions or events in the future

  > They <u>will arrive</u> tomorrow.

- Future progressive

  future action that will continue for some time

  > I <u>will be expecting</u> you.

- Future perfect

  Actions that will be completed by or before a specified time in the future

  > By Monday, I <u>will have cleaned up</u> that cabinet.

● Future perfect progressive

ongoing actions or conditions until a specified time in the future

> She <u>will have been traveling</u> for six months by the time she arrives here.

30b Helping verbs with main verbs

Helping (or auxiliary) verbs combine with other verbs. (See section 13b.)

> **be:** "be," "am," "is," "are," "was," "were," "being," "been"
> **do:** "do," "does," "did"
> **have:** "have," "has," "had"
> **modals:** "can," "could," "may," "might," "must," "shall," "should," "will," "would," "ought to"

Modal verbs are helping verbs that indicate possibility, uncertainty, necessity, or advisability. Use the base form of the verb after a modal.

> <u>May</u> I <u>ask</u> you a question?

30c Two-word (phrasal) verbs

Some verbs are followed by a second (and sometimes a third) word that combine to indicate the meaning. Many dictionaries will indicate the meanings of these phrasal verbs.

> look over (examine): She <u>looked over</u> the contract.
> look up (search): I will <u>look up</u> his phone number.
> look out for (watch for): <u>Look out for</u> the puddle.

The second word of some of these verbs can be separated from the main verb by a noun or pronoun:

> add (it) up put (the phone call) off

In other cases, the second word cannot be separated from the main verb:

> back out of the garage get through the mob

30d Verbs with "–ing" and with "to" + verb form

Some verbs combine only with the "–ing" form of the verb; some verbs combine only with the "to" + verb form (the infinitive form); some verbs can be followed by either form.

Verbs followed only by –ing forms:

admit	enjoy	recall
appreciate	finish	regret
deny	keep	stop
dislike	practice	suggest

He <u>admits spending</u> that money.

Verbs followed only by "to" + verb:

agree	have	plan
ask	mean	promise
claim	need	wait
decide	offer	want

She <u>needs to take</u> that medicine.

Verbs that can be followed by either form:

begin	intend	prefer
continue	like	start
hate	love	try

They <u>begin to sing</u>. (or) They <u>begin singing</u>.

31

NOUNS (COUNT AND NONCOUNT)

There are two kinds of nouns—proper nouns and common nouns. Proper nouns name specific things (such as Lake Michigan or Mexico) and begin with capital letters (see section 24). Other nouns are common nouns, and they are either nouns that can be counted (count nouns) or nouns that cannot be counted (noncount nouns).

Count nouns: name things that can be counted because those things can be divided into separate and distinct units. Count nouns have plurals and usually refer to things that can be seen, heard, touched, tasted, or smelled.

apple:	one apple, some apples
chair:	a chair, six chairs
child:	the child, all of the children

hint

Noncount Nouns

Many foods are noncount nouns:

coffee	tea	corn	water
cereal	milk	candy	flour

Noncount nouns: name things that cannot be counted because they are abstractions or things that cannot be cut into parts. Noncount nouns do not have plurals, do not have "a" or "an" preceding them, and may have a collective meaning.

Some noncount nouns:

air	humor	oil	weather
furniture	money	beauty	clothing

To indicate amounts for noncount nouns, use a count noun that quantifies:

a pound of coffee   a loaf of bread
a quart of milk   a great deal of money

32
ARTICLES ("A", "AN", AND "THE")

A/An

"A" and "an" identify nouns in a general or indefinite way and refer to any member of a group. "A" and "an" are generally used with singular count nouns.

Please hand me <u>a</u> towel.

(This sentence does not specify which towel, just any towel that is handy.)

The

"The" identifies a particular or specific noun in a group or a noun already specified in a previous phrase or sentence. "The" may be used with singular or plural nouns.

Please hand me <u>the</u> towel that is on the table.

(This sentence means that not just any towel is being requested—only the one particular towel that is on the table.)

<u>A</u> new computer model is being introduced. <u>The</u> new model will probably cost more.

("A" is used first in a general way to mention the model, and then, because it has been specified, it is referred to as "the" model.)

Some uses of "the"

- Use "the" when an essential phrase or clause follows the noun.

  <u>The</u> man who addressed the group is my art teacher.

- Use "the" when the noun refers to a class as a whole.

  He explained that <u>the</u> fox is a nocturnal animal.

- Use "the" with names composed partly of common nouns and plural nouns.

  <u>the</u> British Commonwealth   <u>the</u> United States
  <u>the</u> Netherlands   <u>the</u> University of Illinois

- Use "the" with names that refer to rivers, oceans, seas, deserts, forests, gulfs, and peninsulas and with points of the compass used as names.

  <u>the</u> Nile   <u>the</u> Persian Gulf   <u>the</u> South

- Use "the" with superlatives

  <u>the</u> best reporter   <u>the</u> most expensive car

No articles

Articles are not used with names of streets, cities, states, countries, continents, lakes, parks, mountains, names of languages, sports, holidays, universities, and academic subjects.

He traveled to Africa.   She is studying Chinese.
He likes to watch tennis.   He graduated from Brandeis.

33

PREPOSITIONS

Prepositions in English show relationships between words and are difficult to master because they are idiomatic. The following lists some of the most commonly used prepositions and the relationships they indicate.

Prepositions of time

On   used with days

         on Monday

At   used with hours of the day

         at 9 a.m.

In   used with other parts of the day

         in the afternoon

Prepositions of place

On   indicates a surface on which something rests

         The car was parked <u>on</u> the street.

At   indicates a point in relation to another subject

         My sister is <u>at</u> home.

In   indicates a subject is inside the boundaries of
         an area or volume

         The sample is <u>in</u> the bottle.

Prepositions to show logical relationships

Of   shows relationship between a part and the whole

         Two <u>of</u> her teachers gave quizzes today.

         shows material or content

         That basket <u>of</u> fruit is a present.

For   shows purpose

         He bought some plants <u>for</u> the garden.

34
OMITTED/REPEATED WORDS

34a   Omitted words

Subjects and verbs can be omitted in some languages, but
they are necessary in English sentences and must appear.

The only exception in English is the command that has an understood subject: "Put that box here." (The understood subject here is "you.")

Subjects

Include a subject in the main clause and in all other clauses as well. "There" and "it" may sometimes serve as subject words.

All the children laughed while ^they were watching cartoons.

^It is raining today.

Verbs

Although verbs such as "is" and "are" and helping verbs can be omitted in some languages, they must appear in English.

She ^is an effective Spanish teacher.

No one ^has gone to the lecture.

34b Repeated words

In some languages, the subject can be repeated as a pronoun before the verb. However, in English, the subject is included only once.

Bones in the body ~~they~~ become brittle as people grow older.

In some languages, objects of verbs or prepositional phrases are repeated, but not in English.

The woman tried on the hat that I left ~~it~~ on the seat.

The city where I live ~~there~~ has two soccer fields.

35

IDIOMS

An idiom is an expression that means something beyond the simple definition or literal translation into another language. An idiom such as "kick the bucket" (meaning "die") is not understandable from the meanings of the individual words.

Dictionaries of American English idioms can define many of the commonly used ones. The second word in two-word verb phrases (phrasals, see section 30b) is idiomatic and changes meanings.

> dark horse = someone not likely to be the winner
> under the table = something done illegally
> to turn <u>off</u> the light= to shut the light, to stop it
> to set an alarm to go <u>off</u>= to make an alarm work,
>   to start it.

VII RESEARCH

CONTENTS OF THIS SECTION

36 Doing Print and Online Research — 112

36a **Selecting a topic** — 112

36b **Sources of Information** — 113
- Library sources — 114
- Internet sources — 115
- Community sources — 117
- Interviews and surveys — 117

36c **Search engine strategies and options** — 117

36d **Web resources** — 120

36e **Sources in various disciplines** — 126

36f **Taking notes** — 129

37 Evaluating Print and Internet Sources — 129

37a **Getting started** — 130

37b **Evaluating bibliographic citations** — 131

37c **Evaluating content** — 133
- Print sources — 133
- Internet sources — 134

38 Integrating Sources — 137

38a **Showing the relevance** — 138

38b **Writing summaries and paraphrases** — 139

38c **Using quotations** — 140

38d **Using signal words with sources** — 140

38e **Avoiding plagiarism** — 142

39 Document Design — 144

39a **Paper preparation** — 144

39b **Visual elements** — 146

QUESTIONS TO ASK YOURSELF

This section covers the process of doing research in print and online sources, finding and narrowing a topic, using Web resources, evaluating and integrating information, and following document design principles. You'll also find discussions of summaries, paraphrases, and quotations, as well as plagiarism and how to avoid it.

	SECTION	PAGE
● What are some suggestions for finding a topic for my research paper?	36a	112
● What should I do to come up with a thesis statement after I have a topic?	36a	113
● What's the difference between primary and secondary sources?	36b	113
● When I'm looking for information in the library, what are some useful catalogs, databases, and other sources?	36b	114
● In addition to the library, where else can I search for information?	36b	115
● What are some strategies for searching the Web?	36c	117
● What are some useful Web sites to try?	36d	120
● What are some journals and magazines I can search through?	36e	126
● What is a working bibliography?	36f	129
● When I'm collecting information, how should I handle note cards?	36f	129
● What are some criteria to think about when I evaluate whether or not to use a source I find?	37a	130
● What should I consider when I'm deciding if the author is a reliable source of information?	37b	131
● Are there other criteria to keep in mind to evaluate the bibliographic citation before I decide to spend time finding and reading it?	37b	132

- When I'm reading the material, what are some criteria to think about to evaluate it? 37c 133

- What are some ways to include sources smoothly? 38a 137

- What is the difference between a summary, a paraphrase, and a quotation? 38b 139

- How do I smoothly insert a quotation in my paper? 38c 140

- What are signal words, and what are some examples? 38d 140

- What is plagiarism, and how do I avoid it? 38e 142

- What are some guidelines for margins and other matters when I prepare my paper? 39a 144

- What are visual elements and when should I include them? 39b 146

- How and when do I use tables, charts, and so on? 39b 146

DOING PRINT AND ONLINE RESEARCH

Some research papers that present your findings may be objective and discuss only the information you found but not your opinion or perspective on the topic. Other research papers may be persuasive because, after presenting the information you found, you come to conclusions or argue your opinion or viewpoint. Be sure that you know which is the appropriate goal as you write the paper.

Doing research is a process of selecting a topic, formulating the research question(s) you will address, searching for information, taking notes, keeping a list of the citations, evaluating what you have found, organizing the material, writing the paper, including adequate support for your thesis, and citing your sources.

36a Selecting a topic

There are four steps to selecting a topic:

1. **Find** a general subject that interests you (if one has not been assigned).

   One way to locate an interesting subject is to browse through any book or catalog of subject headings such as the *Library of Congress Subject Headings* or the *Reader's Guide to Periodical Literature.* On the Web, you can browse through subject directories (see 36d for specific sites to try). You can also browse through journals in a field you are interested in to look at topics discussed there. (See section 36e for a resource list of journals you are likely to find in your library.) Two examples of general subjects to start with are the following:

   Imagery in Maya Angelou's poetry

   Careers in technical writing

2. **Narrow** that subject to a topic to fit the assignment and the length of the paper that will be written. To narrow a topic, begin by listing some subtopics or smaller aspects of the larger topic, and choose one of those subtopics.

   Maya Angelou's use of fire imagery

   Technical writing jobs in the computer industry

3. **Formulate a research question** about your topic. Your research question will help you decide what information is relevant. Try formulating the question with any of the reporter's "who," "what," "where," "why," "when," and "how" questions.

> Why does Maya Angelou use fire imagery in her poetry?

> What kinds of jobs are available in the computer industry for technical writing majors?

4. **Formulate a thesis statement** that answers your research question.
   After completing your research and reviewing your information, you will be able to formulate a tentative thesis. This statement will answer your research question, but it may need to be revised somewhat as you write your paper.

> Maya Angelou uses images of fire in her poetry to convey cleansing and rebirth.

> In the computer industry, technical writing majors are hired to write documents such as computer manuals, training materials, and in-house newsletters.

36b Sources of information

The two categories of information to use are primary and secondary sources.

- **Primary sources** Primary sources are original or first-hand materials such as the poem or novel by the author you are writing about. Other primary materials are surveys, speeches, interviews you conduct, or firsthand accounts of events. Primary sources are not filtered through a second person. They may be more accurate because they have not been distorted or misinterpreted by others.
- **Secondary sources** Secondary sources are secondhand accounts, information, or reports about primary sources. Typical secondary sources include reviews, biographies about a person you are studying, documentaries, encyclopedia articles, news stories, and other materials interpreted, studied, or reported by others. Remember that secondary sources are interpretations or analyses that may be biased, inaccurate, or incomplete.

> ## hint
>
> **ESL Stating Your Ideas**
>
> Although some cultures place more value on student writing that primarily brings together or collects the thoughts of great scholars or experts, readers of research papers in American institutions value the writer's own interpretations and thinking about the subject.

Library Sources

Your library is most useful for the following kinds of information:

- **Major works in the field (books, journals, references)** Although there are some books, reference works, and other important resources being made available on the Web, most major studies, histories, references, etc. are in the library, not on the Internet. Some scholarly journals are now available on the Web, and there are some electronic journals and magazines too, but they may require readers to subscribe or may make only a sampling of their contents available at no charge. Many major scholarly books and journals, reference works, and magazines are in your library, not on the Internet.

- **Historical sources and textbooks** Most older books and other materials such as textbooks that are important or useful sources of information will be in libraries, not on the Internet.

- **Data bases** Your library is the place to look for those data bases that charge or that require the purchase of a CD-ROM.

Libraries have various printed and online guides for users and an information desk where you can talk with helpful librarians. In addition to the print and online catalogs available through your library, you can access other libraries with online catalogs and data bases (see 36d). Some useful indexes, catalogs, and databases that may be available through your library include the following:

- *Books in Print*
- *Reader's Guide to Periodical Literature*
- Encyclopedias such as *Collier's Encyclopedia* and more specialized ones such as the *Harvard Guide to American History* and the *Oxford Companion to English Literature*

- Abstracts and almanacs such as *Statistical Abstracts of the United States*
- Online searches of the library's holdings by author, title, key word, and subject heading.
- *Library of Congress Subject Headings* (This is helpful for subject heading searches when working online and can suggest alternate ways of phrasing keywords for your topic.)
- The Library of Congress (It's the largest library in the world.)
- Electronic databases such as the following:
    Business and Industry
    Business Periodicals Index
    CINAHL: Cumulative Index to Nursing and Allied Health Literature
    Contemporary Authors
    Contemporary Literary Criticism Select
    Dictionary of Literary Biography
    ERIC (Educational Resources Information Center)
    GPO Index (index of federal government publications)
    Humanities Index
    Literary Resource Center
    MathSciNet
    ModLino
    Newspaper Source
    PsycINFO
    Social Science Index
- Computerized bibliographic utilities such as *FirstSearch* (which accesses databases such as academic journals, corporations, congressional publications, and medical journals) or *Newsbank CD News* (which indexes articles from a variety of newspapers). Nexis/Lexis is a commercial service available online and has abstracts and full texts of magazines, newspapers, publications from industry and government, wire services, and other sources.

Internet sources

Online searching for information can be very fruitful because it connects you to vast resources in distant places that you can access quickly and easily. But it's important to have a clear sense of which kinds of information are available online and which are better searched for in libraries or other sources such as the community or your campus. Specific Web sites to use when searching are listed in 36d.

The Internet is useful when searching for the following kinds of information:

- **Government sources** The Federal Government has numerous sites on the Internet with large quantities of information produced by various government bureaus, departments, and agencies, in addition to information produced by legislative action. The Library of Congress is especially useful because of its huge collection of materials, the largest in the world. You can also check for references to appropriate government publications that your library may have on the shelves.

- **Library catalogs online** You can search many libraries online to find other materials on your topic, materials that your library may not have and may be able to borrow for you. You can also read titles and abstracts to get a sense of what's available on the topic. These online catalogs are especially useful for compiling a working bibliography to start your search. Some of the major libraries online also have searchable databases and lists of resources in various areas that may be useful.

- **Current news** The major American newspapers and magazines have Web sites where you can read about recent events or rapidly changing conditions, and you can search the sites for past information. In most cases, however, these archives go back only a few years, and some newspapers may charge a fee for these materials.

- **Non-profit public interest groups** Although there is a great deal of propaganda on the Internet put up by special-interest groups, some nonprofit organizations collect useful information on issues such as how to organize local citizen action groups, detect propaganda, identify Internet myths, fix various types of electronics, uncover media bias, and so on. However, other special-interest groups promote hate, fraudulent practices, violence, fear, and deception of various types. Be very careful when you enter the world of special-interest Web sites. The section on evaluating Internet sources, in 37c, will help you identify appropriate and unbiased sources. (Some special-interest sites, though, may help you identify arguments on various sides of an issue. For example, if you are researching an issue such as federal regulation of automobile emission standards, you'll find Web sites promoting a number of viewpoints. These will help you locate the arguments being made for and against various aspects of the issue.)

- **Some older books** There are several projects, such as Project Bartleby, the English Server at Carnegie Mellon University, and Project Gutenberg, dedicated to making available online older books whose copyrights have expired. Other projects are dedicated to making rare or hard-to-find older resources available online.
- **Information relevant to a field of study or major** If you start with the sites listed in fields of study in 36d, you'll quickly find the Web sites that have collected links to information about that field.

Community sources

Your community has a variety of resources to tap, including public records and other local government information in a city hall or county courthouse. Other sources are community service workers, social service agencies, school teachers and school administrators, community leaders, religious leaders, coordinators in nonprofit groups, the local chamber of commerce or visitors and convention bureau, local public library, museums or historical societies, the newspaper, and your campus offices and faculty.

Interviews and surveys

You can do field research by interviewing people, sending e-mail messages, conducting surveys, and taking notes on your own observations.

36c Search engine strategies and options

1. **Search Engine Strategies**

- **Different types of tools available**

  - **Search engines** Search engines work by searching among the contents of public sites on the Internet for key terms that you indicate. The search engine returns a list of sites that include the key term. Because various search engines work differently, each will turn up different results. Some results, however, may be prominently displayed because the site owner has paid to be listed at or near the top of the results list. (These are usually referred to as "sponsored links.") Be sure to read the search options the site offers so that you use it effectively. Also, some sites have their own search engines and site maps to help you find information on various parts of that site.

- **Subject categories or directories** These indexes or directories organize Web resources by categories such as "health," "entertainment," and "business." Most have subdirectories under the main headings. These lists are particularly useful when you are looking for suggestions for a topic, for a quick look at the types of information available on that topic, or for ways to phrase key terms for searches. Yahoo.com and Altavista.com are examples of sites with extensive lists of categories and subjects.

- **Newsgroups and listservs** Newsgroups are open forums on the Usenet network where anyone can post a message on the topic of the forum. Listservs are e-mail discussion groups in which participants have to subscribe to the list. Any message from any member of the listserv goes to all the subscribers. The listowner may or may not moderate what appears by controlling which messages get through to the list. On Google.com's home page, you can select the "groups" option to search newsgroups and listservs.

- **Web sites with collections of information** In 36d you will find addresses for many Web sites that compile large quantities of information. For example, under "Fields of Study" there, you will find sites with many links to information in the particular field. The government sites will be collections of documents relevant to various areas of the government such as census data, congressional bills under consideration, world health surveys, and so on.

- **Different ways to search**
  Use your detective skills to think about different ways to start and which leads to follow. When you use some creative thinking, you'll find that you begin to think of a variety of kinds of sites, sites that are beyond the ordinary or expected ones.

  Sample search Suppose your assignment is to research your major, and you want to learn more about job opportunities in that major. Here are some different ways to approach your search:

- Go to general job search sites to see what they have listed.
- Try the resource lists and directories in that academic field (see 36d) because some of the Web sites listed will have relevant job opportunities listed.
- Try university Web sites that have department pages and career centers that will include job opportunities.
- Seek out sites that collect résumés or help companies find employees. (Some sites charge for these services.)
- Look at U.S. Census report data to see what you can find there. In other federal government sites, you'll find government studies of prospects for various fields.
- Try Web sites of large companies in that field to see what they list as job openings. (Some online yellow pages search engines list the Web addresses in addition to the street and city locations.)
- Tune in to listservs and newsgroups of people in that area of work to see what they are discussing.
- Use a few search engines to see what they turn up. Some search engines, such as Altavista.com, include among their categories that of job seeking. (There will be some similarities in search engine listings, but there will also be different ones in each. But be prepared to find that the search engine turns up more items than you want to read.)

2. **Search engine options**

Search engines offer a variety of options when searching the Web. They differ in the ways they search, the categories of sites they search, the results that turn up, and the varieties of options for searching they offer. So, before using any search engine, read any explanations and choices offered on the site that will give you a better idea of how to use it effectively.

As you will find out when you read what the search engine offers as options, you can limit your search by language, date, and so on. For example, Altavista.com can translate short passages from one language to another; Hotbot.lycos.com permits you to specify the date and language to search in, and on Google.com you can choose to search the entire Web, images only, or postings in newsgroups and listservs. Google.com and Yahoo.com offer options such as advanced searching too, which is explained on the site.

When you view the results lists, you need to be aware of policies of the site. Google.com identifies sponsored links (links that companies pay for, to list prominently at the top of the list), but some other search engines may or may not indicate that the first few listings are there because some company paid to have you see them, not because they are the best match for what you are seeking.

36d Web resources

The pages of Web resources listed here are categorized in the following way:

1. **Writing**
   Here you'll find links to style manuals; grammar and writing handouts; MLA, APA, and Chicago Manual sites; dictionaries; a thesaurus; Bartlett's Quotations; and information on business, social science, and technical writing.

   Use these sites for help with writing.

2. **General subjects**
   This is a particularly useful collection of links to huge subject directories; online books, journals, and newspapers; scholarly societies and electronic discussion groups; colleges; and search engines.

   Use these sites for initial searches across a broad area and for links to articles and books available online.

3. **Fields of study**
   Here you'll find links to sites that focus on specific fields of study such as education, history, science, engineering, etc.

   Use these sites for more specialized information in a particular field of study.

4. **Government**
   There are vast sites that link to all the government agencies and have online publications of data collected by all branches of the government, from health to population to governments of other countries.

   Use these sites for data, statistics, or studies you think might have been done by government agencies and for information about all branches of government and the work they do.

5. **Libraries online**
   These are links to online libraries. Many have search engines, data bases that are available to all users, and collections of useful links.

   Use these links to find out what else has been written about your topic and what books and journals can be loaned to your library if it does not have those materials.

1. **Writing**

   ● **Writing guides**
     Strunk and White, *Elements of Style:* <**http://www. bartleby.com/141/**>
     Writing Lab OWLs (Online Writing Labs):
     -International Writing Centers Association OWLs: <**http://iwca.syr.edu/IWCA/IWCAOWLS.html**>
     -Purdue University: <**http://owl.english.purdue.edu**>
     -University of Missouri: <**http://www.missouri.edu/~ writery/index2.html**>

   ● **Writing in special fields**
     Business Writing: Purdue OWL: <**http://owl. english.purdue.edu/handouts/pw/index.html**>
     Engineering and Science Writing: <**http://fbox.vt. edu/eng/mech/writing/**>
     Social Science Writing: <**http://www.emayzine. com/lectures/writing.htm**>
     Scientific Writing: (See Engineering and Science Writing)

   ● **References**
     Bartlett's Familiar Quotations: <**http://www.bartleby. com/100/**>
     Biographical Dictionary: <**http://s9.com/biography**>
     Encyclopedia Britannica: <**http://www.britannica. com/**>

KnowPlay: <**http://www.kplay.cc/reference.html**>

Merriam Webster Dictionary: <**http://www.m-w. com/dictionary**>

Online Dictionaries: <**http://www.yourdictionary. com/**> <**http://www.dictionary.com/**>

Roget's Thesaurus: <**http://www.bartleby.com/ thesauri**>

2. **General subjects**

● **Search engines**

Many of these sites show sponsored links first, that is, links to sites that have paid to have a prominent listing. Google has sponsored links, but it indicates that fact in its results list. It is also perhaps the most comprehensive search engine.

Alta Vista: <**http://www.altavista.com**>

Dogpile: <**http://www.dogpile.com**>

Google: <**http://www.google.com**>

HotBot: <**http://www.hotbot.lycos.com/**>

Yahoo: <**http://www.yahoo.com**>

For a directory of search engines, see AllSearch Engines.com, which briefly describes the largest search engines on the home page, lists all search engines on a separate page and offers a brief note on each, and lists search engines for various categories:

<**http://www.allsearchengines.com/**>

● **General subject directories**

Awesome Library: <**http://www.awesomelibrary. org/**>

Internet Public Library: <**http://www.ipl.org**>

WWW Virtual Library: <**http://vlib.org/**>

● **Books online**

Electronic Text Center: <**www.cs.cmu.edu/afs/cs. cmu.edu/user/ phoebe/mosaic/stuff-to-read.html**>

Online Books Page: <**http://onlinebooks.library. upenn.edu/**>

Project Bartleby: <**http://www.bartleby.com/**>

Project Gutenberg: <**http://promo.net/pg**>

● **Electronic listservs and newsgroups**
<**http://tile.net/lists/**>

Usenet: <**http://www.faqs.org/faqs/**>

● **Journals and periodicals online**
Magazines, Journals, Periodicals Online<**http://www. wam.umd.edu/~mlhall/magazines.html**>

- **Newspapers, news services, e-zines, media, magazines online**
  ABC News:<http://abc.abcnews.go.com/>
  CBS New: <http://www.cbsnews.com/>
  Chronicle of Higher Education: <http://chronicle.com>
  EcolaNewsstand: <http://www.ecola.com>
  Electronic Newsstand: <http://home.worldonline.dk/knud-sor/en/>
  E-Journal Site Guide: <http://www.library.ubc.ca/ejour/>
  FOX News: <http://www.foxnews.com/>
  MSNBC: <http://www.msnbc.com/news/>
  NBC News: <http://nbc.com/>
  New York Times: <http://nytimes.com>
  Reuters News Media: <http://www.reuters.com>
  USA Today: <http://usatoday.com>
  Wall Street Journal: <http://online.wsj.com/public/us>

- **Scholarly electronic conferences**
  Directory of Scholarly and Professional E-Conferences: <http://www.kovacs.com/directory/>

- **Scholarly societies**
  Alliance for Computers and Writing: <http://english.ttu.edu/acw/>
  American Astronomical Society: <http://www.aas.org>
  American Institute of Physics: <http://www.aip.org>
  American Philosophical Society: <http://www.amphilsoc.org/>
  Association of Teachers of Technical Writing: <http://english.ttu.edu/ATTW/>
  Council of Science Editors: <http://www.councilscienceeditors.org/>
  Home Pages of Scholarly Societies Project: <http://www.lib.uwaterloo.ca/society/overview.html>
  National Academy of Sciences: <http://www.nas.edu>
  National Council of Teachers of English: <http://www.ncte.org/>
  Web Pages of Scholarly Societies Project: <http://www.lib.uwaterloo.ca/society/webpages.html>

- **Universities in the United States**
  <http://www.clas.ufl.edu/CLAS/american-universities.html>

3. **Fields of study**

An excellent place to start is the Academic Information Index. It has a rich collection of links for most major academic fields of study:
<**http://www.academicinfo.net/table.html**>

● African American History and Study <**http://www. academicinfo.net/africanam.html**>
● Business
CommerceNet: <**http://www.commerce.net**>
● Education
AskEric: <**http://ericir.syr.edu**>
Education Gateway: <**http://www.academicinfo. net/ed.html**>
Educational Technology: <**http://www.educause.edu/**>
ERIC: <**http://www.eric.ed.gov/**>

● Humanities
American Studies: <**http://www.georgetown.edu/ crossroads/asw**>
Art and Art History: <**http://www.academicinfo. net/art.html**>
Communication: <**http://www.academicinfo.net/ comm.html**>
Education: Ask ERIC: <**http://ericir.syr.edu/**>
English:
-Academic Info English and ESL/EFL: <**http:// www.academicinfo.net/englang.html**>
-American Literature: <**http://www.academicinfo. net/amlit.html**>
-English Literature: <**http://www.academicinfo. net/englit.html**>
-Online Literary Resources: <**http://andromeda. rutgers.edu/~jlynch/Lit/**>
-University of Washington E-Server: <**http:// eserver.org/**>
Foreign Language and Literature:
-Academic Info Foreign Lang Study: <**http:// www.academicinfo.net/lang.html**>
-Foreign Language Resources on the WWW:
<**http://www.itp.berkeley.edu/~thorne/ HumanResources.html**>
History:
-Academic Info History:<**http://www. academicinfo.net/hist.html**>

-World History Archives: <**http://www.hartford-hwp.com/archives/**>

Humanities: Voice of the Shuttles: <**http://www.qub.ac.uk/english/humanitas_home.html**>

Journalism: Journalistic Resources Page: <**http://www.markovits.com/journalism/**>

Philosophy:

-<**http://www.academicinfo.net/phil.html**>

-Philosophy in Cyberspace: <**http://www.personal.monash.edu.au/~dey/phil/**>

Political Science:

-Academic Info Pol Sci: <**http://www.academicinfo.net/polisci.html**>

-Political Science Resources on the Web: <**http://www.lib.umich.edu/govdocs/polisci.html**>

Psychology:

-CyberPsychLink:

<**http://cctr.umkc.edu/user/dmartin/psych2.html**>

-<**http://www.academicinfo.net/psych.html**>

Religion: Academic Info Religion Main Index: <**http://www.academicinfo.net/religindex.html**>

Social Science Information Gateway: <**http://sosig.ac.uk/welcome.html**>

Sociology: Socioweb: <**http://www.socioweb.com/~markbl/socioweb**>

Women's Studies:

-Academic Info Women's Studies: <**http://www.academicinfo.net/women.html**>

-Women's Resource Project: <**http://sunsite.unc.edu/cheryb/women**>

-Women's Studies (R)E-Sources on the Web: <**http://scriptorium.lib.duke.edu/women/cyber.html**>

- Natural Sciences

Chemistry:

-Chemdex: <**http://www.chemdex.org/**>

-Chemistry.Org:

<**http://www.acs.org/portal/Chemistry**>

Computer Science:

-Computer Technology-Engineering and Technology: <**http://galaxy.einet.net/galaxy/Engineering-and-Technology/Computer-Technology.html**>

-EE/CS Mother Site: <**http://www-ee.stanford.edu/~ ieee/eesites.html**>

Environmental Studies:
  -Best Environmental Resources Directory: <http://www.ulb.ac.be/ceese/meta/cds.html>
  -EnviroInfo: <http://www.deb.uminho.pt/fontes/enviroinfo/>
Mathematics:
  -Mathematics Information Servers: <http://www.math.psu.edu/MathLists/Contents.html>
  -MathSearch: <http://www.maths.usyd.edu.au:8000/MathSearch.html>
Medicine:
  -Medscape: <http://www.medscape.com>
  -Medweb: <http://www.medweb.emory.edu>
Physics:
  -Academic Info Physics: <http://www.academicinfo.net/physics.html>
  -PhysicsWeb: <http://physicsweb.org/paw/>

4. **Government**

- Bureau of the Census: <http://www.census.gov>
- CIA: <http://www.odci.gov>
- Fedworld: <http://www.fedworld.gov>
- National Institutes of Health: <http://www.nih.gov>
- Nonprofit Gateway: <http://www.nonprofit.gov>
- Stat USA (business, trade, and economic information): <http://www. stat-usa.gov/>
- Thomas: <http://thomas.loc.gov>
- White House: <http://www.whitehouse.gov>
- World Health Organization: <http://www.who.int/home-page/>

5. **Libraries online**

- American Library Association: <http://www.ala.org>
- Internet Public Library: <http://www.ipl.org>
- Library of Congress: <http://lcweb.loc.gov>
- Libweb: <http://sunsite.berkeley.edu/Libweb>

36e Sources in various disciplines

When you are seeking information in various fields of study, the following lists of journals should help you. Also, check the Web sites listed in 36d to search for those journals and magazines that are also available online.

Research Sources in Various Fields: Journals and Magazines

Art:	• *American Artist* • *Art History*
	• *Artforum* • *Metropolis*

Biology:
- *JAMA: Journal of the American Medical Association*
- *Quarterly Review of Biology*

Business/Economics/Management:
- *Business Week*
- *Economist*
- *Harvard Business Review*
- *Journal of Business*
- *Sloan Management Review*

Communication:
- *Communication Monographs*
- *Journalism & Mass Communication*
- *Quarterly Journal of Speech*

Composition and Rhetoric:
- *College Composition and Communication*
- *College English*

Computer Science:
- *Artificial Intelligence*
- *Byte*
- *Harvard Computer Review*
- *Technical Computing*

Culture:
- *Common Knowledge*
- *Language, Society, and Culture*

Education:
- *Education Research and Perspectives*
- *Education Week*

Engineering:
- *Space Technology*
- *Automotive Engineering*
- *Industrial Engineering*

Environment:
- *Amicus*
- *Atmospheric Environment*
- *Center for Health and the Global Environment Newsletter*
- *The Earth Times*
- *Environmental Health Perspectives Journals*

History:
- *American Historical Review*
- *American History*

- *English Literary History*
- *History Today*
- *Journal of Social History*
- *Journal of Modern History*
- *Journal of World History*

Law:
- *IDEA: The Journal of Law and Technology*
- *Intellectual Property*
- *Journal of Information Law and Technology*

Literature:
- *African-American Review*
- *Journal of Modern Literature*
- *PMLA*

Movies:
- *KINEMA: A Journal for Film and Audiovisual Media*

Music:
- *Journal of Musicology*
- *Musical Quarterly*

Physics:
- *Physical Review*
- *Physics Letters*

Political Science:
- *The Americana*
- *Congressional Quarterly*
- *Foreign Affairs*
- *Harvard Political Review*
- *Political Science Quarterly*
- *Yale Political Monthly*

Psychology:
- *American Journal of Psychology*
- *Counseling Psychologist*
- *Journal of Personality and Social Psychology*
- *Psychological Review*

Religion:
- *Cross Currents*
- *Religion and Literature*

Sociology:
- *American Sociological Review*
- *Human Development and Family Life*
- *Journal of Sociology and Social Welfare*

Women's Studies:
- *Journal of Women's History*
- *Sister*
- *Womanist Theory and Research*
- *Women's Review of Books*

36f   Taking notes

- **Working bibliography** As you collect information, start a
working bibliography that lists all the sources you will
read. See section 37b on evaluating the citation before
you spend time locating it. Some sources won't be as useful, and there are some questions you can ask yourself as
you look at citations to see whether they belong in your
working bibliography.

  Because you may not use all those sources in your paper, the final list of sources is likely to be shorter than the
working bibliography. Make bibliographic entries on separate 3" × 5" cards so that you can easily insert new entries in alphabetical order. If you are using a computer,
construct your list in a file that is separate from the paper. In each entry include all the information you will
need in your bibliography. You may also want to include
information you would need (such as the library call number) to find that source again.

- **Note cards** After you evaluate the source (see section 37)
and decide that the information may be useful, record the
information on note cards (either 3" × 5" or 4" × 6"
cards) to summarize, paraphrase, or record a quotation
(see section 38a). Use parentheses or brackets to record
your thoughts as to how you can use this source in your
paper. It is best to limit each note card to one short aspect of a topic so that you can reorder the cards later as
you organize the whole project.

  Label the note card with the author's last name and
shortened title, if needed, in the upper right-hand corner.
Use a short phrase in the upper left-hand corner as a subject heading. As you write the information, include the
exact page numbers and indicate to yourself whether the
information is a summary, paraphrase, or quotation.

37

EVALUATING PRINT AND
INTERNET SOURCES

We live in an age of information—such vast amounts of information that we cannot know everything about a subject. All of
that information that comes streaming at us in newspapers,

magazines, the media, books, journals, brochures, and Web sites is also of very uneven quality. People want to convince us to depend on their data, buy their products, accept their viewpoints, vote for their candidates, agree with their opinions, and rely on them as experts.

We sift and make decisions all the time about which information we will use based on how we evaluate the information. Evaluating sources, then, is a skill we need all the time, and applying that skill to research papers is equally important. Listed here are some stages in the process of evaluating sources.

37a Getting started

As you begin searching for information, ask yourself what kinds of information you are looking for and where you are likely to find appropriate sources for that kind of information. You want to be sure that you are headed in the right direction as you launch into your search, and this too is part of the evaluation process—evaluating where you are most likely to get the right kind of information for your purpose.

- **What kind of information are you looking for?**

  Do you want facts? Opinions? News reports? Research studies? Analyses? Historical accounts? Personal reflections? Data? Public records? Scholarly essays reflecting on the topic? Reviews?

- **Where would you find such information?**

  Which sources are most likely to be useful? Libraries with scholarly journals, books, and government publications? Public libraries with popular magazines? The Internet? Newspapers? Community records? Someone on your campus?

  If, for example, you are searching for information on some current event, a reliable newspaper such as the *New York Times* will be a useful source, and it is likely to be available in a university library, a public library, and on the Web. If you need some statistics on the U.S. population, government census documents in libraries and on the Internet will be appropriate places to search. But if you want to do research into local history, the archives of the local government offices and local newspaper are better places to start. Consider whether there are organizations designed to gather and publish the kinds of information you are seeking. And be sure to ask yourself if the organization's goal is to be objective or to gain support for its viewpoint.

37b Evaluating bibliographic citations

Before you spend time hunting for a source or read it, begin by looking at the following information in the citation to evaluate whether it's worth finding or reading.

1. **Author**

   - *Credentials*

     How reputable is the person (or organization) listed there?

     -What is the author's educational background?

     -What has the author written in the past about this topic?

     -Why is this person considered an expert or a reliable authority?

     You can learn more about the person by checking the Library of Congress to see what else the person has written, and the *Book Review Index* and *Book Review Digest* may lead you to reviews of other books by this person. Your library may have citation indexes in the person's field that will lead you to other articles and short pieces by this person that have been cited by others.

     For biographical information you can read *Who's Who in America* or the *Biography Index*. There may also be information about the person in the publication such as listing of previous writings, awards, and notes about the author. Your goal is to get some sense of who this person is and why it's worth reading what that person wrote before you plunge in and begin reading. That may be important as you write the paper and build your case. For example, if you are citing a source to show the spread of AIDS in Africa, which of these sentences strengthens your argument?

     "Dr. John Smith notes that the incidence of AIDS in Africa has more than doubled in the last five years."

   (or)

     "Dr. John Smith, head of the World Health Organization committee studying AIDS in African countries, notes that the incidence of AIDS in Africa has more than doubled in the last five years."

- *References*
  - -Did a teacher or librarian or some other person who is knowledgeable about the topic mention this person?
  - -Did you see the person listed in other sources that you've already determined to be trustworthy?

When someone is an authority, you may find other references to this person. Or this person's viewpoint or perspective may be important to read.

- *Institution or affiliation*
  - -What organization, institution, or company is the person associated with?
  - -What are the goals of this group?
  - -Does it monitor or review what is published under its name?
  - -Might this group be biased in some way? Are they trying to sell you something or convince you to accept their views? Do they conduct disinterested research?

2. **Timeliness**
   - -When was the source published? (For Web sites, look at the "last revised" date at the end of the home page.)
   - -Is that date current enough to be useful, or might there be outdated material?
   - -Is the source a revision of an earlier edition? If so, it is likely to be more current, and a revision indicates that the source is sufficiently valuable to revise. Check a library catalog or *Books in Print* to see if you have the latest edition.

3. **Publisher/producer**
   - -Who published or produced the material?
   - -Is that publisher reputable? For example, a university press or a government agency is likely to be a reputable source that reviews what it publishes.
   - -Is the group recognized as being an authority?
   - -Is the publisher or group an appropriate one for this topic?
   - -Might the publisher be likely to have a particular bias? (For example, a brochure printed by an antiabortion, right-to-life group is not going to argue for abortion.)

-Is there any review process or fact checking? (If a pharmaceutical company publishes data on a new drug it is developing, is there evidence of outside review of the data?)

4. **Audience**
    -Can you tell who the intended audience is? Is that audience appropriate for your purposes?
    -Is the material too specialized or too popular or brief to be useful? (A three-volume study of gene splitting is more than you need for a five-page paper on some genetically transmitted disease. But a half-page article on a visit to Antarctica won't tell you much about research into ozone depletion going on there.)

37c   Evaluating content

Print sources

When you have the source in hand, you can evaluate the content by keeping in mind the following important criteria:

● **Accuracy** Are the facts accurate? Do they agree with other information you've read? Are there sources for the data given?
● **Comprehensiveness** Is the topic covered in adequate depth? Or is it too superficial or limited to only one aspect that, therefore, overemphasizes only one part of the topic?
● **Credibility** Is the source of the material generally considered trustworthy? Does the source have a review process or do fact checking? Is the author an expert? What are the author's credentials for writing about this topic?
● **Fairness** If the author has a particular viewpoint, are differing views presented with some sense of fairness? Or are they presented as irrational or stupid?
● **Objectivity** Is the language objective or emotional? Does the author acknowledge differing viewpoints? Are the various perspectives fairly presented? If you are reading an article in a magazine, do other articles in that source promote a particular viewpoint?
● **Relevance** How closely related is the material to your topic? Is it really relevant or merely related? Is it too general or too specific? Too technical?
● **Timeliness** Is the information current enough to be useful? How necessary is timeliness for your topic?

To help you determine the degree to which the criteria listed above are present in the source, try the following:

- Read the preface. What does the author want to accomplish?
- Browse through the table of contents and the index. Is the topic covered in enough depth to be helpful?
- Is there a list of references that look as if the author has consulted other sources and that may lead you to useful related material?
- Are you the intended audience? Consider the tone, style, level of information, and assumptions the author makes about the reader. Are they appropriate to your needs?
- Is the content of the source fact, opinion, or propaganda? If the material is presented as factual, are the sources of the facts clearly indicated? Do you think there's enough evidence offered? Is the coverage comprehensive? (As you learn more about the topic, you will notice that this gets easier as you become more of an expert.) Is the language emotional or objective?
- Are there broad, sweeping generalizations that overstate or simplify the matter?
- Does the author use a mix of primary and secondary sources?
- To determine accuracy, consider whether the source is outdated. Do some cross-checking. Do you find some of the same information elsewhere?
- Are there arguments that are one-sided with no acknowledgement of other viewpoints?

Internet sources

Evaluating Internet sources is particularly difficult because anyone can put up anything he or she wants to on the Internet. There is no way to monitor or to check facts, though there are some site ratings you can check. At the end of the essay by Hope Tillman (listed below in section 4), you will find a discussion of various ratings given to sites by companies that issue awards (some of which are objective ratings for quality and some of which are merely to promote the company issuing the award)

Some criteria to consider as you read Internet sources:

1. **Authorship**

    -Is there an author or organization clearly indicated?
        If so, review the questions about authorship listed in 37b. Can the author be contacted?

-*What can you find out about the author?*

If there is no information on the site, use a search engine or search Usenet for the person. You may find the author's home page or other documents that mention this person. If the person is associated with a university, look at the university Web site.

-*If there is an organization sponsoring the page, what can you learn about the organization and who they are?*

You can search the site by following links to the home page or going back a previous level on the site by deleting the last part of the address, after the various "/" marks. Or try contacting the person who maintains the site if a name, title, or e-mail address is included. Or there may be a "contact us" link to which you can send an e-mail.

Does the organization take responsibility for what's on the site? Does it monitor or review what's there? Look at the address. If it ends in ".edu," that indicates it's an educational institution. If it ends in ".gov," whatever you find should be a fairly objective government-sponsored material. Addresses with ".org" are usually nonprofit organizations that are advocacy groups. For example, the Sierra Club, at **http://www.sierra.org**, is an advocacy group whose postings will conform to their goals of environmental protection. Information posted by advocacy groups may be accurate but not entirely objective. If the site has a ".com" address, it's more likely to be promoting or selling something.

2. **Accuracy of information**

-Is there documentation to indicate the source of the information? There may be a link to the original source of the information.
-Can you tell how well researched the information is?
-Are criteria for including information offered?
-Is there a bibliography or links to other useful sites? Has the author considered information on those sites or considered viewpoints represented there?
-Is the information current? When was it updated? (Check at the bottom of the page for a "last revised" date. If there are numerous dead links, that's a clue that the page has not been updated recently.)

-Is there an indication of bias on the site?

-Does the site have any credentials such as being rated by a reputable rating group? If you see a high rating, is that because of the reliability of the content or the quality of the graphics? (An attractive page is not a reason for accepting its information as reliable.)

3. **Goals of the site**

-What is the purpose of the site? Advertise? Persuade? Provide information? Provide disinformation? For example, some groups intent on helping their candidate get elected put up sites that emphasize the opponent's weaknesses or that ridicule the opponent. Some sites are owned by hate groups that manage to disguise their real purpose, and some sites appear to be objective but are promoting some product or service.

-Are the goals of the site clearly indicated?

-Who is the intended audience?

-Is there a lot of flash and color and gimmicks to attract attention? Is that masking a lack of sound information or a blatant attempt to get you to buy or do something?

4. **Access**

-How did you find the site? Were there links from reputable sites? From ads? If you found the site through a search engine, that means only that the site has the keywords in your search term prominently placed or used with great frequency. It could also mean that the site owner paid to be listed at or near the top of the results list. If sites are prominently listed because they have paid to be seen on the results lists, they are sometimes identified as "sponsored links." If you found the site by browsing through a subject directory, that may mean only that someone at that site registered it with that directory.

Internet Resources on Evaluation

Some Web sites that have useful materials on evaluating sources and links to other useful sites are the following:

• Alexander, Jan, and Marsha Tate. "Evaluating Web Resources": <**http://www2.widener.edu/Wolfgram-Memorial-Library/webevaluation/webeval.htm**>

- Barker, Joe, and Saifon Obromsook. "Evaluating Web Pages": <**http://www.lib.berkeley.edu/TeachingLib/Guides/ Internet/EvalQuestions.html**>
- Engle, Michael. "Evaluating Web Sites: Criteria and Tools": <**http://www.library.cornell.edu/okuref/research/ webeval.html**>
- Harris, Robert. "Evaluating Internet Research Sources": <**http://www.virtualsalt.com/evalu8it.htm**>
- Henderson, John R. "The ICYouSee Critical Thinking Guide": <**http://www.ithaca.edu/library/Training/hott.html**>
- Jacobson, Trudi and Laura Cohen. "Evaluating Internet Resources": <**http://library.albany.edu/internet/evaluate. html**>
- Kirk, Elizabeth. "Evaluating Information Found on the Internet": <**http://www.library.jhu.edu/elp/useit/evaluate/ index.html**>
- Richmond, Betsy. "Ten C's for Evaluating Internet Resources": <**http://www.uwec.edu/library/Guides/tencs.html**>
- Smith, Alastair. "Criteria for Evaluation of Internet Information Sources": <**http://www.vuw.ac.nz/~agsmith/ evaln/index.htm**>
- Tillman, Hope. "Evaluating Quality on the Net": <**http:// www.hopetillman.com/findqual.html**>
- UCLA Biomed Library. "Searching for and Evaluating Web Resources": <**http://www.library.ucla.edu/libraries/biomed/ tutorials/searchweb.html**>

38

INTEGRATING SOURCES

As you write your paper, you will be including material from the sources you found during your research. As you include those sources, you have several important writing tasks:

- You have to help the reader see why the source is being quoted or referred to so that the reader sees the relevance (see 38a).
- Because you may also be incorporating summaries, paraphrases, and quotations, you need to be able to distinguish between them. It is also important to weave these in smoothly and to distinguish for the reader as to whether you are summarizing, paraphrasing, or quoting (see 38b and 38c).

- A very useful way to integrate references to source material, summaries, paraphrases, and quotations is to signal your reader by using signal words (see 38d) to introduce and smoothly blend these sources into your writing.
- Finally, as you use sources in your writing, you want to be sure that you are not plagiarizing the material (see 38e).

38a Showing the relevance

Suppose you read a paragraph that dealt with genetically modified foods and saw the following two sentences:

> Biologists are working toward developing a strain of corn that can withstand drought. Gerritson notes that the drought in Africa will most likely continue through this decade (81).

Did it take you a moment to figure out the connection? The writer of those sentences failed to help us see the relevance of the second sentence. The sentence was just dropped in, and the reader was left to figure out the point being made.

Notice the difference in this revised version:
Revised: Biologists are working toward developing a strain of corn that can withstand drought. This will be needed in the near future because, as Gerritson notes, the drought in Africa will most likely continue through this decade (81).

The revised version adds an explanation to the reader as to how the source material is connected to the rest of the paragraph. One way to check that you have integrated a source effectively is to ask yourself if you have explained the relevance of the material you are including. Put the explanation before the source material so that the reader can move forward easily.

Here's another example in which a quotation is dropped awkwardly in a paragraph:
Marketing research has shown that college-bound first-year students spend millions in furnishing their residence hall rooms. "Milgrim will be launching a funky line of colorful bedding exclusively for Hines" (27), says Feliz Morrano, design coordinator at Hines.

Does this revised version clarify that quotation?

Revised: Marketing research has shown that college-bound first-year students spend millions in furnishing their residence hall rooms. To cash in on this market, large discount chains are eager to introduce the work of well-known clothing designers such as Tom Milgrim. For example, Feliz Morrano, design coordinator at Hines, a major discount retailer, recently announced that "Milgrim will be launching a funky line of colorful bedding exclusively for Hines" (27).

38b Writing summaries and paraphrases

As you gather information from your sources, you may need to summarize or paraphrase them when you include them in your writing.

1. **Summaries**

A summary is a brief statement of the main idea in a source, using your own words. Include a citation to the source.

Characteristics of summaries:
● Are written in your own words
● Include only the main points, omitting details, facts, examples, illustrations, direct quotations, and other specifics
● Use fewer words than the source
● Do not have to be in the same order as the source
● Are objective and do not include your own interpretation

Good reasons for using summaries are that the source has unnecessary detail, that the writing is not particularly memorable or worth quoting, or that you want to keep your writing concise.

2. **Paraphrases**

A paraphrase restates the information from a source, using your own words. Include a citation to the source.

Characteristics of paraphrases:

- Have approximately the same number of words as the source
- Include all main points and important details in the source
- Use your own words, not those of the source
- Keep the same organization as the source
- Are more detailed than a summary
- Are objective and do not include your interpretation

38c Using quotations

> A quotation is the record of the exact words of a written or spoken source and is set off by quotation marks. All quotations should have citation to the source.

Guidelines for using quotations:

- Use quotations as evidence, support, or further explanation of what you have written. Quotations are not substitutes for stating your point in your own words.
- Before you include the quotation, indicate the point the quotation is making and why that quotation is relevant.
- Use quotations sparingly. Too many quotations strung together with little of your own writing can make a paper look like a scrapbook of pasted-together sources, not a thoughtful integration of what is known about a subject.
- Use quotations that illustrate an authority's viewpoint or style or that would not be as effective if rewritten in different words.
- Introduce quotations with signal words (see 38d).

For guidelines on punctuating quotations, see section 22.

38d Using signal words with sources

As you include summaries, paraphrases, and quotations in your papers, you need to integrate them smoothly so that there is no sudden jump or break between the flow of your words and the source material. Use the following strategies to prepare your readers and to create that needed smooth transition into the inserted material:

* *Use signal phrases*

  Signal words or phrases let the reader know a quotation will follow. Choose a phrase or word that is appropriate to the quotation and indicates the relationship to the ideas being discussed.

  > In 1990 when the United Nations International Human Rights Commission predicted "there will be an outburst of major violations of human rights in Yugoslavia within the next few years" (14), few people in Europe or the United States paid attention to the warning. (United Nations International Human Rights Commission. *The Future of Human Rights in Eastern Europe.* New York: United Nations, 1990.)

SOME COMMON SIGNAL WORDS

according to	considers	observes
acknowledges	denies	points out
admits	describes	predicts
argues	disagrees	proposes
asserts	emphasizes	rejects
comments	explains	reports
complains	finds	responds
concedes	insists	suggests
concludes	maintains	thinks
condemns	notes	warns

---

* *Explain the connection with signal words*

  Do not let the quotation make a point by itself. Explain to your reader what the quotation indicates or adds to your explanation or argument. When you explain the connection between a quotation you use and the point you are making, you are showing the logical link. If it is appropriate, you can add a follow-up comment that continues to integrate the quotation into your paragraph.

  Quotation not integrated into the paragraph:

  Modern farming techniques are different from those used twenty years ago. John Hession, an Iowa soybean grower, says, "Without a computer program to plan my crop allotments or to record my expenses, I'd be back in the dark ages of guessing what to do." New computer software programs are being developed commercially and are selling well.
  (Hession, John. Personal interview. 27 July 1998.)

The quotation here is abruptly dropped into the paragraph, without an introduction and without a clear indication from the writer as to how Mr. Hession's statement fits into the ideas being discussed.

> **Revised:**
>
> Modern farming techniques differ from those of twenty years ago, *particularly in the use of computer programs for planning and budgeting.* John Hession, an Iowa soybean grower *who relies heavily on computers, confirms this* when he notes, "Without a computer program to plan my crop allotments or to record my expenses, I'd be back in the dark ages of guessing what to do." Commercial software programs *such as those used by Mr. Hession, for crop allotments and budgeting,* are being developed and are selling well.

The added words in italics explain how Mr. Hession's statement confirms the point being made.

38e Avoiding plagiarism

> Plagiarism results when writers fail to document a source so that the words and ideas of someone else are presented as the writer's own work.

- *What information needs to be documented?*

  When we use the ideas, findings, data, conclusions, arguments, and words of others, we need to acknowledge that we are borrowing their work and inserting it in our own by documenting. Consciously or unconsciously passing off the work of others as our own results in the very serious form of stealing known as plagiarism, an act that has serious consequences for the writer who plagiarizes.

  If you summarize, paraphrase, or use the words of someone else (see 38b), you need to provide documentation for those sources.

- *What information does not need to be documented?*

  Common knowledge, that body of general ideas we share with our readers, does not have to be documented. Common knowledge consists of the following:

  - Standard information on a subject that your readers know
  - Information that is widely shared and can be found in numerous sources

> ## *hint*
> ### ESL Citing Sources
> In some cultures, educated writers are expected to
> know and incorporate the thinking of great scholars. It
> may be considered an insult to the reader to mention
> the names of the scholars, implying that the reader is
> not educated enough to recognize the references.
> However, in American writing, this is not the case, and
> writers are always expected to acknowledge their
> sources and give public credit to the source.

> ## *hint*
> ### Avoiding Plagiarism
> To avoid plagiarism, read over your paper and ask
> yourself whether your readers can properly identify
> which ideas and words are yours and which are from
> the sources you cite. If that is clear, then you are not
> plagiarizing.

For example, it is common knowledge among most Amer-
icans aware of current energy problems that solar power
is one answer to future energy needs. But forecasts about
how widely solar power may be used in twenty years or
estimates of the cost-effectiveness of using solar energy
would be the work of some person or group studying the
subject, and documentation would be needed.

Field research you conduct also does not need to be
documented, though you should indicate that you are re-
porting your own findings.

Original source:
Researchers studying human aggression are discovering that, in contrast to the usual stereotypes, patterns
of aggression among girls and women under some circumstances may mirror or even exaggerate those seen
in boys and men. And while women's weapons are often words, fists may be used too.

-Abigail Zuger, "A Fistful of Hostility Is Found In Women."
New York Times 28 Jul. 1998, B9.

Plagiarized version:
Women can be as hostile as men. According to Abigail Zuger, researchers studying human aggression are discovering that, in contrast to the usual stereotypes, patterns of aggression among girls and women under some circumstances may mirror or even exaggerate those seen in boys and men. And while women's weapons are often words, fists may be used too (B9).

Revision:
An acceptable revision of the plagiarized version above would have either a paraphrase or summary in the writer's own words or would indicate, with quotation marks, the exact words of the source. (See 38a.)

39

DOCUMENT DESIGN

As we write, we think about the words and ideas we are composing and the grammatical correctness of the language used. But in an age of so much visual communication, we also have to be concerned with the visual presentation of our writing. This is necessary because readers need clear visual markers to help understand the information on the page and because we want readers to read our documents. When readers see overcrowded pages with little white space and long, unbroken sections of text, they are likely to react negatively. This section will offer guidelines for paper presentation and for ways to make your writing more visually effective.

39a Paper presentation

Your instructor may request that you follow specific guidelines for papers in that course. But if not, you can follow these general guidelines:

Paper: Use 8 1/2″ × 11″ white, unlined paper. Print or write on one side only.
Line spacing: Double-space throughout, including every line in the title, the text of the paper, headings, quotations, and bibliography.
Margins: Allow one inch at the top and bottom and at both sides of the page, but put page numbers one-half inch

from the top at the right side of the page. Justify margins at the left, but not at the right side of the page.

Indentation: Indent the first line of every paragraph one-half inch or five spaces from the left margin. For long quotations within paragraphs, indent one inch or ten spaces from the left margin.

Title: For MLA format, research papers and reports do not need a title page. Leave a margin of one inch from the top, and then on separate lines, double-spaced, at the left side of the page, put your name, your instructor's name, the course number, and date submitted. Then, double-space and type the paper title, centered on the page. If a second line is needed, double-space between lines. For APA format, the title page includes an abbreviated title and page number one-half inch from the top of the page, at the upper left-hand corner. The title is centered and double-spaced in the middle of the page, with your name, instructor's name, course number, and date double-spaced and centered under the title.

Page ordering: For MLA format, start with the first page with the title, then the text, and then end notes on a separate page, with the Works Cited (on a separate page) at the end. For APA format, place the title page first and then the text of the paper. Following that, starting on separate pages for each, put references, appendices, footnotes, tables, figure captions, and at the end, figures (each on a separate page).

Font: Use ten- to twelve-point type and a standard font with serifs, such as Helvetica, Times New Roman, or Palatino. Do not use fonts that resemble cursive writing, that do not have serifs, or that are unusually shaped and difficult to read.

Headings and subheadings: These are short titles that define sections and subsections in long reports or papers. They provide visual emphasis by breaking the paper into manageable portions that are easily seen and identified. For MLA format, put top-level headings in boldface type, capitalized (except for short prepositions and articles), and centered on the page. Second-level headings for subsections are boldfaced at the left margin, with only the first word capitalized. For APA, one level of heading is recommended for short papers, centered on the page, with each word capitalized (except short prepositions and articles that are not the first word of the heading title).

Visuals: For MLA, place visuals at the point in the text where the reader may benefit by consulting it. Be sure to include a caption that explains the chart, table, diagram, or graph. In APA, all visuals are placed on separate pages, at the end of the paper, with tables first and then figures. (See 39b for more on visuals.)

39b Visual elements

Visual appearance has always been important, but it is becoming even more so because people are regularly being overloaded with a great deal of information. To get our readers' attention, we have to present them with attractive pages and help them get through the documents we give them. And we can condense some information and make it clearer with visual elements such as lists, graphs, and tables. We aren't all artists, but we have the technological tools to word process and have our writing printed out neatly and attractively. With a few basic principles in mind, we can produce documents that our readers find attractive and readable.

Include white space. Well-used white space on the page invites readers into the page and offers some relief from the heaviness of blocks of print. Leave open space around margins and between sections of a document. Indent where it's appropriate, and add other visuals such as photographs and color.

Use headings and subheadings. Announce new topics or segments of a topic, especially in long essays and reports.

Use lists wherever possible. Instead of long paragraphs discussing many related items, group the items in lists with bullets, dashes, or numbers. This also adds white space, especially if you indent the list.

Use contrast to add emphasis. Show differences between elements and indicate more important from less important elements with a few different type sizes, indentations, graphics, and background shading. Boldface type can also help, but don't overdo it so that the page looks darker and more cluttered.

Use visuals such as tables and charts. Tables and charts can convey information easily and succinctly.

Tables

Tables present information in columns and rows and can include numbers or words.

Visuals

To present data in visual form, you can also use various kinds of figures, such as pie charts (especially for per-

TABLE 39–1

EXPECTATION	WOMEN	MEN
Starting salary	$49,190	$55,950
Signing bonus an important factor	31%	42%
Signing bonus expected	27%	51%
Signing bonus expectation	$7,000	$ 7,900
Year end bonus an important factor	38%	47%
Year end bonus expected	33%	49%
Year end bonus expectation	$8,400	$13,300
Health insurance an important factor	72%	52%
Entrepreneurial environment preferred	35%	55%
Stock option an important factor	33%	46%

centages or fractions of a whole), bar graphs and line graphs (especially for comparative data or change over time), images (such as diagrams, drawings, and photographs), and flowcharts (to help readers follow a process or show options in making decisions).

- **Use appendixes for detailed information.** In documents with detailed information such as tables, figures, questionnaires, lists, photographs, cost estimates, and so on, don't interrupt the flow of the document by including such material there. Instead, move the information to appendixes (you can have more than one) so that readers who do not need that data can skip it. Refer to each appendix in your document. If you have only one appendix, label it Appendix. If you have more than one, label them Appendix A, Appendix B, and so on. Give each appendix a title.

- **Avoid busy, cluttered pages.** Although you want your documents to have variety and interest, you also have to avoid creating pages that are too busy and cluttered. That can happen when there are too many different font types and sizes and too much use of boldface or italics. Try to limit your fonts to two or, at most, three different ones.

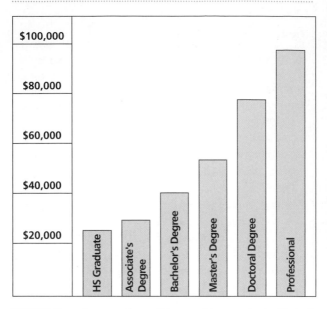

FIGURE 1 ● Average Annual Personal Income in the United States.
Source: "The Value of a College Education." Maint. Jeremy Parish. Rev. 23 May 2001. Abilene Christian College. 24 July 2001 <http://www.acu.edu/admissions/ugrad/yei/ed-value.html>. Reprinted with permission.

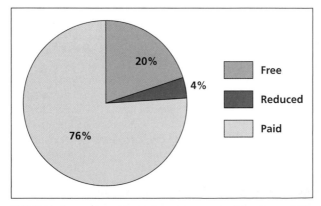

FIGURE 2 ● Free and Reduced Lunch (Total = 645), Grades 1–5
Source: Douglas MacArthur Elementary School. "School Improvement Plan." 24 July 2001 <http://dm.msdpt.k12.in.us/NCA%20Self-Study%20and%20SIP/NCA%205.24.00.html>. Reprinted with permission.

VIII
DOCUMENTATION

CONTENTS OF THIS SECTION

40 MLA Style   152

  40a In-text citations   153

  40b Endnotes   157

  40c Works Cited list   158

    • Books   162

    • Articles in periodicals   166

    • Electronic sources   167

    • Other sources   178

  40d Sample pages   182

41 APA Style   185

  41a In-text citations   186

  41b Footnotes   190

  41c References list   190

    • Books   192

    • Articles in periodicals   194

    • Electronic sources   195

    • Other sources   198

  41d Sample pages   199

42 Chicago Manual of Style   203

43 CSE (Council of Science Editors)   212

44 COS and Style Manuals for Various Fields 217

  44a Columbia Online Style (COS)   217

  44b Style manuals for various fields   225

QUESTIONS TO ASK YOURSELF

This section contains information on documenting your sources in your paper, in endnotes or footnotes, and in the list of works cited (or reference list) at the end of the paper. The formats for MLA, APA, *Chicago Manual of Style,* and Council of Science Editors (CSE) are explained and illustrated. Indexes to the examples for the notes and bibliographies will lead you to the ones you need, and there is also a list of style manuals for fields which use other documentation formats and some information on Columbia Online Style (COS).

	SECTION	PAGE

For Modern Language Association (MLA):

- What are the major features of MLA documentation? — 40 — 152

- How do I refer to the sources in the paper ["in-text citations"] for MLA? — 40a — 153

- When do I use notes (or endnotes) in MLA, and what is the appropriate way to type them? — 40b — 157

- What are the parts of a citation in the Works Cited list for MLA at the end of the paper? — 40c — 158

- How do I cite Internet sources in the Works Cited list? — 40c — 168

- What do the title page, first page, and Works Cited page in MLA look like? — 40d — 182

For American Psychological Association (APA):

- How are APA and MLA similar and different? — 41 — 185

- How do I refer to the sources in the paper ["in-text citations"] for APA? — 41a — 186

- When do I use footnotes in APA, and what is the appropriate way to type them? — 41b — 190

- What are the parts of a citation in the References list for APA at the end of the paper? — 41c — 190

- How do I cite online sources in the references? — 41c — 195

- What do the title page, first page, and Reference page in APA look like? — 41d — 199

For other formats (Chicago Manual, CSE, COS, etc.):

- How and when do I use *Chicago Manual*   42 203
  style for notes and a bibliography?

- How and when do I use the two CSE styles
  for notes and the Reference list?   43 212

- What is COS (Columbia Online Style), when
  should I use it, and is it helpful with online
  sources?   44a 217

- What are some style manuals with formats
  for writing in other fields?   44b 225

When you research a topic, you are building on the work of others, and your work, in turn, contributes to the pool of knowledge about the topic for others who will read and depend on your research. Thus, it is necessary to give credit to those whose work you use and to document your sources so completely that readers of your work can find the sources you used.

Documentation formats vary, depending on the field of study. Organizations such as newspapers and other publishing companies, businesses, and large organizations often have their own formats that are explained in their style manuals.

40

MLA STYLE

For English and other humanities, use the format of the Modern Language Association (MLA):

> Gibaldi, Joseph. *MLA Handbook for Writers of Research Papers.* 6th ed. New York: MLA, 2003.

Some of the major features of MLA style are as follows:

- For in-text citations, give the author's last name and page number of the source, preferably within the sentence rather than after it.
- Use full first and last names and middle initials of authors.
- Capitalize all major words in titles, and underline titles or put them in italics. Enclose article titles in quotation marks.
- In "Works Cited" list at the end of the paper, give full publication information, alphabetized by author.

THREE ASPECTS OF MLA FORMAT TO CONSIDER

- **In-text citations**
  In your paper you need parenthetical references to your sources to acknowledge wherever you use the words, ideas, and facts you've taken from your sources.

- **Endnotes**
  If you need to add material that would disrupt your paper if it were included in the text, include such notes at the end of the paper.

- **Works cited**
  At the end of your paper, include a list of the sources from which you have quoted, summarized, or paraphrased.

40a In-text citations

The purpose of in-text citations is to help your reader find the appropriate reference in the list of works cited at the end of the paper. Current MLA format recommends parenthetical references (not footnotes), depending on how much information you include in your sentence or in your introduction to a quotation. Try to be brief, but not at the expense of clarity, and remember to use signal words and phrases (see 38d).

INDEX TO EXAMPLES OF MLA IN-TEXT CITATIONS

1. Author's name not given in the text — 154
2. Author's name given in the text — 154
3. Two or more works by the same author — 154
4. Two or three authors — 154
5. More than three authors — 154
6. Unknown author — 155
7. Corporate author or government document — 155
8. An entire work — 155
9. A work in an anthology — 155
10. A literary work — 155
11. A multivolume work — 156
12. Indirect source — 156
13. Two or more sources — 156
14. Electronic sources — 157

1. Author's name not given in the text

If the author's name is not in your sentence, put the last name in parentheses, leave a space with no punctuation, and then put the page number.

> Recent research on sleep and dreaming indicates that dreams move backward in time as the night progresses (Dement 72).

2. Author's name given in the text

If you include the author's name in the sentence, only the page number is needed in parentheses.

> Freud states that "a dream is the fulfillment of a wish" (154).

3. Two or more works by the same author

If you used two or more different sources by the same author, put a comma after the author's last name and include a shortened version of the title and the page reference. If the author's name is in the text, include only the title and page reference.

> One current theory emphasizes the principle that dreams express "profound aspects of personality" (Foulkes, <u>Sleep</u> 144). Foulkes' investigation shows that young children's dreams are "rather simple and unemotional" ("Children's Dreams" 90).

4. Two or three authors

If your source has two or three authors, either name them in your sentence or include the names in parentheses.

> Jeffrey and Milanovitch argue that the recently reported statistics for teenage pregnancies are inaccurate (112).

(or)

> The recently reported statistics for teenage pregnancies are said to be inaccurate (Jeffrey and Milanovitch 112).

5. More than three authors

If your source has more than three authors, either use the first author's last name followed by "et al." (which means "and others") or list all the last names.

The conclusions drawn from a survey on the growth of the Internet, conducted by Martin et al., are that global usage will double within two years (36).

(or)

Recent figures on the growth of the Internet indicate that global usage will double within two years (Martin, Ober, Mancuso, and Blum 36).

6. Unknown author

If the author is unknown, use a shortened form of the title in your citation.

More detailed nutritional information in food labels is proving to be a great advantage to diabetics ("New Labeling Laws" 3).

7. Corporate author or government document

Use the name of the corporation or government agency, shortened or in full. It is better to include long names in your sentence to avoid extending the parenthetical reference.

The United Nations Regional Flood Containment Commission has been studying weather patterns that contribute to flooding in Africa (4).

8. An entire work

For an entire work, it is preferable to include the author's name in the text.

Lafmun was the first to argue that small infants respond to music.

9. A work in an anthology

Cite the name of the author of the work, not the editor of the anthology, in the sentence or in parentheses.

When Millet refers to her childhood, she uses vague references such as "in my younger days" (14) rather than specific ages or dates.

10. A literary work

For classic prose works, such as novels or plays available in several editions, it is helpful to provide more information than a page reference to the edition you used. A chapter number, for example, might help readers locate the reference in any copy.

Give the page number first, add a semicolon, and then give other identifying information.

> In <u>The Prince</u>, Machiavelli reminds us that although some manage to jump from humble origins to great power, such people find their greatest challenge to be staying in power: " Those who rise from private citizens to be princes merely by fortune have little trouble in rising but very much trouble in maintaining their position" (23; Ch. 7).

For verse plays and poems, omit page numbers and cite by division (act, scene, canto, etc.) and line, with periods separating the various numbers. For lines, initially use the word *line* or *lines* and then afterwards, give the numbers alone.

> Eliot again reminds us of society's superficiality in "The Lovesong of J. Alfred Prufrock": "There will be time, there will be time/To prepare a face to meet the faces that you meet" (lines 26–27).

11. A multivolume work

When you cite a volume number as well as a page reference for a multivolume work, separate the two by a colon and a space. Do not use the words "volume" or "page."

> In his <u>History of the Civil War</u>, Jimmersen traces the economic influences that contributed to the decisions of several states to stay in the Union (3: 798–823).

12. Indirect source

If you have to rely on a secondhand source in which someone's quoted words appear in a source written by someone else, start the citation with the abbreviation "qtd. in."

> Although Newman has established a high degree of accuracy for such tests, he reminds us that "no test like this is ever completely and totally accurate" (qtd. in Mazor 33).

13. Two or more sources

If you cite more than one work in your parenthetical reference, separate the references by a semicolon.

> Recent attempts to control the rapid destruction of the rain forests in Central America have met with little success (Costanza 22; Kinderman 94).

MLA Style **157**

MLA
MLA
MLA
MLA
MLA
MLA

14. Electronic sources

For electronic sources, start with the word by which the source is alphabetized in your Works Cited list (see 40c). For Columbia Online Style (COS) in the humanities, see 44a.

> The World Wide Web is a helpful source for community groups seeking information on how to protest projects that damage the local environment ("Environmental Activism").

40b Endnotes

When you have additional comments or information that would disrupt the paper, cite the information in endnotes numbered consecutively through the paper. Put the number at the end of the phrase, clause, or sentence containing the material you are referring to. Use a superscript (raised) number above the line, with no punctuation. Leave no extra space before the number and one extra space after if the reference is in the middle of the sentence and two extra spaces when the reference number is at the end of the sentence.

> The treasure hunt for sixteenth-century pirate loot buried in Nova Scotia began in 1927,[3] but hunting was discontinued when the treasure seekers found the site flooded at high tide.[4]

At the end of your paper, begin a new sheet with the heading "Notes," but do not underline or put the heading in quotation marks. Leave a one-inch margin at the top, center the heading, double-space, and then begin listing your notes. For each note, indent five spaces, use a superscript (the number raised above the line), and begin the note. Double-space, and if the note continues on the next line, begin that line at the left margin. The format is slightly different from that used in the Works Cited section in that the author's name appears in normal order, followed by a comma, the title, publisher and date in parentheses, and a page reference.

> [3] Some historians argue that this widely accepted date is inaccurate. See Jerome Flynn, <u>Buried Treasures</u> (New York: Newport, 1978) 29–43.

> [4] Avery Jones and Jessica Lund, "The Nova Scotia Mystery Treasure," <u>Contemporary History</u> 9 (1985): 81–83.

If you are asked to use footnotes instead of endnotes, place them at the bottoms of pages, beginning four lines (two double spaces) below the text. Single-space footnotes, but double-space between them. Number them consecutively through the paper.

40c Works Cited list

The Works Cited is a list of all the sources cited in your paper, not other materials you read but didn't refer to. Arrange the list alphabetically by the last name of the author, and if there is no author, alphabetize by the first word of the title (but not the articles *a, an,* or *the*).

For the Works Cited section, begin a new sheet of paper, leave a one-inch margin at the top, center the heading "Works Cited" (with no underline or quotation marks), and then double-space before the first entry. For each entry, begin at the left margin for the first line and indent five spaces (or one-half inch) for additional lines in the entry. Double-space throughout. Place the Works Cited list at the end of your paper after the notes, if you have any.

There are three parts to each reference: 1) author, 2) title, and 3) publishing information. Each part is followed by a period and two spaces.

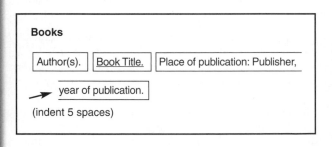

Books

Author(s). | Book Title. | Place of publication: Publisher,

year of publication.

(indent 5 spaces)

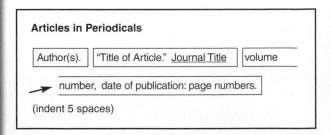

Articles in Periodicals

Author(s). | "Title of Article." | Journal Title | volume

number, | date of publication: page numbers.

(indent 5 spaces)

INDEX TO EXAMPLES OF MLA WORKS CITED

Books

1. One author 162

2. Two or three authors 162

3. More than three authors 162

4. More than one work by the same author 162

5. A work that names an editor 163

6. A work with an author and an editor 163

7. A work that names a translator 163

8. A work by a corporate author 163

9. A work by an unknown author 163

10. A work that has more than one volume 163

11. A work in an anthology 164

12. Two or more works in the same anthology 164

13. An article in a reference book 164

14. Introduction, foreword, preface, or afterword 164

15. A work with a title within a title 164

16. Second or later edition 165

17. Modern reprint 165

18. A work in a series 165

19. A work with a publisher's imprint 165

20. Government publication 165

21. Proceedings of a conference 165

Articles in Periodicals **166**

22. Scholarly journal with continuous paging 166

23. Scholarly journal that pages each issue
   separately 166

24. Monthly or bimonthly magazine article 166

25. Weekly or biweekly magazine article — 166

26. Newspaper article — 166

27. Unsigned article — 167

28. Editorial or letter to the editor — 167

29. Review of a work — 167

30. Article in microform collection of articles — 167

Electronic Sources
CD-ROMs and other portable databases — **167**

31. Material accessed from a periodically published database on CD-ROM — 167

32. Publication on CD-ROM — 168

33. Publication on diskette — 168

34. Work in more than one published medium — 168

The Internet and online databases — **168**

35. Entire Internet site — 171

   a. Home page for a course — 172

   b. Home page for academic department — 172

   c. Personal home page — 172

36. Online book — 173

   a. Entire online book — 173

   b. Part of an online book — 173

   c. Online government publication — 174

37. Article in an online periodical — 174

   a. Article in a scholarly journal — 174

   b. Article in a newspaper or newswire — 175

   c. Article in a magazine — 175

   d. Anonymous article — 175

   e. Letter to the editor — 175

38. Work from a library or personal
   subscription service   175

   a. Library subscription service   176

   b. Personal subscription service   176

39 Other electronic sources   176

   a. Television or radio   177

   b. Sound recording or clip   177

   c. Film or film clip   177

   d. Painting, sculpture, or photograph   177

   e. Interview   177

   f. Cartoon   177

   g. Advertisement   178

   h. E-mail   178

   i. Online posting   178

   j. Synchronous communication   178

Other Sources   **178**

40. Computer software   178

41. Television or radio program   178

42. Record, tape cassette, or CD   179

43. Film or video recording   179

44. Live performance of a play   179

45. Musical composition   180

46. Work of art   180

47. Letter or memo   180

48. Personal interview   180

49. Published interview   180

50. Radio or television interview   180

51. Map or chart   180

52. Cartoon   181

53. Advertisement	181
54. Lecture, speech, or an address	181
55. Pamphlet	181
56. Published dissertation	181
57. Abstract of a dissertation	181
58. Unpublished dissertation	181

Books

1. One author

> Joos, Martin. <u>The Five Clocks</u>. New York:
> Harcourt, 1962.

2. Two or three authors

> Mellerman, Sidney, John Scarcini, and Leslie Karlin.
> <u>Human Development: An Introduction to
> Cognitive Growth.</u> New York: Harper, 1981.

3. More than three authors
Either name only the first and add "et al." ("and
others") or give all names in the order they appear
on the title page.

> Spiller, Robert, et al. <u>Literary History of the United
> States</u>. New York: Macmillan, 1960.

(or)

> Spiller, Robert, Harlan Minton, Michael Upta, and
> Gretchen Kielstra. <u>Literary History of the
> United States</u>. New York: Macmillan, 1960.

4. More than one work by the same author
Use the author's name in the first entry only. From
then on, type three hyphens and a period and then
begin the next title. Alphabetize by title.

> Newman, Edwin. <u>A Civil Tongue</u>. Indianapolis:
> Bobbs-Merrill, 1966.

> — <u>Strictly Speaking</u>. New York: Warner Books, 1974.

5. A work that names an editor

Use the abbreviation "ed." for one editor (for "edited by") and "eds." for more than one editor.

> Kinkead, Joyce A., and Jeanette Harris, eds. <u>Writing Centers in Context: Twelve Case Studies</u>. Urbana: NCTE, 1993.

6. A work with an author and an editor

Give the editor's name after the title. Before the name or names (if there is more than one editor) put the abbreviation "Ed." (for "Edited by").

> Frankfurter, Felix. <u>The Diaries of Felix Frankfurter</u>. Ed. Thomas Sayres. Boston: Norton, 1975.

7. A work that names a translator

Use the abbreviation "Trans." (for "Translated by").

> Sastre, Alfonso. <u>Sad Are the Eyes of William Tell</u>. Trans. Leonard Pronko. Ed. George Wellwarth. New York: New York UP, 1970.

8. A work by a corporate author

> United States Capitol Society. <u>We, the People: The Story of the United States Capitol</u>. Washington, National Geographic Soc., 1964.

9. A work by an unknown author

> <u>Report of the Commission on Tests</u>. New York: College Entrance Examination Board, 1970.

10. A work that has more than one volume

For two or more volumes of a work cited in your paper, put references to volume and page numbers in the parenthetical references. If you are citing only one of the volumes in your paper, state the number of that volume in the Works Cited list and give publication information for that volume alone.

> Rutherford, Ernest. <u>The Collected Papers</u>. 3 vols. Philadelphia: Allen and Unwin, 1962–65.

> Stowe, Harriet Beecher. "Sojourner Truth, the Libyan Sibyl." 1863. <u>The Heath Anthology of American Literature</u>. Ed. Paul Lauter et al. 2nd ed. Vol. 1. Lexington: Heath, 1994. 2425–33.

11. A work in an anthology

State the author and title of the work first, then the title and other information about the anthology, including page numbers on which the selection appears.

> Dymvok, George E., Jr. "Vengeance." <u>Poetry in the Modern Age</u>. Ed. Jason Metier. San Francisco: New Horizons. 1994. 54.

> Licouktis, Michelle. "From Slavery to Freedom." <u>New South Quarterly</u> 29 (1962): 87–98. Rpt. in <u>Voices of the Sixties: Selected Essays</u>. Ed. Myrabelle McConn. Atlanta: Horizons, 1995. 12–19.

12. Two or more works in the same anthology

Include a complete entry for the collection and then cross-reference the works to that collection. In the cross-reference include the author and title of the work, the last name of the editor of the collection, and the inclusive page numbers.

> Batu, Marda, and Hillary Matthews, eds. <u>Voices of American Women</u>. New York: Littlefield, 1995.

> Jamba, Shawleen. "My Mother's Not Going Home." Batu and Matthews 423–41.

13. An article in a reference book

If the article is signed, give the author first. If it is unsigned, give the title first. If articles are arranged alphabetically, omit volume and page numbers. When citing familiar reference books, list only the edition and year of publication.

> "Bioluminescence." <u>The Concise Columbia Encyclopedia</u>. 2nd ed. 1983.

14. Introduction, foreword, preface, or afterword Start the entry with the author of the introductory part.

> Bruner, Jerome. Introduction. <u>Thought and Language</u>. By Lev Vygotsky. Cambridge: M.I.T., 1962. v–xiii.

15. A work with a title within a title

If a title normally underlined appears within another title, do not underline it or put it inside of quotation marks.

Lillo, Alphonso. <u>Re-Reading Shakespeare's</u> Hamlet
   <u>from the Outside</u>. Boston: Martinson, 1995.

16. Second or later edition

Ornstein, Robert E. <u>The Psychology of
   Consciousness</u>. 2nd ed. New York: Harcourt,
   1977.

17. Modern reprint

After the title of the book state the original
publication date. In the publication information that
follows, put the date of publication for the reprint.

Weston, Jessie L. <u>From Ritual to Romance</u>. 1920.
   Garden City: Anchor-Doubleday, 1957.

18. A work in a series

If the title page or preceding page of the book
indicates it is part of a series, include the series
name, without underlines or quotation marks, and
the series number, followed by a period, before the
publication information.

Waldheim, Isaac. <u>Revisiting the Bill of Rights</u>.
   Studies of Amer. Constitutional Hist. 18. New
   York: Waterman, 1991.

19. A work with a publisher's imprint

For books under imprints or special names that
usually appear with the publisher's name on the title
page, include the imprint name and then a hyphen
and the name of the publisher.

Tamataru, Ishiko. <u>Sunlight and Strength</u>. New
   York: Anchor-Doubleday, 1992.

20. Government publication

United States. Office of Education. <u>Tutor-Trainer's
   Resource Handbook</u>. Washington: GPO, 1973.

21. Proceedings of a conference

Treat the published proceedings of a conference like
a book and include information about the conference
if such information isn't included in the title.

Esquino, Luis. <u>Second Language Acquisition in the
   Classroom</u>. Proc. of the Soc. for Second
   Language Acquisition Conference, Nov. 1994,
   U of Texas. Dallas: Midlands, 1995.

Articles in periodicals

22. Scholarly journal with continuous paging
Most scholarly journals have continuous pagination throughout the whole volume for the year. To find a particular issue on the shelf, you need only the volume number and the page, not the issue number.

> Delbruch, Max. "Mind from Matter." <u>American Scholar</u> 47 (1978): 339–53.

23. Scholarly journal that pages each issue separately
If each issue of the journal starts with page 1, then include the issue number.

> Barthla, Frederick, and Joseph Murphy. "Alcoholism in Fiction." <u>Kansas Quarterly</u> 17.2 (1981) : 77–80.

24. Monthly or bimonthly magazine article

> Lillio, Debra. "New Cures for Migraine Headaches." <u>Health Digest</u> Oct. 1995: 14–18.

25. Weekly or biweekly magazine article
For a magazine published every week or every two weeks, give the complete date beginning with the day and abbreviating the month. Do not give the volume and issue numbers.

> Isaacson, Walter. "Will the Cold War Fade Away?" <u>Time</u> 27 Feb. 1987: 40–45.

26. Newspaper article
Provide the author's name and the title of the article, then the name of the newspaper as it appears on the masthead, omitting any introductory article such as *The*. If the city of publication is not included in the name, add the city in square brackets but not underlined, after the name: <u>Journal-Courier</u> [Trenton]. If the paper is nationally published, such as <u>Wall Street Journal</u>, do not add the city of publication.

> Strout, Richard L. "Another Bicentennial." <u>New York Times</u> 10 Nov. 1994, late ed.: A9+.

27. Unsigned article

> "Trading Lives." <u>Newsweek</u> 21 Apr. 1993: 87–89.

28. Editorial or letter to the editor

If you are citing an editorial, add the word
"Editorial," without an underline or quotation marks,
after the title of the editorial.

> "Watching Hillary's Defense Team at Play." Editorial.
> <u>Washington Times</u> 5 Jan. 1996, late ed.: A18.

29. Review of a work

Include the reviewer's name and title of the review, if
any, followed by the words "Rev. of" (for "Review of"),
the title of the work being reviewed, a comma, the
word "by," and then the author's name. If the work
has no title and is not signed, begin the entry with
"Rev. of" and in your list of Works Cited alphabetize
under the title of the work being reviewed.

> Kauffmann, Stanley. "Cast of Character." Rev. of
> <u>Nixon</u>, dir. Oliver Stone. <u>New Republic</u> 22
> Jan. 1996: 26–27.

> Rev. of <u>The Beak of the Finch</u>, by Jonathan Weiner.
> <u>Science Weekly</u> 12 Dec. 1995: 36.

30. Article in microform collection of articles

> Gilman, Elias. "New Programs for School Reform."
> <u>Charleston Herald</u> 18 Jan. 1991: 14. <u>Newsbank:</u>
> <u>School Reform</u> 14 (1991): fiche 1, grids A7–12.

Electronic sources

CD-ROMs and other portable databases

Sources in electronic form that are stored on CD-ROMs,
diskettes, and magnetic tapes and have to be read on computers are portable databases. State the medium of publication (such as CD-ROM or diskette), the vendor's name, and
the date of electronic publication.

31. Material accessed from a periodically published database on CD-ROM

If no printed source is indicated, include author, title
of material (in quotation marks), date of material (if

given), title of database (underlined), publication medium, name of vendor, electronic publication date.

> Anstor, Marylee. "Nutrition for Pregnant Women."
> <u>New York Times</u> 12 Apr. 1994, late ed.: C1.
> <u>New York Times Ondisc</u>. CD-ROM. UMI-
> Proquest. Oct. 1994.

32. Publication on CD-ROM

For CD-ROM publications without updates or regular revisions, cite like books, and add the medium of publication.

> Mattmer, Tobias. "Discovering Jane Austen."
> <u>Discovering Authors</u>. Vers. 1.0. CD-ROM.
> Detroit: Gale, 1992.

33. Publication on diskette

Diskette publications are cited like books with an added description of the medium of publication.

> Lehmo, Jarred. <u>Ethnicity in Dance</u>. Diskette.
> Chicago: U of Chicago P, 1995.

34. Work in more than one published medium

Some electronic publications appear as packages of materials in different publication media. For example, a CD-ROM may be packaged with a diskette. Cite such publication packages as you would a CD-ROM product, specifying the media in the package.

> <u>History of Stage Costuming in Europe</u>. CD-ROM,
> videodisc. Philadelphia: Michelson, 1995.

The Internet and online databases

Both the Internet and online databases are useful resources. Online databases, like the Internet, are accessed electronically, but online databases may not be linked to the Internet. For example, your library may have purchased databases for some of their computers that are not connected to the Internet.

When you cite sources from the Internet and online databases, you have the same goals as you do when citing print sources: to identify your sources and to help your reader find your sources. But citing electronic sources can be confusing because people who develop sites do not universally agree upon what information to include on the site. Moreover, Internet sources change more easily than print sources, and many will not contain all the information you need for a citation. But your aim is to be as complete as possible, to include as much of the information as is available. You may also want to consult the Columbia Online Style (COS) guidelines in humanities, in section 44a, which some instructors turn to when MLA guidelines do not specifically offer a format for a particular type of source.

The basic entry for *print* sources normally has three main divisions (author, title, and publication information), but a citation for an *electronic* publication may have as many as five divisions (with periods between each division):

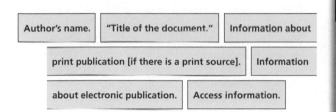

Author's name

Follow the recommendations for citing the names of authors of books.

Title of the document

State the full title of a document that is part of an entire Internet site, and enclose it in quotation marks. (To cite the entire Internet site, see entry 35.)

Information about print publication (if there is a print source)

If the document indicates there is a previous or simultaneous print form of the publication, follow the guidelines for print publications for that part of the citation.

Information about electronic publication

Internet sites vary greatly as to the amount of information provided. Typically you will find the title of the site (underlined in your citation), the date of electronic publication or the latest update, and the name of any institution or organization that sponsors the site. If you see an editor's name or a version number, include that information directly following the title of the site.

Access information

Date of access: Print sources include only one date for publication, but citations to electronic works normally include two (or more) dates, the date for the source and the date on which you viewed the site. If you access the site more than once, include the latest date of access because sites change easily. For a work with a print or simultaneous print existence, it may be necessary to include three dates: the date of print publication, the date of the site, and the date you viewed the site.

URL: The most efficient way to find an online site is to use its network address, known as a URL (uniform resource locator). The 6th edition of the <u>MLA Handbook</u> recommends including URLs when citing online works, though URLs are often complex and need to be copied carefully. Because URLs change, include as much other information as you can so that readers can find the site if it has a new address. The <u>MLA Handbook</u> also recommends that you print out or download sites you are citing because they might disappear completely from the Internet. Include the URL immediately following the date of access, and enclose the URL in angle brackets. If you need to divide the URL between two lines, break only after a slash and don't include a hyphen at the break. Include the access-mode identifier (http, ftp, gopher, telnet, or news). If the URL you need to include is unusually complicated and lengthy and if there is a search page on the site, give the URL of the site's search page.

Examples of entries for documents found on the Internet:

"Chat Room Libel Case Goes Before State High Court."
<u>CNN.com.</u> 2003. Cable News Network. 4 March 2003
<http://www.cnn.com/2003/US/Northeast/03/04/
internet.defamation.ap/index.html>.

Gray, Martin. "Machu Picchu, Peru." <u>Places of Peace
and Power.</u> 2003. 28 Feb. 2003 <http://
www.sacredsites.com/2nd56/21422.html>.

Lizza, Ryan. "State of Peace." <u>The New Republic.</u> 10
March 2003: 14–17.5 March 2003 <http://
www.tnr.com/
doc.mhtml?i520030310&s5lizza031003>.

Because there will be citations requiring additional information, the following list includes most of the possible types of
information that may be needed, listed here in the order
they are normally arranged.

- **Name** of author, editor, compiler, or translator, in
  reversed order, followed by an abbreviation, if needed,
  such as "ed." or "trans."
- **Title of the work** enclosed in quotation marks. Or the title of a posting to a discussion list or forum (taken from
  the subject line and enclosed in quotation marks) followed by the description "Online posting" (not enclosed
  in quotation marks or underlined)
- **Title of book** (underlined)
- **Name of editor, compiler, etc.** if not already included as
  the first entry, preceded by an abbreviation such as "Ed."
  or "Trans."
- **Publication information** for any print version of the source
- **Title of the Internet project or site** (such as a database,
  online periodical, scholarly project, or personal site), underlined. For a professional or personal site with no title,
  a description such as "Home page" (not underlined or
  enclosed in quotation marks)
- **Name of editor,** if available
- **Version number of the source** or, for a journal, volume
  number, issue number, or other identifying number
- **Date of electronic publication** of the latest update or of
  the posting
- **Name of the subscription service** and if a library or con-
  sortium of libraries is the subscriber, name and geographical location (city, state abbreviation) of the
  subscriber (see entry 38)
- **List or forum name** for posting to a discussion list or forum
- **Numbers** (total) of pages, paragraphs, or other sections,
  if numbered
- **Organization or institution name** that sponsors the site
  (if not cited earlier)
- **Date of access** (when you accessed the source)
- **Electronic address (URL)** in angle brackets: < > If a URL
  must be divided between two lines, break it only after a
  slash, and do not add a hyphen at the break

Kinds of Electronic Publications

35. Entire Internet site

Typically, to cite an entire online scholarly project,
information database, journal, or professional site,

include the following items. If you can't find some of this information, cite what is available.

a. Title of the site (underlined)
b. Name of the editor of the site (if given)
c. Electronic publication information, including version number (if relevant and if not part of the title), date of electronic publication or of the latest update, and name of any sponsoring institution or organization
d. Date of access and URL

> CompPile. Ed. Rich Haswell. Feb. 2003. 9 March
>   2003 <http://comppile.tamucc.edu/index.html>.

> Herbalgram.org. American Botanical Council. 2002.
>   18 Feb. 2003 <http://www.herbalgram.org>.

35a. Home page for a course Begin the entry with the name of the instructor, reversed, followed by a period, and the title of the course (neither underlined nor in quotation marks). Continue with a description such as "Course home page" (neither underlined nor in quotation marks), dates of the course, names of the department and institution, the date of access, and the URL.

> Feluga, Dino F. Nineteenth-Century
>   English Literature. Course home page.
>   Aug. 2002–Dec. 2002. Dept. of English,
>   Purdue U. 9 March 2003 <http://
>   web.ics.purdue.edu/~felluga/337.html>.

35b. Home page for an academic department Give the name of the department, a description such as "Dept. home page" (neither underlined nor in quotation marks), the name of the institution, the date of access, and the URL.

> Horticulture and Landscape Architecture.
>   Dept. home page. Purdue U School of
>   Agriculture. 10 March 2003 <http://
>   www.hort.purdue.edu/hort/>.

35c. Personal home page Begin with the name of the person who created it, reversed, followed by a period. Continue with the title of the site (underlined) or, if there is no title, with the description "Home page" (neither underlined nor in quotation marks), date of the last update, if given, the date of access, and the URL.

> Harris, Muriel. <u>Meet Muriel Harris.</u> 18 June 2002. 6 March 2003 <http:// owl.english.purdue.edu/lab/staff/ homepages/mickey.html>.

36. Online book

36a. Entire online book For printed books available online, follow the recommendations for citing books (see entries 1–21), modifying them as appropriate to the electronic source. The following items are typically included:

1. Name of the author or, if only an editor, compiler, or translator is listed, include that as an abbreviation (for example, "ed." or "trans.")
2. Title of the work (underlined)
3. Name of the editor, compiler, or translator of the book if that's appropriate, with "Ed.," "Comp.," or "Trans." before the name
4. Publication information for the original print version, if that is included (city of publication, name of publisher, year of publication)
5. Electronic publication information:
   a. title of the Internet site (underlined)
   b. editor of the site
   c. version number
   d. date of electronic publication
   e. name of any sponsoring organization
   f. date you access the site and the URL for the work

> Yonge, Charlotte. <u>Henrietta's Wish: or, Domineering: A Tale.</u> 2nd ed. London. 1853. <u>Victorian Women Writers Project. Indiana U.</u> Ed. Perry Willett. 28 Aug. 1997. Indiana University Library Electronic Text Resource Service. 9 Aug. 2002 <http://www.indiana.edu/~letrs/ vwwp/yonge/henrietta.html>.

36b. Part of an online book Put the title or name of the part between the author's name and title of the book. If the part is a work like a poem or essay, put quotation marks around the title of the part.

> Eliot, T[homas] S[terns]. "Whispers of
> Immortality." <u>Poems.</u> New York. 1920.
> <u>Project Bartleby Archive.</u> 1994.
> Columbia U. 6 Feb. 1999 <http://
> www.columbia.edu/acis/bartleby/
> eliot/22.html>.

36c. Online government publication

> United States. Department of Defense.
> Air Force, Air University.
> <u>Development of Military Night
> Aviation to 1919.</u> By William Edward
> Fischer, Jr. 1998. U.S. Government
> Online Bookstore. 10 March 2003
> <http://bookstore.gpo.gov/>.

37. Article in an online periodical

Online periodicals include scholarly journals, newspapers, and magazines, and works within such publications include articles, reviews, editorials, and letters to the editor. Follow the guidelines for citing parts of print periodicals, modifying them as needed for an electronic source. Include the author's name; title of the article or other work (enclosed in quotation marks); name of the periodical (underlined); volume number, issue number, or other identifying number; date of publication; number of pages or other sections, if numbered; date of access; and URL. If you can't find all this information, cite what is available.

37a. Article in a scholarly journal
Scholarly journals may be available independently on their own sites or as part of databases. If the journal is included in a database, cite the name of the database (underlined) after the print information, and follow this with the date of access and URL.

> Carmean, Colleen, and Jeremy Haefner.
> "Next-Generation Course
> Management Systems." <u>Educause
> Quarterly</u> 26.1 (2003): 10–13.
> <u>Educause.</u> 11 March 2003
> <http://www.educause.edu/ir/
> library/pdf/eqm0311.pdf>.

37b. Article in a newspaper or newswire

> "Microsoft Testimony Continues." <u>AP Online</u> 3 Dec. 1998. 10 Dec. 1998 <http://www.nytimes.com/ aponline/e/AP-Carter.html>.

37c. Article in a magazine

> Palmentier, Marianne. "Today's Children." <u>Parents Online</u> 4.7 (1998): 18 pars. 21 Nov. 2000 <http:// www.parentstoday.com/issue4.7html>.

37d. Anonymous article

> "Senate Votes to Slash Bush Tax Cut Plan." <u>NYTimes.com</u> 25 March 2003. 26 March 2003 <http:// www.nytimes.com/aponline/national/ AP-Budget. html>.

37e. Letter to the editor

> Cripps, Camilla. Letter <u>Lafayette Journal and Courier Online</u> 25 March 2003. 26 March 2003 <http:// www.lafayettejc.com/news20030325/ 200303252local_opinion1048569904. shtml>.

38. Work from a library or personal subscription service

Two types of online subscription services are those that libraries or library systems typically subscribe to (such as InfoTrac or Lexis-Nexis) and those to which users personally subscribe to (such as America Online). When you document sources from either type, begin the entry as shown in entry 35, with the title of the site, name of the editor, electronic publication information, and date of access and URL.

The format of the entry depends on whether your source was taken from an information database, an online book, article from a periodical, and so on. When citing material that originally had a print source, begin with the information about the print publication, omitting whatever is not given in the online version. If you can, conclude with a URL or, if that is complicated and very long, with the URL for the site's search page. If there is no URL, finish your citation as described here.

38a. Library subscription service When you cite a source from a service to which a library or library system subscribes, end the citation with the name of the database you used (underlined), if known; the name of the service; name of the library or library system (with a city, a state abbreviation, or both if it is useful); and date of access. If you know the URL of the service's home page, include that, in angle brackets, immediately after the date of access. If the service provides only the starting page number of an article's original print version (for example, page 18), include the number followed by a hyphen, a space, and a period: "18- ."

> Gelerntner, David. "Replacing the United Nations" <u>Weekly Standard</u> 17 March 2003: 23–29. <u>Current Affairs.</u> Lexis-Nexis. Purdue U Lib., West Lafayette, IN. 14 March 2003 <http://web.lexis-nexis.com/universe>.

38b. Personal subscription service If you use a source from a personal subscription service that retrieves material for you when you enter a keyword or similar designation, complete the citation by writing "Keyword" (not underlined or enclosed in quotation marks), with a colon, and the word itself following the name of the service and date of access. If you follow a series of topic labels, write the word "Path" (with no underline and not enclosed in quotation marks), with a colon, and list the sequence of topics you followed; use semicolons to separate topics.

> "White and Bleiler Win X-Games." <u>Extreme Sports.</u> America Online. 28 Feb. 2003. Keyword: Action sports.

39. Other electronic sources

To document other electronic sources, follow the guidelines for print and nonprint sources, and modify as needed. Some kinds of sources will need labels, such as "Interview," "Map," or "Online posting," but do not underline or enclose in quotation marks. If there is an archive available, cite it so that your reader can consult that source.

39a. Television or radio

> Sorkin, Aaron. <u>The West Wing</u>. With Martin
> Sheen. 5 March 2003. National
> Broadcasting Company. 12 March
> 2003 <http://www.nbc.com/
> The_West_Wing/index.html>.

39b. Sound recording or clip

> Nussbaum, Felicity, Joanne Braxton,
> Susan Stanford Friedman. "Women's
> Life Writing" <u>What's the Word?</u> 2001.
> <u>Modern Language Association</u>. 5
> March 2003 <http://www.mla.org/>.
> Path: MLA Radio Show; Browse
> Shows and Listen; 2001.

39c. Film or film clip

> Moore, Michael, dir. <u>Bowling for Columbine.</u>
> 2002. <u>Film Clips & Soundtrack.</u> 12
> March 2003 <http://
> www.bowlingforcolumbine.com/
> media/clips/index.php>.

39d. Painting, sculpture, or photograph

> Gursky, Andreas. <u>Shanghai.</u> 2000. Museum
> of Mod. Art, New York. 15 Feb. 2003
> <http://www.moma.org/exhibitions/
> 2001/gursky/index.html>.

39e. Interview

> Rice, Condoleezza. Interview. <u>National
> Public Radio.</u> 12 March 2003. 14 March
> 2003 <http://www.npr.org/
> display_pages/features/
> feature_1189368.html>.

39f. Cartoon

> Oliphant, Pat. "Oliphant." Cartoon.
> <u>Washingtonpost.com</u> 11 March 2003.
> 15 March 2003 <http://
> www.washingtonpost.com/wp-dyn/
> opinion/?nav5hpleft1>.

39g. Advertisement

> The 2003 Demotivators Calendar.
> Advertisement. 4 March 2003
> <http://www.despair.com/>.

39h. E-mail To cite electronic mail, include the name of the writer; the title of the message (if any) from the subject line and enclosed in quotation marks; description of the message that includes the name of the person receiving it; and the date of the message.

> Harris, David. "Madeleine Albright's State-
> ment." E-mail to the author. 5 Dec. 2000.

39i. Online posting

> Maxon, Don. "Blending ESL and Bilingual
> Education." Online posting. 5 Jan.
> 1998. Dave Sperling Presents ESL
> Discussion Center Forum for Teachers:
> Bilingual Education. 6 Feb. 1998
> <http://www.eslcafe.com/discussion/
> ds/index.cgi?read52>.

39j. Synchronous communication When you cite a synchronous communication, give the name of the speaker, a description of the event, date of the event, the forum for the communication, date of access, and the URL, with the prefix "telnet://."

> Garlenum, Karl. Online discussion of peer
> tutoring. 22 Nov. 1998. WRITE-C/MOO.
> 27 Nov. 1998 <telnet://
> write-c.udel.edu: 2341>.

Other sources

40. Computer software
Citations are similar to citations for CD-ROM or diskette materials

> McProof. Vers. 3.2.1. Diskette. Salt Lake City:
> Lexpertise, 1987.

41. Television or radio program
Include the episode title (in quotation marks), program title (underlined), series title (no underline or quotation marks), name of the network, call letters

and city of the local station, broadcast date. If pertinent, add information such as names of performers, director, or narrator.

> "Tall Tales from the West." <u>American Folklore</u>. Narr. Hugh McKenna. Writ. Carl Tannenberg. PBS. WFYI, Indianapolis. 14 Mar. 1995.

42. Record, tape cassette, or CD
Depending on which is emphasized, cite the composer, conductor, or performer first. Then list the title (underlined), artist, medium—if not a compact disc (no underline or quotation marks), manufacturer, year of issue (if unknown, include "n.d." for "no date"). Place a comma between manufacturer and date, with periods following all other items.

> Perlman, Itzhak. <u>Mozart Violin Concertos Nos. 3 & 5</u>. Weiner Philarmoniker Orch. Cond. James Levine. Deutsche Grammophon, 1983.

> Schiff, Heinrich. <u>Five Cello Concertos</u>. By Antonio Vivaldi. Academy of St. Martin-in-the-Fields. Dir. Iona Brown. Audiocassette. Philips, 1984.

43. Film or video recording
Begin film citations with the title (underlined), include the director, distributor, and the year, and perhaps the names of the writer, performers, and producer. Treat a videocassette, videodisc, slide program, or filmstrip like a film, and give the original release date and the medium before the name of the distributor.

> <u>Richard III</u>. By William Shakespeare. Dir. Ian McKellen and Richard Loncrain. Perf. Ian McKellen, Annette Bening, Jim Broadbent, and Robert Downey, Jr. MGM/UA, 1995.

> Renoir, Jean, dir. <u>The Rules of the Game</u> [<u>Le Regle du Jeu</u>]. Perf. Marcel Dalio and Nora Gregor. 1937. Videocassette. Video Images, 1981.

44. Live performance of a play
Include the theater and city where the performance was given, separated by a comma and followed by a period, and the date of the performance.

Inherit the Wind. By Jerome Lawrence and Robert
E. Lee. Dir. John Tillinger. Perf. George
C. Scott and Charles Durning. Royale
Theatre, New York. 23 January 1996.

45. Musical composition

If the composition is known only by number, form, or
key, do not underline or use quotation marks. If the
score is published, cite it like a book and capitalize
abbreviations such as "no." and "op."

Bach, Johann Sebastian. Brandenburg Concertos.

Bach, Johann Sebastian. Orchestral Suite No. 1 in
C Major.

46. Work of art

Monet, Claude. Rouen Cathedral. Metropolitan
Museum of Art, New York. Masterpieces of
Fifty Centuries. New York: Dutton, 1970. 316.

47. Letter or memo

Blumen, Lado. Letter to Lui Han. 14 Oct. 1990.
Lado Blumen Papers. Minneapolis Museum
of Art Lib., Minneapolis.

48. Personal interview

Kochem, Prof. Alexander. Personal interview. 18
Apr. 2002.

49. Published interview

Goran, Nadya. "A Poet's Reflections on the End of
the Cold War." By Leonid Tuzman.
International Literary Times 18 Nov. 1995:
41–44.

50. Radio or television interview

Netanyahu, Benyamin. Interview with Ted Koppel.
Nightline. ABC. WABC, New York. 18 Aug.
1995.

51. Map or chart

Treat a map or chart like a book without an author
(#9), but add the descriptive label (Map or Chart).

New York. Map. Chicago: Rand, 1995.

52. Cartoon

> Adams, Scott. "Dilbert." Cartoon. <u>Journal and Courier</u> [Lafayette] 20 Jan. 1996: B7.

53. Advertisement

> Apple Computer. Advertisement. <u>GQ</u>, Dec. 1999: 145–46.

54. Lecture, speech, or an address

> Lihandro, Alexandra. "Writing to Learn." Conf. on Coll. Composition and Communication. Palmer House, Chicago. 23 Mar. 1990.

> Trapun, Millicent. Address. Loeb Theater. Indianapolis. 16 Mar. 2001.

55. Pamphlet

> <u>Thirty Food for Your Health</u>. New York: Consumers Health Soc., 1996.

56. Published dissertation

If the work was published by University Microfilms International (UMI), add the order number as supplementary information.

> Blalock, Mary Jo. <u>Consumer Awareness of Food Additives in Products Offered as Organic</u>. Diss. U Plainfield, 1994. Ann Arbor: UMI, 1995. 10325891.

57. Abstract of a dissertation

Begin with the publication information for the original work, and then add the information for the journal that includes the abstract.

> McGuy, Timothy. "Campaign Rhetoric of Conservatives in the 1994 Congressional Elections." Diss. Johns Hopkins U, 1995. <u>DAI</u> 56 (1996): 1402A.

58. Unpublished dissertation

> Tibbur, Matthew. "Computer-Mediated Intervention in Early Childhood Stuttering." Diss. Stanford U, 1991.

40d Sample pages

Included here are

1. a sample title page

2. a first page for a paper that does not have a title page

3. a first page for the Works Cited list

Research papers that follow MLA style generally do not need a title page, but if you are asked to include one, follow the format shown.

1. Sample title page using MLA style

(center title one-third down the page)

A Miracle Drug to Keep Us Young

or Another False Hope?

Michael G. Mitun   *(name)*

Professor Jomale   *(instructor)*

English 102, Section 59   *(course)*

18 November 2001   *(date)*

1″

2. Sample first page using MLA style

Michael G. Mitun

Professor Jomale

English 102

18 November 2001

A Miracle Drug to Keep Us Young

or Another False Hope?

Even before Ponce de Leon landed in Florida in 1513, searching for a fountain of youth, people looked for ways to resist the aging process. Among the unsuccessful cures that we find in history records are ice baths, gold elixirs, and holding one's breath. But now modern medicine is opening the door to new therapies that might work, pills based on hormones that our bodies produce when we're young but that decrease as we grow old. At the moment, the most promising of these hormones is DHEA. But most physicians are unwilling to prescribe DHEA for their patients, and the U.S. Food and Drug Administration has not approved its sale in the United States. At the present time, DHEA shows promise but is not yet the miraculous "fountain of youth" people have been waiting for.

At a recent conference hosted by the New York Academy of Sciences, titled "Dehydroepiandrosterone (DHEA) and Aging," medical researchers reported on their studies of DHEA. Burkhard Bilger, one of the people attending that conference, heard vivid testimonials about this compound which he describes as "the most plentiful steroid hormone in the human body—and the most poorly understood" (26). The promise of DHEA suggests that we take a closer look at the evidence to see if medicine really can offer us a new fountain of youth, though the chief of biology Dr. Anna McCormick at the National Institute on Aging warns that there are potential harmful effects (Jaroff).

3. Sample Works Cited page using MLA format

1″

Works Cited

Ames, Donna Spahn. "The Effects of Chronic Endurance

Training on DHEA and DHEA-S Levels in Middle-Aged Men."

Diss. U. of New Hampshire, 1991.

Bilger, Burkhard. "Forever Young." The Sciences

Sept./Oct. 1998: 26–30.

Eye to Eye. CBS. WCBS, New York. 15 June 1995.

Fahey, Thomas D. "DHEA." Joe Weider's Muscle and Fitness Aug.

1995: 94–97.

Garcia, Homer. "Effects of Dehydroepiandrosterone

(DHEA) on Brain Tissue." DHEA Transformations in Target

Tissue. Ed. Milan Zucheffa. London: Binn, 1994: 36–45.

— "Estrogens in Target Tissues." Endocrinology 136 (1997): 3247–56.

Health and Aging. Prod. Hormone Therapy Project, Middleton Medical

School. Videodisc. Middleton, 1997.

Jaroff, Leon. "New Age Therapy." Time 23 Jan. 1996: 52.

Li, Min Zhen, ed. The Biologic Role of Dehydroepiandrosterone

(DHEA). Berlin: de Gruyter, 1990.

Mindell, Earl L. "Stay Healthy." Let's Live Sept. 2000: 8–14.

"Nature's Other Time Stopper." Newsweek 7 Aug. 1995: 49.

Oppenheim, Edgar. "DHEA Offers Promise." Springfield Courier 22

June 1995, late ed.: B1. Current News Ondisc. CD-ROM. New

York: Qube, 1995.

Rabin, Prof. Jonathan. Personal interview. 21 Oct. 2001.

Rosch, Paul J. "DHEA, Electrical Stimulation, and the Fountain of

Youth." Stress Medicine 11.4 (1995): 211–27.

Whaum, Ken. "Re: DHEA testimonials." Online posting. 23 Oct. 1998.

Newsgroup alt. health.aging. natural. 2 Nov. 1998. <http://www.

dhea.com/discussion/dheabenefits.html>

1″

41

APA STYLE

American Psychological Association (APA) format is used to document papers in the behavioral and social sciences. If you are asked to use APA format, consult *The Publication Manual of the American Psychological Association,* 5th ed. Washington, D.C.: American Psychological Association, 2001. For updates and additions, see the APA Web site: **www.apastyle.org.**

APA/MLA similarities

- Both have parenthetical references in the paper to refer readers to the list at the end of the paper.
- Both have numbered notes to include information that would disrupt the writing if included there.
- Both have a reference list of works cited at the end of the paper.
- For both, references include only the sources used in the research and preparation of the paper.

APA/MLA differences

- In APA, the date of publication is included in parenthetical references in the paper and appears after the author's name in the reference list.
- In APA, authors' first and middle names are indicated by initials only.
- In APA, capitalization and use of quotation marks and underlines are different. (See the box below.)
- In APA put signal words (see 38d) in past tense ("Smith reported") or present perfect tense ("as Smith has reported").

IMPORTANT FEATURES OF APA STYLE

- For in-text citations, give the author's last name and publication year of the source.
- Use full last names and initials of first and middle names of authors.
- Capitalize only the first word and proper names in book and article titles, but capitalize all major words

in journal titles. Use italics for titles of books and journals; do not put article titles in quotation marks.

● In "References" list at the end of the paper, give full
publication information, alphabetized by author.

41a In-text citations

Include the author's name and date of publication. For direct
quotations, include the page number also.

EXAMPLES OF APA IN-TEXT CITATIONS

1. Direct quotations	186
2. Author's name given in the text	187
3. Author's name not given in the text	187
4. Work by multiple authors	187
5. Group as author	188
6. Work with unknown author	188
7. Authors with the same last name	188
8. Two or more works in same parentheses	188
9. Classical works	188
10. Specific parts of a source	189
11. Personal communications	189
12. World Wide Web and other electronic sources	189

1. Direct quotations

When you quote a source, end with quotation marks
and give the author, year, and page number in
parentheses.

Many others agree with the assessment that "this
is a seriously flawed study" (Methasa, 1994, p. 22)
and do not include its data in their own work.

2. Author's name given in the text

Cite only the year of publication in parentheses. If the year also appears in the sentence, do not add parenthetical information. If you refer to the same study again in the paragraph, with the source's name, you do not have to cite the year again if it is clear that the same study is being referred to.

> When Millard (1970) compared reaction times among the participants, he noticed an increase in errors.

> In 1994 Pradha found improvement in short-term memory with accompanying practice.

3. Author's name not given in the text

Cite the name and year, separated by a comma.

> In a recent study of reaction times (Millard, 1970) no change was noticed.

4. Work by multiple authors

For two authors, cite both names every time you refer to the source. Use "and" in the text, but an ampersand (&) in parenthetical material, tables, captions, and the References list.

> When Glick and Metah (1991) reported on their findings, they were unaware of a similar study (Grimm & Tolman, 1991) with contradictory data.

For three, four, or five authors, include all authors (and date) the first time you cite the source. For additional references, include only the first author's name and "et al." (for "and others"), with no underline or italics.

> Ellison, Mayer, Brunerd, and Keif (1987) studied supervisors who were given no training. Later, when Ellison et al. (1987) continued to study these same supervisors, they added a one-week training program.

For six or more authors, cite only the first author and "et al." and the year for all references.

> Mokach, et al. (1989) noted no improvement in norms for participant scores.

5. Group as author

The name of the group that serves as the author (for example, a government agency or a corporation) is usually spelled out every time it appears in a citation. If the name is long but easily identified by its abbreviation and you want to switch to the abbreviation, give the abbreviation in parentheses when the entire name first appears.

> In 1992 when the National Institute of Mental Health (NIMH) prepared its report, no field data on this epidemic were available. However, NIMH agreed that future reports would correct this.

6. Work with unknown author

When a work has no author, cite the first few words of the reference list entry and the year.

> One newspaper article ("When South Americans," 1987) indicated the rapid growth of this phenomenon.

7. Authors with the same last name

If two or more authors in your References list have the same last name, include their initials in all text citations.

> Until T. A. Wilman (1994) studied the initial survey (M. R. Wilman, 1993), no reports were issued.

8. Two or more works in the same parentheses

When two or more works are cited within the same parentheses, arrange them in the order they appear in the reference list, and separate them with semicolons.

> Several studies (Canin, 1989; Duniere, 1987; Pferman & Chu, 1991) reported similar behavior patterns in such cases.

9. Classical works

Reference entries are not necessary for major classical works such as ancient Greek and Roman works and the Bible, but identify the version you used in the first citation in your text. If appropriate, in each citation, include the part (book, chapter, lines).

This was known (Aristotle, trans. 1931) to be prevalent among young men with these symptoms.

10. **Specific parts of a source**

To cite a specific part of a source, include the page, chapter, figure, or table, and use the abbreviation "p." (for "page") and "chap." (for "chapter").

No work was done on interaction of long-term memory and computer programming (Sitwa & Shiu, 1993, p. 224), but recently (Takamuru, 1996, chap. 6) reported studies have considered this interaction.

For an electronic source that contains no page number, cite the paragraph number with the paragraph symbol (¶) or abbreviation for paragraph (para.). When no paragraph number is given, cite the heading and then number of the paragraph.

The two methods showed a significant difference (Smith, 2000, ¶ 2) when repeated with a different age group.

No further study indicated any change in the results (Thomasus, 2001, Conclusion, para. 3).

11. **Personal communications**

Personal communications include letters, memos, some electronic communications (e.g., e-mail, discussion groups, messages on electronic bulletin boards), telephone conversations, and other similar communications. Because the data cannot be recovered, these are included only in the text and not in the reference list. Include the initials and last name of the communicator and as exact a date as possible. (For electronic sources that can be documented, see 41c.)

According to I. M. Boza (personal communication, June 18, 2001), no population studies of the problem were done before 1999.

12. **World Wide Web and other electronic sources**

To cite a Web site in the text (but not a specific document), include the Web address. No reference entry is needed in the References.

The Web site for the American Psychological Association (**http://www.apastyle.org**) has listed an update on how to cite information found on the World Wide Web.

When paraphrasing or quoting electronic sources with no page numbers, use paragraph numbers if they are visible. Use the paragraph symbol (¶) or the abbreviation "para."

Medawar declared the results "inadequate" (2002, ¶ 6).

If there are headings but no page or paragraph numbers visible, cite the heading and the number of the paragraph following it.

"Emotional interference made the outcome questionable" (Lintona, 2002, Conclusion section, ¶ 3).

41b Footnotes

Content footnotes add important information that cannot be integrated into the text, but they are distracting and should be used only if they strengthen the discussion. Copyright permission footnotes acknowledge the source of quotations that are copyrighted. Number the footnotes consecutively with superscript arabic numerals and include the footnotes on a separate page after the reference list. Indent the first line of each footnote.

41c References list

Arrange entries in alphabetical order by the author's last name, and for several works by one author, arrange by year of publication with the earliest one first. For authors' names, give all surnames first and then the initials. Use commas to separate a list of two or more names, and use an ampersand (&) before the last name in the list. Capitalize only the first word of the title and the subtitle (and any proper names) of a book or article, but capitalize the name of the journal. Italicize book titles, names of journals, and the volume number of the journal.

Start the References list on a new page, with *References* centered at the top of the page, and double-space all entries. For each entry in the list, the first line begins at the left margin and all following lines are indented five spaces.

EXAMPLES OF APA REFERENCES

Books **192**

1. One author 192

2. Two or more works by the same author 192

3. Two or more authors 193

4. Group or corporate author 193

5. Unknown author 193

6. Edited volume 193

7. Translation 193

8. Article or chapter in an edited book 193

9. Article in a reference book 193

10. Revised edition 194

11. Multivolume work 194

12. Technical and research report 194

13. Report from a university 194

Articles in Periodicals **194**

14. Article in a journal paged continuously 194

15. Article in a journal paged separately by issue 194

16. Article in a magazine 194

17. Article in a newspaper 194

18. Unsigned article 194

19. Monograph 195

20. Review of a book, film, or video 195

Electronic sources **195**

21. Journal article 195

22. Article in an Internet-only journal 196

23. Newspaper article 196

24. Chapter or section in an Internet document 196

APA
APA
APA
APA
APA

25. Stand-alone document, no author identified, no date   196

26. Abstract   196

27. U.S. government report available on the Web   197

28. Message posted to a newsgroup   197

29. Message posted to an electronic mailing list   197

30. E-mail   197

31. Electronic database   197

32. CD-ROM   197

33. Computer program or software   197

Other Sources   **198**

34. Information service   198

35. Dissertation abstract   198

36. Government document   198

37. Conference proceedings   198

38. Interview   198

39. Film, videotape, performance, or artwork   198

40. Recording   199

41. Cassette recording   199

42. Television broadcast, series, and single episode from a series   199

43. Unpublished paper presented at a meeting   199

Books

1. One author

Rico, G. L. (1983). *Writing the natural way.* Los Angeles: J. P. Tarcher.

2. Two or more works by the same author

Include the author's name in all references and arrange by year of publication, the earliest first.

Kilmonto, R. J. (1983). *Culture and ethnicity*. Washington, D.C.: American Psychiatric Press.

Kilmonto, R. J. (1989). Comparisons of cultural adaptations. *Modern Cultural Studies, 27,* 237–43.

3. Two or more authors

Strunk, W., Jr., & White, E. B. (1979). *The elements of style* (3rd ed.). New York: Macmillan.

4. Group or corporate author

If the publication is a brochure, list this in brackets.

Mental Health Technical Training Support Center. (1994). *Guidelines for mental health nonprofit agency staffs* (2nd ed.) [Brochure]. Manhattan, KS: Author.

5. Unknown author

Americana collegiate dictionary (4th ed.). (1995). Indianapolis, IN: Huntsfield.

6. Edited volume

Griffith, J. W., & Frey, C. H. (Eds.). (1996). *Classics of children's literature* (4th ed.). Upper Saddle River, NJ: Prentice Hall.

7. Translation

Lefranc, J. R. (1976). *A Treatise on Probability* (R. W. Mateau & D. Trilling, Trans.). New York: Macmillan. (Original work published 1952)

8. Article or chapter in an edited book

Riesen, A. H. (1991). Sensory deprivation. In E. Stellar & J. M. Sprague (Eds.), *Progress in physiological psychology* (pp. 24–54). New York: Academic Press.

9. Article in a reference book

Terusami, H. T. (1993). Relativity. In *The new handbook of science* (Vol. 12, pp. 247–249). Chicago: Modern Science Encyclopedia.

10. Revised edition

> Telphafi, J. (1989). *Diagnostic techniques* (Rev. ed.). Newbury Park: CA: Pine.

11. Multivolume work

> Donovan, W. (Ed.). (1979–1986). *Social sciences: A history* (Vols. 1–5). New York: Hollins.

12. Technical and research report

> Birney, A. F. & Hall, M. M. (1981). *Early identification of children with written language disabilities* (Report No. 81–502). Washington, D.C.: National Education Association.

13. Report from a university

> Lundersen, P. S., McIver, R. L., & Yepperman, B. B. *Sexual harassment policies and the law* (Tech. Rep. No. 9). Springfield, IN: University of Central Indiana, Faculty Affairs Research Center.

Articles in periodicals

14. Article in a journal paged continuously

> Schaubroeck, J., Sime, W. E., & Mayes, B. T. (1991). The nomological validity of the type A personality. *Journal of Applied Psychology, 76,* 143–168.

15. Article in a journal paged separately by issue

> Timmo, L. A., & Kikovio, R. (1994). Young children's attempts at deception. *Research in Early Childhood Learning, 53*(2), 49–67.

16. Article in a magazine

> Simmons, H. (1995, November 29). Changing our buying habits. *American Consumer, 21,* 29–36.

17. Article in a newspaper

> Leftlow, B. S. (1993, December 18). Corporate takeovers confuse stock market predictions. *Wall Street Journal,* pp. A1, A14.

18. Unsigned article

> New study promises age-defying pills. (1995, July 27). *The Washington Post,* p. B21.

19. Monograph

> Rotter, P. B., & Stolz, G. (1966). Generalized
> expectancies of early childhood speech
> patterns. *Monographs of the Childhood
> Education Society, 36* (2, Serial No. 181).

20. Review of a book, film, or video

If the review is untitled, use the material in brackets
as the title and indicate if the review is of a book,
film, or video; the brackets indicate the material is a
description of form and content, not a title.

> Carmody, T. P. (1982). A new look at medicine from
> the social perspective [Review of the book
> *Social contexts of health, illness, and patient
> care*]. *Contemporary Psychology, 27,* 208–209.

Electronic sources

Electronic correspondence (e-mail, electronic discussion
groups, and so on) is cited as personal communication in
your text but does not need to be included in your reference
list.

All references begin with the same information (or as
much as possible) that is included for a print source. World
Wide Web information is placed at the end of the reference.
Use "Retrieved from" and the date of retrieval because the
content of documents can be changed or revised and can
be removed from the site. If you have to divide the URL so
that it starts on one line and continues on to the next line,
break the address before a period or after a slash, and
never add a hyphen. Do not use underlining or italics for
the URL.

21. Journal article

If the article appears online exactly as it appears in
the print source, use the following format:

> Majitsu, K. (2001). Necessary intervention in
> teenage depression [Electronic version].
> *Behavior Intervention, 6,* 36–54.

If you read an article online from a print source, but
you think the online version may have been revised,
or if you notice the format differs from the print
source or page numbers are not indicated, use the
following format:

APA

APA

APA

APA

APA

Klein, D. F. (1997). Control groups in pharmacotherapy and psychotherapy evaluations. *Treatment, 1.* Retrieved February 9, 1998, from http://journals .apa.org/treatment/vol1/97_a1.html

22. Article in an Internet-only journal

For articles retrieved via file transfer protocol (FTP), use that URL.

Greenberg, M. T., Domitrovich C., & Bumbarger, B. (2001). The prevention of mental disorders in school-aged children: Current state of the field. *Prevention & Treatment, 4.* Retrieved July 18, 2001, from http://journals.apa.org/ prevention/volume4/pre0040001a.html

23. Newspaper article

Berke, R. L. (2001, July 14). Lieberman put Democrats in retreat on military vote. *New York Times.* Retrieved July 18, 2001, from http://www.nytimes.com.

24. Chapter or section in an Internet document

Berwick, D. M. (n. d.). As good as it should get: Making health care better in the new millennium. In *Policy studies, national coalition on health care* (sec. Adding it up). Retrieved August 1, 2001, from http://www. nchc.org/berwick.html#ADDING

25. Stand-alone document, no author identified, no date

Associative learning (n. d.). Retrieved July 18, 2001, from http://psy.soton.ac.uk/RGdata/ lbarg/Associative%20Learning.htm

26. Abstract

Dukas, R. (2001). Effects of perceived danger on flower choice by bees. Abstract retrieved July 18, 2001, from http://www.sfu.ca/ biology/faculty/ dukas/abstracts .htm#hbpred

27. U.S. government report available on the Web

National Institutes of Health. Stem cells: Scientific progress and future research. Retrieved July 19, 2001, from http:// www.nih.gov/news/ stemcell/scireport.htm

28. Message posted to a newsgroup

Woodgate, J. (2001, July 16). Calif to change their voltage? [Msg. 1]. Message posted to sci.electronics.design

29. Message posted to an electronic mailing list

Fischer, K. (2000, January 31). RE: writing assessment. Message posted to WCenter electronic mailing list, archived at http:// www.ttu.edu/wcenter/0002/msg00014.html

30. E-mail

Personal e-mail and other electronic communications that are not archived are listed as a personal communication in the paper and are not listed in the References list.

31. Electronic database

Center for Public Policy Study. (1994). *Survey of public response to terrorism abroad: 1992–93.* Retrieved October 20, 2000, from USGOV database.

32. CD-ROM

Culrose, P., Trimmer, N., & Debruikker, K. (1996). Gender differentiation in fear responses [CD-ROM]. *Emotion and Behavior, 27,* 914–937. Abstract retrieved July 7, 2001, from FirstSearch (PsycLIT Item: 900312) database.

33. Computer program or software

Gangnopahdhav, A. (1994). Data analyzer for e-mail usage [Computer software]. Princeton, NJ: MasterMinders.

Other sources

34. Information service

> Mead, J. V. (1992). *Looking at old photographs: Investigating the teacher tales that novice teachers bring with them* (Report No. NCRTL-RR-92-4). East Lansing, MI: National Center for Research on Teacher Learning. (ERIC Document Reproduction Service No. ED 346 082)

35. Dissertation abstract

> Rosen, P. R. (1994). Learning to cope with family crises through counselor mediation (Doctoral dissertation, Clairemont University, 1994). *Dissertation Abstracts International, 53,* Z6812.

36. Government document

> United States Bureau of Statistics. (1994). *Population density in the contiguous United States* (No. A1994-2306). Washington, D.C.: Government Printing Office.

37. Conference proceedings

> Cordulla, F. M., Teitelman, P. J., & Preba, E. E. (1995). Bio-feedback in muscle relaxation. *Proceedings of the National Academy of Biological Sciences, USA, 96,* 1271–1342.

38. Interview

Personal interviews are not included in the reference list. Instead, use a parenthetical citation in the text. List published interviews under the interviewer's name.

> Daly, C. C. (1995, July 14). [Interview with Malcolm Forbes]. *International Business Weekly, 37,* 34–35.

39. Film, videotape, performance, or artwork

Start with the name and, in parentheses, functions of the originators or primary contributors; put the medium, such as film, videotape, slides, etc., in brackets after the title; give the name and location of the distributor, and if the company is not well known, include the address.

Weiss, I. (Producer), & Terris, A. (Director). (1992).
Infant babbling and speech production [Film].
(Available from Childhood Research
Foundation, 125 Marchmont Avenue, Suite
224, New York, NY 10022)

40. Recording

Totonn, R. (1993). When I wander [Recorded by
A. Lopper, T. Seagrim, & E. Post]. On *Songs
of our age* [CD]. Wilmington, ME: Folk
Heritage Records.

41. Cassette recording

Trussler, R. W., Jr. (Speaker). (1989). *Validity of
mental measurements with young children*
(Cassette Recording No. 21-47B).
Washington, DC: American Psychological
Measurements Society.

**42. Television broadcast, series, and single episode
from a series**

Widener, I. [Executive Producer]. (1995, October 21).
Window on the world. New York: Public
Policy Broadcasting.

Biaccio, R. (Producer). (1994). *The mind of man.*
New York: WNET.

Nostanci, L. (1994). The human sense of curiosity
(R. Mindlin, Director). In R. Biaccio (Producer),
The mind of man. New York: WNET.

43. Unpublished paper presented at a meeting

Lillestein, M. A. (1994, January). *Notes on inter-
racial conflict in college settings.* Paper
presented at the meeting of the American
Cultural Studies Society, San Antonio, TX.

41d Sample pages

If you are using APA style and asked to include a title page,
follow the format shown here for a title page. Included also
are a first page and a first page for the References list. For
all pages, leave a margin of at least one inch on all sides.

1. Title page following APA style

1/2″

(*abbreviated title*)   Militia Organizations   1

(*page numbering
begins on first
page*)

(*center and*   Militia Organizations: (*title*)
double-space)
      Their Attractions and Appeal

            Leila Koach   (*name*)

            Prof. McIver   (*instructor*)

            Humanities 204   (*course*)

            March 22, 2002   (*date*)

2. First page following APA style

1" *1/2"*

Militia Organizations: Their Attractions and Appeal

As the number of militia organizations continues to increase (Billman, R. T., 1995), their members are being studied to learn more about the attraction of such groups. A number of factors have surfaced in such interviews. R. Rudner (1994) finds that the publicity surrounding such groups gives meaning to the lives of the members. Other studies (Lattner, 1994; Tobias & Klein, 1994) focus on the feelings of frustration expressed by militia members who typically work in jobs which keep them in lower socio-economic groups. The research project completed by R. Mintz and A. H. Prumanyhuma (1995) indicates that a major attraction of militia groups is their ability to provide members with a strong sense of belonging. These people, who often express accompanying feelings of alienation from society, typically have trouble fitting in elsewhere, a trait noted in several studies (Mukiyama, 1993; Tobias &, Klein, 1994). P. Jukan's study (1995) reveals another dimension to the appeal of militias, their announced interest in "getting the government off their backs" (p. 121). A discussion of the results of these studies will provide a profile of typical militia members and their motivations for joining these organizations.

When members profess allegiance to the goals of organizations, they are also giving significance to lives that may otherwise have little meaning. However, as Bryan Liftner, the chair of a recent government task force on terrorism, notes, "allegiance to a group that moves outside of the law or that tries to operate at the thin edges of legality usually reveals a deep sense of allegiance to group goals that, in turn, define the member" (1994, p. 21). This group allegiance is strengthened when militia groups operate in remote areas, thereby placing themselves even farther

1"   *1"*

1"

3. References page following APA style

References

Billman, R. T., (1995, April 14). Paramilitary groups on the increase. *American Public Policy, 21,* 47–53.

Calmanov, K., Messer, P. B., & Nocatio, L. (1993). *Public Response to Terrorism: 1992–93.* [Electronic database]. (1994). Washington, D.C.: Center for Public Policy Study [Producer and Distributor].

Defense responses of paramilitary groups. (1991). (Report No. 27). Washington, DC: National Crime Prevention Research Project.

Farmer, P. L., Melson, W. W., & Audati, C. J. (1998). Threatening behaviors exhibited by unemployed vs. underemployed individuals. *Current Studies in Psycho- social Behavior, 2.* Retrieved November 12, 1998 from http://www.apa.org/studies/vol2/98_a2.html.

Gumper, M., & Stark, P. T. (1993). *The warrior in postwar culture.* New York: Mayfair.

Jukan, P. (1995). Factors contributing to anti-government organizations' threats of violence. *Journal of Culture and Contem- porary Society, 23,* 78–103.

Liftner, B. (1994). *Report on terrorism and weapon use: 1992–1993.* (U. S. Senate Task Force on Terrorism Publication No. 7). Wash- ington, D.C.: Government Printing Office.

Mintz, R., & Prumanyhuma, A. H. (1995). *Social alienation in members of paramilitary groups* (Commission on violence in America Rep. No. 45). Washington, D.C.: U.S. Government Printing Office.

R. Rudner, R. (1994). *Paramilitary doctrines and personal goals, beliefs, and fears.* (Rep. No. 19). New York: City University of New York, Center for the Study of Social Action.

Tamar, R., Sylman, A., Bentur, W., & Foturin, L. (1992). *Paramilitary cultures in post-Vietnam America.* New York: Hampton.

Tobias, C. & Klein, J. T. (1994). Socioeconomic factors in feelings of alienation. *American Journal of Psychiatric Studies, 33,* 256–73.

42

CHICAGO MANUAL OF STYLE

In disciplines such as history and other fields of study in the humanities, the preferred style is the *Chicago Manual*. The most recent guide for this format is *The Chicago Manual of Style* (14th ed., 1993). A shorter volume on Chicago style, for student writers, is the following:

> Turabian, Kate L. *A Manual for Writers of Term Papers, Theses, and Dissertations*. 6th ed. Rev. John Grossman and Alice Bennett. Chicago: U of Chicago P, 1996.

When you use *Chicago Manual* style, include (1) notes (or endnotes) to cite references in the text and (2) a bibliography at the end of the paper to list those works referred to in the notes.

Notes in Chicago Style:

Numbering in the text
- Number citations consecutively with superscript numbers ([1]) for publication information or for explanations and additional material that would interrupt the main text if inserted there.
- Put the note number at the end of the citation following the sentence punctuation with no space between the last letter or punctuation mark.

> The violence in the Raj at that time was more pronounced than it had been in the previous conflict.[4] But, as has been noted by Peter Holman, "the military police were at a loss to stem the tide of bloodshed."[5]

Placing Notes
- List notes at the bottom of the page as footnotes or at the end of the essay as endnotes.

Spacing Notes
- Single-space individual notes, with the first line indented five spaces.
- Double-space between notes.

Ordering the Parts of Notes
- Begin with the author's first name and then last name.

- Then add the title(s).
- Then include the publishing information and page numbers.

Punctuating, Capitalizing, and Abbreviating
- Use commas between elements, and put publishing information within parentheses.
- Include the page number, but omit the abbreviation "p" or "pp."
- Underline or italicize titles of books and periodicals.
- Capitalize titles of articles, books, and journals.
- Use quotation marks around parts of books or articles in periodicals.
- Do not abbreviate the name of the publisher.

Later Notes:
- The first time a source is cited, all the relevant information is included. Later citations for that source are shortened.
- For most cases, note the author's last name, then insert a comma, and then the page(s) cited, but omit "p." or "pp."
- If you cite more than one work by the same author, use a shortened form of the title.
- If you wish, use "ibid." to refer to the work in the previous note or, if the page is different, use "ibid." followed by a comma and the page number.

  6. Peter Holman, <u>The History of the Raj: Nineteenth and Twentieth Centuries</u> (New York: Dorset Press, 1996), 18.

  7. Holman, 34–36.

  8. Ibid., 72.

Bibliography in Chicago Style:

- Differences between the notes and the bibliography:

  –Notes have names in natural order (first name, then last name); the bibliography inverts the first author's name, with last name first.
  –Elements in the bibliography are separated by periods, not commas and parentheses.

Holman, Peter. <u>The History of the Raj: Nineteenth and Twentieth Centuries</u>. New York: Dorset Press, 1996.

- Use the title "Bibliography," but it can also be "Select Bibliography," "Works Cited," or "References."
- Start with the first line at the left margin and indent other lines in the entry. Double-space throughout.
- Include all the elements that were in the first note for that source but do not put parentheses around the publishing information.
- Underline or italicize titles of books and periodicals.
- Use quotation marks around parts of books or articles in periodicals.
- Do not abbreviate the name of the publisher.

Parts of the bibliography (in the order they appear):

Author:	–full name of author(s), editor(s), and translator(s)
Title:	–full title, including subtitle
Editor, compiler, or translator:	–if any and if in addition to the author
Volume:	–total number of volumes if referred to as a whole
Volume number:	–if a single volume in the whole work is cited
Title of individual volume:	–if applicable
Facts of publication:	–city, publisher's full name, and date
Page number(s):	or volume and page number if any

EXAMPLES OF CHICAGO STYLE NOTES AND BIBLIOGRAPHY

Books	207
1. One author	207
2. Two or three authors	207
3. Four or more authors	207
4. Unknown author	207
5. Editor or translator	207

CMS CMS CMS

6. Edition other than the first one   208

7. Selection or book chapter in an anthology   208

8. Multivolume book   208

9. Reference book   208

10. Biblical or other scriptural reference   208

Periodicals   **209**

11. Article in a journal paginated by volume   209

12. Article in a journal paginated by issue   209

13. Article in a magazine   209

14. Article in a newspaper   209

15. Book review   209

Electronic sources   **209**

16. Information service   210

17. Online database   210

18. Electronic documents   210

19. Computer software   211

Other sources   **211**

20. Government publication   211

21. Unpublished dissertation   211

22. Interview   211

23. Personal communication   211

24. Film or videotape   212

25. Sound recording   212

26. Source quoted from another source   212

(N=Note; B=Bibliography)

Books

1. One author
- **N:** 1. George Frederick Abbot, <u>Israel in Europe</u> (New York: Humanities Press, 1972), 18.
- **B:** Abbot, George Frederick. <u>Israel in Europe.</u> New York: Humanities Press, 1972.

2. Two or three authors
- **N:** 2. A. Y. Yodfat and Y. Arnon-Channa, <u>P.L.O. Strategy and Tactics</u> (London: Croom Helm, 1981), 45.
- **B:** Yodfat, A. Y. and Y. Arnon-Channa. <u>P.L.O. Strategy and Tactics.</u> London: Croom Helm, 1981.

3. Four or more authors
- **N:** 3. John K. Fairbank, Edwin O. Reischauer, George Allen, and Albert Craig, <u>East Asia: Tradition and Transformation</u> (Boston: Houghton, Mifflin Co., 1973), 274–5.

  (Chicago Style also permits giving the name of the first author followed by "et al." or "and others" with no intervening punctuation.)

- **B:** Fairbank, John K, Edwin O. Reischauer, George Allen, and Albert Craig. <u>East Asia: Tradition and Transformation</u>. Boston: Houghton, Mifflin, 1973.

4. Unknown author.
- **N:** 4. <u>The Chicago Manual of Style</u>, 14th ed. (Chicago: University of Chicago Press, 1993) 420.
- **B:** <u>The Chicago Manual of Style</u>. 14th ed. Chicago: University of Chicago Press, 1993.

5. Editor or translator
- **N:** 5. Dan Caspi, Abraham Diskin, and Emmanuel Gutmann, eds., <u>The Roots of Begin's Success</u> (New York: St. Martin's Press, 1984), 36.
- **B:** Caspi, Dan, Abraham Diskin, and Emmanuel Gutmann, eds. <u>The Roots of Begin's Success</u>. New York: St. Martin's Press, 1984.

6. Edition other than the first one

N: 6. John Joseph Mathews, <u>The Osages: Children of the Middle Waters</u>, 2nd ed. (Norman, OK: University of Oklahoma Press, 1963), 145-47.

B: Mathews, John Joseph. <u>The Osages: Children of the Middle Waters</u>. 2nd ed. Norman, OK: University of Oklahoma Press, 1963.

7. Selection or book chapter in an anthology

N: 7. Emmanuel Anati, "The Prehistory of the Holy Land (Until 3200 BC)," in <u>A History of the Holy Land</u>, ed. Michael Avi-Yonah (Jerusalem: The Jerusalem Publishing House Ltd., 1969), 33–41.

B: Anati, Emmanuel. "The Prehistory of the Holy Land (Until 3200 BC)." In <u>A History of the Holy Land</u>, edited by Michael Avi-Yonah. Jerusalem: The Jerusalem Publishing House Ltd., 1969.

8. Multivolume book

N: 8. Cao Xuequin, <u>The Story of Stone</u>, trans. David Hawkes (Harmondsworth: Penguin Books, 1977), 2:150–51.

B: Xuequin, Cao, <u>The Story of Stone</u>, translated by David Hawkes. Vol. 2. Harmondsworth: Penguin Books, 1977.

9. Reference book

N: 9. <u>Encyclopedia Britannica</u>, 15th ed., s.v. "Henry Clay."

(Do not include the volume or page number. Instead, cite the term in the reference book under which the information is contained. Use the abbreviation "s.v." for "sub verbo," meaning "under the word.")

B: Well known reference books are not usually listed in the bibliography.

10. Biblical or other scriptural reference

N: 10. Gen. 21:14–18.

(Include the book in Roman type, abbreviated with no underline or italics, chapter, and verse. No page number.)

B: Scriptural references are usually cited only in the notes.

Periodicals

11. Article in a journal paginated by volume

N: 11. Russell Reid, "Journals of the Atkinson-O'Fallon Expedition," <u>North Dakota Historical Quarterly</u> 4 (1929): 5–56.

B: Reid, Russell. "Journals of the Atkinson-O'Fallon Expedition." <u>North Dakota Historical Quarterly</u> 4 (1929): 5–56.

12. Article in a journal paginated by issue

N: 12. Carl Coke Rister, "The Significance of the Destruction of the Buffalo in the Southwest," <u>Southwestern Historical Society</u> 33, no. 1 (1929): 44.

B: Rister, Carl Coke. "The Significance of the Destruction of the Buffalo in the Southwest." <u>Southwestern Historical Society</u> 33, no. 1 (1929): 44–57.

13. Article in a magazine

N: 13. Jacob Schlesinger, "Sundown," <u>The New Republic</u>, 3 August 1998, 12.

B: Schlesinger, Jacob. "Sundown." <u>The New Republic</u>, 3 August 1998, 12.

14. Article in a newspaper

N: 14. Barbara Crossette, "New U.N. Push to Urge Iraq to Cooperate with Inspectors," <u>New York Times</u>, 8 August 1998, sec. A.

B: Crossette, Barbara. "New U.N. Push to Urge Iraq to Cooperate with Inspectors." <u>New York Times</u>, 8 August 1998, sec. A.

15. Book review

N: 15. Bernard Lewis, review of <u>Autumn of Fury: The Assassination of Anwar Sadat</u>, by Mohamed Heikal, <u>New York Review of Books</u>, 31 May 1984, 25–27.

B: Lewis, Bernard. Review of <u>Autumn of Fury: The Assassination of Anwar Sadat</u>, by Mohamed Heikal. <u>New York Review of Books</u>, 31 May 1984, 25–27.

Electronic sources

The Chicago Manual of Style recommends following the latest documentation system of the International Standards

Organization (ISO). The ISO is constructing and continues to modify a uniform system of citing electronic documents.

16. Information service

N: 16. Linda Flower, "Diagnoses in Revision: The Experts' Option," Communications Design Center Technical Report No. 27 (Pittsburgh: Carnegie Mellon University, 1986), OVID, ERIC ED 266 464.

B: Flower, Linda. "Diagnosis in Revision: The Experts' Option." Communications Design Center Technical Report No. 27. Pittsburgh: Carnegie Mellon University, 1986. OVID, ERIC ED 266 464.

17. Online database

N: 17. Pennti Aalto, "Swells of the Mongol-Storm around the Baltic." Acta Orientalia 36 (Budapest,1982): 5–15, in Bibliography of Asian Studies [database online] [cited 24 August 1998]; available from OVID Information Services, Inc., Murray, Utah, identifier no. 19980218.232.

B: Aalto, Pennti. "Swells of the Mongol-Storm around the Baltic." Acta Orientalia 36 (Budapest, 1982): 5–15. In Bibliography of Asian Studies [database online] [cited 24 August 1998]. Murray, Utah: OVID Information Services, Inc. Identifier no. 19980218.232.

18. Electronic documents

Listserv:

N: 18. John Murray, "Economic Historians in the News," in EH.T [electronic bulletin board] [cited 12 March 1998]); available from EH.T@cs.muohio.edu; INTERNET.

B: Murray, John. "Economic Historians in the News." In EH.T [electronic bulletin board]. [cited 12 March 1998]. Available from EH.T@cs.muohio.edu; INTERNET.

Electronic journal:

N: 18. Lucia Sommer, "Simon Penny's Electronic Critique: Notes on the Politicization of Art Against the Aestheticization of Politics," Cultronix 1 [electronic journal] (Pittsburgh: Carnegie Mellon University, 1994

[cited 27 August 1998]); available from
http://eserver.org/cultronix/sommer.

B: Sommer, Lucia. "Simon Penny's Electronic
Critique: Notes on the Politicization of Art
Against the Aestheticization of Politics."
<u>Cultronix</u> 1 [electronic journal].
Pittsburgh: Carnegie Mellon University,
1994 [cited 27 August 1998]. Available
from http://eserver.org/cultronix/sommer.

19. Computer software

N: 19. CensusCounts. Ver. 2.1, Decisionmark
Corporation, Cedar Rapids, Iowa.

B: CensusCounts. Ver. 2.1. Decisionmark
Corporation, Cedar Rapids, Iowa.

Other sources

20. Government publication

N: 20. William Lilley, <u>The State Atlas of
Political and Cultural Diversity</u> (Washington,
D.C.: Congressional Quarterly, 1997), 31–45.

B: Lilley, William. <u>The State Atlas of Political and
Cultural Diversity</u>. Washington, D.C.:
Congressional Quarterly, 1997.

21. Unpublished dissertation

N: 21. Arnold Mayniew, "Historical
Perceptions of Royal Prerogative" (Ph.D. diss.,
University of Illinois, 1991), 32–37.

B: Mayniew, Arnold. "Historical Perceptions of
Royal Prerogative." Ph.D. diss.,
University of Illinois, 1991.

22. Interview

N: 22. David Gergen, interview by Ted
Koppell, <u>Nightline</u>, American Broadcasting
Company, 18 August 1998.

B: Gergen, David. Interview by Ted Koppell.
<u>Nightline</u>. American Broadcasting
Company, 18 August 1998.

23. Personal communication (including e-mail)

N: 23. Maynard Jimmerson, telephone
interview by author, 27 July 1998.

N: 24. Daniel Kaplan, e-mail to author, 15
September 1998.

B: Personal communications are not usually
included in the bibliography.

24. Film or videotape

N: 25. <u>The Luttrell Psalter: Everyday Life in Medieval England</u>, prod. and dir. Martin Shuman, 1 hr. 22 min., Films for the Humanities & Sciences, 1996, videocassette.

B: <u>The Luttrell Psalter: Everyday Life in Medieval England</u>. Produced and directed by Martin Shuman. 1 hr. 22 min. Films for the Humanities & Sciences, 1996. Videocassette.

25. Sound recording

N: 26. J. S. Bach, <u>Four Concerti for Various Instruments</u>, Orchestra of St. Luke's, Michael Feldman, Musical Heritage Society, Inc. compact disk 512268T.

B: Bach, J. S. <u>Four Concerti for Various Instruments</u>. Orchestra of St. Luke's. Michael Feldman. Musical Heritage Society, Inc. compact disk 512268T.

26. Source quoted from another source

N: 27. H.H. Dubs, "An Ancient Chinese Mystery Cult," <u>Harvard Theological Review</u>, 35 (1942): 223, quoted in Susan Naquin, <u>Millenarian Rebellion in China: The Eight Trigrams Uprising of 1813</u> (New Haven and London: Yale University Press, 1976), 288.

B: Dubs, H.H. "An Ancient Chinese Mystery Cult." <u>Harvard Theological Review</u>, 35 (1942): 223. Quoted in Susan Naquin, <u>Millenarian Rebellion in China: The Eight Trigrams Uprising of 1813</u> (New Haven and London: Yale University Press, 1976), 288.

43

CSE (Council of Science Editors)

Writers in the physical sciences and life sciences follow the documentation style developed by the Council of Science Editors (CSE) and found in *Scientific Style and Format: The CBE Manual for Authors, Editors, and Publishers*. 6th ed. New York: Cambridge UP, 1994. (The Council of Science Editors, which had previously been known as the Council of Biology Editors, CBE, is currently preparing a seventh edition of this book. See their Web site, **http://www.cbe.org/ pubs_ssf.shtml.**) Mathematicians use either this style or the style in the book listed in 44b, under the entry for "Mathematics." (Section 44 also has style manuals for other scientific fields.)

The CBE Style Manual offers two documentation styles, and you can ask your instructor which one is preferred for your papers. Or you can check a current journal in the field. The two styles are:

● *Authors' names and publication dates*

Here, authors' names and publication dates are included in parenthetical citations in the text, closely resembling the APA style (see section 41).

In-text citation:

The earlier studies done on this virus (Fong and Townes 1992; Mindlin 1994) reported similar results. However, one of these studies (Mindlin 1994) noted a mutated strain.

In the list of references at the end, the names are listed alphabetically with the date after the name.

Reference list:

1. Fong L, Townes HC. (1992). Viral longevity. Biological Reports 27: 129–45.

● *In-text numbered references*

In this format, references are listed with in-text superscript numbers (numbers set above the line, such as [1] and [2]) that refer to a list of numbered references at the end. The references are numbered according to the order in which they are used in the text, and later references to the same work use the original number. When you have two or more sources cited at once, put the numbers in sequence and separate them with commas but no spaces.

In-text citation:
The earlier studies done on this virus[1,4,9] reported similar results. However, one of these studies[4] noted a mutated strain.

In the list of references at the end, list the entries in numerical order, according to the order in which they are cited in the paper, not alphabetically.

Reference list:

> 1. Fong L, Townes H. Viral longevity. Biological
>   Reports 1992; 27: 129–45.

CSE Reference List
At the end of the paper, include a list entitled "References" (or "Cited References"). The placement of the date will differ, depending on which format you use.

Name and publication date format:
- Put the date after the author's name.
- Arrange the list alphabetically by last names.
- Do not indent any lines in the entries.

In-text numbered references
- Put the date after the publisher's name for books.
- Put the date after the periodical name for references to periodicals.
- Arrange the list by number.
- Put the number at the left margin, followed by the authors' last names. For the second and following lines, align beneath the first letter of the line above.

> 1. xxxxxxxxxxxxxxxxxxx
>   xxxxxxxxxx
>
> 2. xxxxxxxxxxxxxxxxxxx
>   xxxx

Parts of the reference:
(Use periods between major divisions of the entry):

Author's name	–Start with last name first, no comma, and initials without periods for first and middle names. Separate authors' names with commas. End the list of authors' names with a period.
Title	For books and article titles, use capitals only for the first word and proper nouns. No underline, italics, or quotation marks. For journals, abbreviate titles and capitalize all major words.

Place of publication (colon), publisher (semicolon), and publication date (period)	Include a space between the full name of the publisher and date. Use a semicolon with no space between the date and volume number of the journal. Abbreviate months.
Number of pages	For books, include the total number of pages in the book, with a space and then a "p" after the number. End the entry with a period. For journal articles, show the total number of pages of the article, and for the second number use only numbers not already included in the first number (for example: 122–7; 49–51; 131–8; 200–9). End with a period.

EXAMPLES OF CSE FORMAT FOR REFERENCE LIST

1. Books with one author   216

2. Books with more than one author   216

3. Books with an editor   216

4. Organization as author   216

5. Section of a book   216

6. Article in scholarly journal   216

7. Newspaper or magazine article   216

8. Article with no author   216

9. Editorial   216

10. Audiovisual materials   217

11. Electronic journal articles   217

12. Web sources   217

CSE CSE

CSE CSE

CSE

1. Books with one author

Glenn EP. Encyclopedia of environmental biology. San Diego: Academic Press; 1995. 1289 p.

2. Books with more than one author

Rouse Ball WW, Coxeter HSM. Mathematical recreations and essays. 13 ed. Mineola, NY: Dover Publications; 1987. 381 p.

3. Books with an editor

Estes JW, Smith BG, editors. A melancholy scene of devastation: the public response to the 1793 Philadelphia yellow fever epidemic. Philadelphia: Science History Publications/USA; 1997. 436 p.

4. Organization as author

Council of Science Editors. Scientific style and format: the CSE manual for authors, editors, and publishers. 6ed. New York: Cambridge UP; 1994. 704 p.

5. Section of a book

Saari JC. Retinoids in photosensitive systems. In: Sporn MB, editor. The retinoids. 2nd ed. New York: Raven Press: 1994. p 351–78.

6. Article in scholarly journal

Adleman LM. Molecular computation of solutions to combinatorial problems. Science 1994;266:1021–4.

7. Newspaper or magazine article

Allen A. Mighty mice: the perils of patenting genes. The New Republic 1998 Aug 10; 16–8.

8. Article with no author

Begin the entry with "[Anonymous]."

9. Editorial

After the title, add "[editorial]."

10. Audiovisual materials

The CSE Manual does not have guidelines for CD-ROM sources, but the format shown here is a suggested model to follow.

> Recent developments in DNA models [videocassette]. Miletius T, editor. DistanceED Productions, producer. [San Diego]: Media Forum; 1997. 3 videocassettes: 315 min, sound, color, 1/2 in. (Genetics laboratories; Nr. 9). Accompanied by: 3 guides. Available from: Boston National Visual Instruction Library, Boston, MA.

11. Electronic journal articles

> Arlinghaus SL, Drake WD, Nystuen, JD. Animaps. Solstice: an electronic journal of geography and mathematics 1998;9(1): Available from: http://www- personal.umich.edu/~sarhaus/ image/animaps.html. Accessed 1998 Aug.16.

12. Web sources

The CSE Manual does not have guidelines for citing Web sources. The following suggested format follows the journal article format and includes the date of Internet publication, the Web address, and your date of access.

> Finn R. DNA vaccines generate excitement as human trials begin. The Scientist 1998 Mar.16; 12(16):http://www.the-scientist.library. upenn.edu/yr1998/mar/research_980316.html. Accessed 2002 Aug. 16.

44

COS AND STYLE MANUALS FOR VARIOUS FIELDS

44a Columbia Online Style (COS)

The Columbia Guide to Online Style (COS) by Janice R. Walker and Todd Taylor (Columbia UP, 1998) is a guide for citing sources you find online for research papers in the humanities and sciences. For humanities, it uses elements from MLA (see Chapter 40) and *Chicago Manual* (see 42a), and for the sciences, it adapts from APA (see section 41) and CSE (see section 43). COS style offers formats for documenting a variety of new online sources not yet covered by other documentation forms that are used primarily for print documents. COS also offers formats for how to document electronic sources in which some of the standard information for print sources, such as author's name, date, publisher, and so on, are missing. For a more complete description of COS style, visit the Web site for the guide, which also has a link to updates in COS style:

<http://www.columbia.edu/cu/cup/cgos/idx_basic.html>

Check with your instructor to see which documentation style you should use.

In-Text Citation:

When print sources are cited in a humanities paper, the author's last name and page number of the reference are put in parentheses. In science papers, the author's last name, date of publication, and page number of the reference appear in parentheses.

But often, for electronic sources one or more of these elements may be missing.

- If the author's name is available, cite the last name. If there is no name, cite the organization. If no author or organization's name is listed, cite the file name.
- When using scientific style, include a comma after the name or title and then the date of publication. If no date is available, put the date of access in day, month, year format: 25 Feb. 2001.
- When citing periodicals in science format, include the month. Put a comma after the year, and then include the month. For newspapers, put year first, then month, and then day.
- If there are navigational aides such as page, paragraph, or section numbers, separate them with a comma and include them in the parentheses as well.

Humanities:

As recent studies have shown, there are fewer advertisements on the World Wide Web because advertisers doubt that users notice their banner ads (Majabi).

Sciences:

Because Malberg's study indicates the incidence of childhood allergies is increasing rapidly, pharmaceutical manufacturers are searching for more medications that are safe for young children (Belin, 2001, June).

Bibliography Citation:

In general, follow the order shown in the following examples for humanities and the sciences. A few considerations to keep in mind are the following:

- For titles of complete works, such as books and periodicals, use italics instead of underlining because your readers may mistakenly think the underline is a hypertext link.
- Italicize titles of online sites and names of information services.
- Cite a page's publication date or date of last revision only if it is different from the date you accessed the site.
- Always include the date you accessed the file. If there is no date of publication or last modification, use the date you accessed the site.
- For a Web address longer than the line on which it starts, break after a slash or before a period, and do not hyphenate.

Humanities Style

1. Author's last name, first name.

2. "Title of Document." *Title of Complete Work* [if applicable]. (Capitalize all major words in both the document title and title of the complete work, and enclose the title of the document in quotation marks. For the complete work, use italics, not underlining.)

3. Version or file number [if applicable].

4. Document date or date of last revision [if different from the date you accessed the file].

5. Protocol (such as http) and address, access path, or directories (date of access).

Scientific Style

1. Author's last name, initial(s).

2. (Date of document [if different from date accessed].)

3. Title of document. *Title of complete work* [if applicable]. (Capitalize only the first word and proper

nouns in the document title and the title of the complete work. Do not use quotation marks for the title of the document, but use italics for titles of complete works or periodicals.)

4. Version or file number [if applicable].

5. Edition or revision [if applicable].

6. Protocol (such as http) and address, access path, or directories (date of access).

EXAMPLES OF COS CITATIONS

Web sites   **221**

  1. Web site   221

  2. Article from a periodical   221

  3. Article in an online journal   221

  4. Web site—group or organization   222

  5. Web site—government   222

  6. Book   222

    a. A book previously published in print   222

    b. An online book   222

  7. Graphic, video, audio file   223

E-mail, Discussion Group, Newsgroup   **223**

  8. Personal e-mail   223

  9. Posting to a discussion list   223

  10. Posting to a newsgroup or forum   224

  11. An archived posting   224

Reference, Database   **224**

  12. Online reference source   224

  13. Computer information services and
online databases   225

Synchronous Communication Site	**225**
14. Synchronous communication site	225
Software	**225**
15. Software	225

Web sites

1. **Web site:**
   Humanities Style:
   Blackmon, Samantha. *Cows in the Classroom? MOOs and MUDs and MUSHes . . . Oh My!* 24 Aug. 2000. http://www.sla.purdue.edu/people/engl/blackmon/moo/index.html (11 Mar. 2002).

   Science Style:
   Blackmon, S. (2000, August 24). Cows in the classroom? MOOs and MUDs and MUSHes . . . oh my! http://www.sla.purdue.edu/people/engl/blackmon/moo/index.html (11 Mar. 2002).

2. **Article from a periodical**
   Humanities Style:
   Kaplan, Carl S. "Suit Considers Computer Files." *The New York Times.* 28 Sep. 2000: http://www.nytimes.com/2000/09/28/technology/29CYBERLAW.html (13 Jan. 2001).

   Science Style:
   Kaplan, C. S. (2000, September 28). Suit considers computer files. *The New York Times.* http://www.nytimes.com/2000/09/28/technology/29CYBERLAW.html (13 Jan. 2001).

3. **Article in an online journal**
   Humanities Style:
   Winickoff, Jonathan P., et al. "Verve and Jolt: Deadly New Internet Drugs." *Pediatrics* 106: 4 (May 2000). http://www.pediatrics.org/cgi/content/abstract/106/4/829 (10 Oct. 2002).

   Science Style:
   Winickoff, J. P., et al. (2000, May). Verve and jolt: Deadly new internet drugs. *Pediatrics, 106* (4).

COS COS

COS

COS

http://www.pediatrics.org/cgi/content/abstract/
106/4/829 (10 Oct. 2002).

4. Web site—group or organization
Humanities Style:

SIL International. "Ethnomusicology: 'Studying
Music from the Outside In and from the Inside
Out'" 7 May 1999. http://www.sil.org/anthro/
ethnomusicology.htm (20 Feb. 2000).

Science Style:

SIL International. (1999, May 7). Ethnomusicology:
"Studying music from the outside in and from
the inside out." http://www.sil.org/anthro/
ethnomusicology.htm (20 Feb. 2000).

5. Web site—government
Humanities Style:

Central Intelligence Agency. "Speeches and
Testimony." 6 Oct. 2002. http://www.cia.gov/
cia/public_affairs/speeches/speeches.html
(18 Dec. 2002).

Science Style:

Central Intelligence Agency. (2002, October 6).
Speeches and testimony. http://www.cia.gov/
cia/public_affairs/speeches/speeches.html
(18 Dec. 2002).

6. Book

a. Book previously published in print:

Humanities Style:

Brontë, Charlotte. *Jane Eyre.* London: Service &
`Paton, 1887. 1999. *University of Maryland
ReadingRoom.* http://www.inform.umd.edu/
EdRes/ReadingRoom/Fiction/Cbronte/JaneEyre/
(15 Sep. 2001).

Science Style:

Brontë, C. (1887). *Jane Eyre.* London: Service & Paton
(1999). *University of Maryland ReadingRoom.*
http://www.inform.umd.edu/EdRes/
ReadingRoom/Fiction/Cbronte/JaneEyre/
(15 Sep. 2001).

b. Online book:

Humanities Style:

Shires, Bob. *CPR (Cardiopulmonary Resuscitation)
Guide.* 17 Jan. 2000. http://www.memoware
.com/Category5Medicine_ResultSet51.htm
(17 Apr. 2000).

Science Style:

Shires, B. (2000, January 17). *CPR (cardiopulmonary
resuscitation) guide.* http://www.memoware
.com/Category5Medicine_ResultSet51.htm
(17 Apr. 2000).

7. **Graphic, video, or audio file**
   Humanities Style:

   owl.gif. 2000. "Original Free Clipart." *Clipart.com.*
   http://www.free-clip-art.net/index4.shtml
   (27 Oct. 2000).

   Science Style:

   owl.gif [graphic file]. (2000). Original free clipart.
   Clipart.com. http://www.free-clip-art.net/
   index4.shtml (27 Oct. 2000).

E-mail, Discussion Group, Newsgroup

8. **Personal e-mail**
   Humanities Style:

   Torres, Elizabeth. "Re: Puerto Rican Baseball
   History." Personal e-mail (11 Sep. 2000).

   Science Style:

   Following APA style, COS scientific style does not
   include personal e-mail in the References.

9. **Posting to a discussion list**
   Humanities Style:

   Sheldon, Amy. "Re: Request for Help on Sexism
   Inscription." 2 Jan. 2000. *FLING List for
   Feminists in Linguistics.* http://listserv
   .linguistlist.org (14 Nov. 2000).

   Science Style:

   Sheldon, A. (2000, January 2). Re: request for help on
   sexism inscription. *FLING List for Feminists in
   Linguistics.* http://listserv.linguistlist.org
   (14 Nov. 2000).

10. Posting to a newsgroup or forum
Humanities Style:

Markowitz, Al. "The Changing Face of Work: A Look
at the Way We Work" 28 Sep. 2000.
http://yourturn.npr.org/cgi-bin/
WebX?50@121.HjNGardZdaj^0@.ee7a9aa
(8 Jan. 2001).

Science Style:

Markowitz, A. (2000, September 28). The changing
face of work: a look at the way we work.
http://yourturn.npr.org/cgi-bin/
WebX?7@141.MM4qaoT6dgK^3@.ee7a9aa/12
(8 Jan. 2001).

11. Archived posting
Humanities Style:

Radev, Dragomir R. "Natural Language Processing
FAQ" 16 Sep. 1999. *Institute of Information and
Computing Sciences.* http://www.cs.ruu.nl/wais/
html/na-dir/natural-lang-processing-faq.html
(27 Jan. 2000).

Science Style:

Radev, D. R. (1999, September 16). Natural language
processing FAQ. *Institute of Information and
Computing Sciences.* http://www.cs.ruu.nl/wais/
html/na-dir/natural-lang-processing-faq.html
(27 Jan. 2000).

Reference, Database
12. Online reference sources (encyclopedias, dictionaries, thesauri, and style manuals)
Humanities Style:

Nordenberg, Tamar. "Make No Mistake! Medical
Errors Can Be Deadly Serious." *Brittanica.com*
Sep./Oct., 2000. Ebsco Publishing.
http://britannica.com/bcom/original/article/
0,5744,12430,00.html (16 Nov. 2000).

Science Style:

Nordenberg, T. (October, 2000). Make no mistake!
Medical errors can be deadly serious.
Brittanica.com. Ebsco Publishing.
http://britannica.com/bcom/original/article/
0,5744,12430,0s.html (16 Nov. 2000).

13. **Computer information services and online databases**
    Humanities Style:
    Raintree Nutrition, Inc. "Pata de Vaca" Jun. 2000. *Raintree Tropical Plant Database.* http://www.rain-tree.com/patadevaca.htm (9 Sep. 2000).

    Science Style:
    Raintree Nutrition Inc. (2000, June). Pata de Vaca. *Raintree Tropical Plant Database.* http://www.rain-tree.com/patadevaca.htm (9 Sep. 2000).

Synchronous Communication Site

14. **Synchronous communication site**
    Humanities Style:
    Dominguez, Jose. "Interchange." *Daedalus Online.* http://daedalus.pearsoned.com (11 Mar. 2001).

    Science Style:
    Dominguez, J. Interchange. *Daedalus Online.* http://daedalus.pearsoned.com (11 Mar. 2001).

Software

15. **Software**
    Humanities Style:
    Wresch, William. *Writer's Helper* Vers. 4.0. Upper Saddle River, NJ: Prentice Hall, 1998.

    Science Style:
    Wresch, W. (1998). *Writer's Helper* (Vers. 4.0). Upper Saddle River, NJ: Prentice Hall.

44b Style Manuals for Various Fields

Anthropology
Uses *Chicago Manual of Style* (see section 42) and *Webster's 10th New Collegiate Dictionary*

On its Web site, the American Anthropological Association offers a brief "AAA Style Guide" :
http://www.aaanet.org/pubs/style_guide.htm

COS COS COS

Astronomy
See entry for *Physics*

Biology
Council of Biology Editors. *Scientific Style and Format: The CBE Manual for Authors, Editors, and Publishers.* 6th ed. New York: Cambridge UP, 1994.

Chemistry
Dodd, Janet S., Ed. *The ACS Style Guide: A Manual for Authors and Editors.* 2nd ed. Washington: Amer. Chemical Soc., 1997.

Education
Uses APA (see section 41) and MLA (see section 40).

English
Gibaldi, Joseph, and Walter S. Achert. *MLA Handbook for Writers of Research Papers.* 5th ed. New York: Modern Language Association of America, 1999.
(See section 40.)

History
Uses *The Chicago Manual of Style,* 14th ed. Chicago: U of Chicago P, 1993.
(See section 42.)

Journalism
Goldstein, Norm, Ed. *Associated Press Style Book and Briefing on Media Law.* Rev. and updated Ed. Portland: Perseus Press, 2002.
Siegal, Allan, and William Connolly. *New York Times Manual of Style and Usage.* NY: Times Books, 1999.

Mathematics
American Mathematical Society. *The AMS Author Handbook: General Instructions for Preparing Manuscripts.* Providence: AMS, 1996.

Medicine
Iverson, Cheryl, et al. *American Medical Association Manual of Style.* 9th ed. Baltimore: Williams and Wilkins, 1998.

Music
Holoman, D. Kern, Ed. *Writing about Music: A Style Sheet from the Editors of 19th-Century Music.* Berkeley: U of California P, 1988.

Philosophy

Guidebook for Publishing in Philosophy. Newark, DE:
American Philosophy Association, 1997.

Physics and Astronomy

American Institute of Physics. *AIP Style Manual.* 4th ed.
College Park, MD: AIP, 1990.

Political Science

Sigleman, Lee. Ed. American Political Science Associa
tion. *Style Manual for Political Science.* rev. ed.
Washington: Amer. Political Science Assn., 2001.

Psychology

American Psychological Association. *Publication Man
ual of the American Psychological Association.* 5th
ed. Washington: APA, 2001.

(See section 41.)

GLOSSARY OF USAGE

This list includes words and phrases you may be uncertain about when writing. If you have questions about words not included here, try the index at the back of this book to see whether the word is discussed elsewhere. You can also check a recently published dictionary.

A, An   Use a before words beginning with a consonant and before words beginning with a vowel that sounds like a consonant:

> a cat   a house   a one-way street   a union   a history

Use an before words that begin with a vowel and before words with a silent *h*.

> an egg   an ice cube   an hour   an honor

Accept, Except   *Accept,* a verb, means to agree to, to believe, or to receive.

> The detective **accepted** his account of the event.

Except, a verb, means to exclude or leave out, and except, a preposition, means leaving out.

> Because he did not know the answers, he was **excepted** from the list of contestants and asked to leave.

Except for brussel sprouts, I eat most vegetables.

Advice, Advise   *Advice* is a noun, and *advise* is a verb.

> She always offers too much **advice.**

Would you **advise** me about choosing the right course?

Affect, Effect   Most frequently, *affect,* which means to influence, is used as a verb, and *effect,* which means a result, is used as a noun.

> The weather **affects** my ability to study.

> What **effect** does coffee have on your concentration?

However, *effect,* meaning to cause or bring about, is also used as a verb.

> The new traffic enforcement laws **effected** a change in people's driving habits.

Common phrases with *effect* include the following:

> in effect   to that effect

Ain't   This is a nonstandard way of saying *am not, is not, has not, have not*, and so on.

All Ready, Already   *All ready* means prepared; *already* means before or by this time.

> The courses for the meal are **all ready** to be served.

> When I got home, she was **already** there.

All Right, Alright   *All right* is two words, not one. *Alright* is an incorrect form.

All Together, Altogether   *All together* means in a group, and *altogether* means entirely, totally.

> We were **all together** again after having separate vacations.

> He was not **altogether** happy about the outcome of the test.

Alot, A Lot   *Alot* is an incorrect form of *a lot*.

a.m., p.m. (or) A.M., P.M.   Use these with numbers, not as substitutes for the words *morning* or *evening*.

> *morning at 9 a.m.*
> We meet every a.m. for an exercise class.

Among, Between   Use *among* when referring to three or more things and *between* when referring to two things.

> The decision was discussed **among** all the members of the committee.

> I had to decide **between** the chocolate mousse pie and the almond ice cream.

Amount, Number   Use *amount* for things or ideas that are general or abstract and cannot be counted. For example, *furniture* is a general term and cannot be counted. That is, we cannot say *one furniture* or *two furnitures*. Use *number* for things that can be counted (for example, *four chairs or three tables*).

> He had a huge **amount** of work to finish before the deadline.

> There were a **number** of people who saw the accident.

An   See the entry for **a, an.**

And   Although some people discourage the use of *and* as the first word in a sentence, it is an acceptable word with which to begin a sentence.

And Etc.   Adding *and* is redundant because *et* means *and* in Latin. See the entry for **etc.**

Anybody, Any Body   See the entry for **anyone, any one.**

Anyone, Any One   *Anyone* means *any person at all. Any one* refers to a specific person or thing in a group. There are similar distinctions for other words ending in *-body* and *-one* (for example, *everybody, every body, anybody, any body, someone,* and *some one*).

> The teacher asked if **anyone** knew the answer.

> **Any one** of those children could have taken the ball.

Anyways, Anywheres   These are nonstandard forms for *anyway* and *anywhere.*

As, As if, As Though, Like Use *as* in a comparison (not *like*) when there is an equality intended or when the meaning is in the *function of*.

> Celia acted **as** [not like] the leader when the group was getting organized. (Celia = leader)

Use *as if* or *as though* for the subjunctive.

> He spent his money **as if** [or **as though**] he were rich.

Use *like* in a comparison (not as) when the meaning is *in the manner of* or *to the same degree as*.

> The boy swam **like** a fish.

Don't use *like* as the opening word in a clause in formal writing:

Informal: **Like** I thought, he was unable to predict the weather.

Formal: **As** I thought, he was unable to predict the weather.

Assure, Ensure, Insure *Assure means to declare or promise, ensure means to make safe or certain, and insure means to protect with a contract of insurance.*

> I **assure** you that I am trying to find your lost package.

> Some people claim that eating properly **ensures** good health.

> This insurance policy also **insures** my car against theft.

Awful, Awfully *Awful is an adjective meaning inspiring awe or extremely unpleasant.*

> He was involved in an **awful** accident.

Awfully is an adverb used in very informal writing to mean *very*. Avoid it in formal writing.

Informal: The dog was **awfully** dirty.

Awhile, A While *Awhile is an adverb meaning a short time* and modifies a verb:

> He talked **awhile** and then left.

A *while* is an article with the noun *while* and means *a period of time:*

> I'll be there in a **while.**

Bad, Badly *Bad is an adjective and is used after linking verbs. Badly is an adverb.* (See section 15.)

> The wheat crop looked **bad** [not *badly*] because of lack of rain.

> There was a **bad** flood last summer.

> The building was **badly** constructed and unable to withstand the strong winds.

Beside, Besides *Beside is a preposition meaning at the side of, compared with,* or *having nothing to do with. Besides is a* preposition meaning *in addition to* or *other than*. *Besides* as an adverb means *also* or *moreover*. Don't confuse *beside* with *besides*.

That is **beside** the point.

Besides the radio, they had no other means of contact with the outside world.

Besides, I enjoyed the concert.

Between, Among   See the entry for **among, between.**

Breath, Breathe   *Breath* is a noun, and *breathe* is a verb.

She held her **breath** when she dived into the water.

Learn to **breathe** deeply when you swim.

But   Although some people discourage the use of *but* as the first word in a sentence, it is an acceptable word with which to begin a sentence.

Can, May   Can is a verb that expresses *ability, knowledge,* or *capacity:*

He **can** play both the violin and the cello.

May is a verb that expresses possibility or permission. Careful writers avoid using *can* to mean permission:

May [not *can*] I sit here?

Can't Hardly   This is incorrect because it is a double negative.

She ~~can't~~ ^{can} hardly hear normal voice levels.

Choose, Chose   *Choose* is the present tense of the verb, and *chose* is the past tense:

Jennie should **choose** strawberry ice cream.

Yesterday, she **chose** strawberry-flavored popcorn.

Cite, Site   *Cite* is a verb that means *to quote an authority or source; site* is a noun referring to a place.

Be sure to **cite** your sources in the paper.

That is the **site** of the new city swimming pool.

Cloth, Clothe   *Cloth* is a noun, and *clothe* is a verb.

Here is some **cloth** for a new scarf.

His paycheck helps to feed and **clothe** many people in his family.

Compared to, Compared with   Use *compared to* when showing that two things are alike. Use *compared with* when showing similarities and differences.

The speaker **compared** the economy to a roller coaster because both have sudden ups and downs.

The detective **compared** the fingerprints with other sets from a previous crime.

Could of   This is incorrect. Instead use *could have.*

Data   This is the plural form of *datum*. In informal usage, *data* is used as a singular noun, with a singular verb. However, because dictionaries do not accept this, use *data* as a plural form for academic writing.

Informal Usage: The **data** is inconclusive.
Formal Usage: The **data** are inconclusive.

Different from, Different than   *Different from* is always correct, but some writers use *different than* if a clause follows this phrase.

This program is **different** from the others.

That is a **different** result **than** they predicted.

Done   The past tense forms of the verb *do* are *did* and *done*. *Did* is the simple form that needs no additional verb as a helper. *Done* is the past form that requires the helper *have*. Some writers make the mistake of interchanging *did* and *done*.

They ~~done~~ *did* it again.   (or)   They ~~done~~ *have done* it again.

Effect, Affect   See the entry for **affect, effect.**

Ensure   See the entry for **assure, ensure, insure.**

Etc.   This is an abbreviation of the Latin *et cetera,* meaning *and the rest*. Because it should be used sparingly if at all in formal academic writing, substitute other phrases such as *and so forth* or *and so on*.

Everybody, Every Body   See the entry for **anyone, any one.**

Everyone, Every One   See the entry for **anyone, any one.**

Except, Accept   See the entry for **accept, except.**

Farther, Further   Although some writers use these words interchangeably, dictionary definitions differentiate them. *Farther* is used when actual distance is involved, and *further* is used to mean *to a greater extent, more*.

The house is **farther** from the road than I realized.

That was **furthest** from my thoughts at the time.

Fewer, Less   *Fewer* is used for things that can be counted (*fewer trees, fewer people*), and *less* is used for ideas, abstractions, things that are thought of collectively, not separately (*less trouble, less furniture*), and things that are measured by amount, not number (*less milk, less fuel*).

Fun   This noun is used informally as an adjective.

Informal: They had a **fun** time.

Goes, Says   *Goes* is a nonstandard form of *says*.

Whenever I give him a book to read, he ~~goes~~ *says*, "What's it about?"

Gone, Went   Past tense forms of the verb *go*. *Went* is the simple form that needs no additional verb as a helper. *Gone* is the past form that requires the helper *have*. Some writers make the mistake of interchanging *went* and *gone*. (See section 13b.)

went (or) have gone
They ~~gone~~ away yesterday.

Good, Well   *Good* is an adjective and therefore describes only nouns. *Well* is an adverb and therefore describes adjectives, other adverbs, and verbs. The word *well* is used as an adjective only in the sense of *in good health*. (See section 15.)

well   well
The stereo works ~~good~~. I feel ~~good~~

She is a **good** driver.

Got, Have   *Got* is the past tense of *get* and should not be used in place of *have*. Similarly, *got to* should not be used as a substitute for *must*. *Have got* to is an informal substitute for *must*.

have
Do you ~~got~~ any pennies for the meter?

must
I ~~got to~~ go now.

Informal: You have **got to** see that movie.

Great   This adjective is overworked in its formal meaning of *very enjoyable*, *good*, or *wonderful* and should be reserved for its more exact meanings such as of *remarkable ability*, *intense*, *high degree of*, and so on.

Informal: That was a **great** movie.
More exact uses of great:

The vaccine was a **great** discovery.

The map went into **great** detail.

Have, Got   See the entry for **got, have.**

Have, Of   *Have*, not *of*, should follow verbs such as *could*, *might*, *must*, and *should*.

have
They should ~~of~~ called by now.

Hisself   This is a nonstandard substitute for *himself*.

Hopefully   This adverb means *in a hopeful way*. Many people consider the meaning *it is to be hoped* as unacceptable.

Acceptable: He listened **hopefully** for the knock at
                          the door.
Often considered

unacceptable: **Hopefully,** it will not rain tonight.

I   Although some people discourage the use of *I* in formal essays, it is acceptable. If you wish to eliminate the use of *I*, see section 7 on passive verbs.

Imply, Infer   Some writers use these interchangeably, but careful writers maintain the distinction between the two words. *Imply* means *to suggest without stating directly, to hint. Infer* means *to reach an opinion from facts or reasoning.*

The tone of her voice **implied** he was stupid.

The anthropologist **inferred** this was a burial site for prehistoric people.

Insure   See the entry for **assure, ensure, insure.**

Irregardless   This is an incorrect form of the word *regardless.*

Is When, Is Why, Is Where, Is Because   These are incorrect forms for definitions. See section 6 and the Glossary of Grammatical Terms on faulty predication.

| **Faulty predication:** | Nervousness is when my palms sweat. |
| **Revised:** | When I am nervous, my palms sweat. |

(or)

Nervousness is a state of being very uneasy or agitated.

Its, It's   *Its* is a personal pronoun in the possessive case. *It's* is a contraction for *it is.*

The kitten licked **its** paw.

It's a good time for a vacation.

Kind, Sort   These two forms are singular and should be used with *this* or *that.* Use *kinds* or *sorts* with *these* or *those.*

This **kind** of cloud indicates heavy rain.

These **sorts** of plants are regarded as weeds.

Lay, Lie   *Lay* is a verb that needs an object and should not be used in place of *lie,* a verb that takes no direct object. (See section 13b.)

He should ~~lay~~ *lie* down and rest awhile.

You can ~~lie~~ *lay* that package on the front table.

Leave, Let   *Leave* means *to go away,* and *let* means to permit. It is incorrect to use *leave* when you mean let:

~~Leave~~ *Let* me get that for you.

Less, Fewer   See the entry for **fewer, less.**

Let, Leave   See the entry for **leave, let.**

Like, As   See the entry for **as, as if, like.**

Like for   The phrase "I'd *like for* you to do that" is incorrect. Omit *for.*

May, Can   See the entry for **can, may.**

Most   It is incorrect to use *most* as a substitute for *almost.*

Nowheres   This is an incorrect form of *nowhere.*

Number, Amount   See the entry for **amount, number.**

Of, Have   See the entry for **have, of.**

Off of   It is incorrect to write *off of* for *off* in a phrase such as *off* the table.

O.K., Ok, Okay   These can be used informally but should not be used in formal or academic writing.

Reason ... Because   This is redundant. Instead of *because*, use *that:*

> The reason she dropped the course is ~~because~~ *that*
>
> she couldn't keep up with the homework.

Less wordy revision: She dropped the course **because** she couldn't keep up with the homework.

Reason Why   Using *why* is redundant. Drop the word *why.*

> The reason ~~why~~ I called is to remind you of your promise.

Saw, Seen   Past tense forms of the verb *see. Saw* is the simple form that needs no additional verb as a helper. *Seen* is the past form that requires the helper *have.* Some writers make the mistake of interchanging *saw* and *seen.* (See section 13b.)

> They ~~seen~~ *saw* it happen. (or) They ~~seen~~ *have seen* it happen.

Set, Sit   *Set* means *to place* and is followed by a direct object. *Sit* means *to be seated.* It is incorrect to substitute *set* for *sit.*

> Come in and ~~set~~ *sit* down.

> *Set*
> ~~Sit~~ the flowers on the table.

Should of   This is incorrect. Instead use *should have.*

Sit, Set   See the entry for **set, sit.**

Site, Cite   See the entry for **cite, site.**

Somebody, Some Body   See the entry for **anyone, any one.**

Someone, Some One   See the entry for **anyone, any one.**

Sort, Kind   See the entry for **kind, sort.**

Such   This is an overworked word when used in place of *very* or *extremely.*

Suppose to, Use to These are nonstandard forms for *supposed to* and *used to.*

Sure The use of *sure* as an adverb is informal. Careful writers use *surely* instead.

Informal: I **sure** hope you can join us.

Revised: I **surely** hope you can join us.

Than, Then *Than* is a conjunction introducing the second element in comparison. *Then* is an adverb meaning *at that time, next, after that, also,* or *in that case.*

She is taller **than** I am.

He picked up the ticket and **then** left the house.

That There, This Here, These Here, Those There These are incorrect forms for *that, this, these, those.*

That, Which Use *that* for essential clauses and *which* for nonessential clauses. Some writers, however, also use *which* for essential clauses. (See section 19c.)

Their, There, They're *Their* is a possessive pronoun; *there* means *in, at,* or *to that place;* and *they're* is a contraction for *they are.*

Their house has been sold.

There is the parking lot.

They're both good swimmers.

Theirself, Theirselves, Themself These are all incorrect forms for *themselves.*

Them It is incorrect to use this in place of either the pronoun *these* or *those.*

Look at ~~them~~ *those* apples.

Then, Than See the entry for **than, then.**

Thusly This is an incorrect substitute for *thus.*

To, Too, Two *To* is a preposition; *Too* is an adverb meaning *very* or *also;* and *two* is a number.

He brought his bass guitar **to** the party.

He brought his drums **too.**

He had **two** music stands.

Toward, Towards Both are accepted forms with the same meaning although *toward* is preferred in American usage.

Use to This is incorrect for the modal meaning *formerly.* Instead, use *used to.*

Use to, Suppose to See the entry for **suppose to, use to.**

Want for Omit the incorrect *for* in phrases such as "I want *for you* to come here."

Well, Good See the entry for **good, well.**

Went, Gone   See the entry for **gone, went.**

Where   It is incorrect to use *where* to mean *when* or *that.*

> The Fourth of July is a holiday ~~where~~ ^when^ the town council shoots off fireworks.

> I see ~~where~~ ^that^ there is now a ban on shooting panthers.

Where . . . at   This is a redundant form. Omit *at.*

> This is where the picnic is ~~at~~.

Which, That   See the entry for **that, which.**

While, Awhile   See the entry for **awhile, a while.**

Who, Whom   Use *who* for the subject case; use *whom* for the object case.

> He is the person **who** signs that form.

> He is the person **whom** I asked for help.

Who's, Whose   *Who's* is a contraction for *who is; whose* is a possessive pronoun.

> **Who's** included on that list?

> **Whose** wristwatch is this?

Your, You're   *Your* is a possessive pronoun; *you're* is a contraction for *you are.*

> **Your** hands are cold.

> **You're** a great success.

GLOSSARY OF GRAMMATICAL TERMS

Absolutes   Words or phrases that modify whole sentences rather than parts of sentences or individual words. An absolute phrase, which consists of a noun and participle, can be placed anywhere in the sentence but needs to be set off from the sentence by commas.

> **The snow having finally stopped,** the football
>
> *(absolute phrase)*
>
> game began.

Abstract Nouns   Nouns that refer to ideas, qualities, generalized concepts, and conditions and do not have plural forms. (See section 31.)

> happiness, pride, furniture, trouble, sincerity

Active Voice See **Voice.**

Adjectives Words that modify nouns and pronouns. (See section 15.)

Descriptive adjectives (*red, clean, beautiful, offensive,* for example) have three forms:

Positive: red, clean, beautiful, offensive

Comparative (for comparing two things): cleaner, more beautiful, less offensive

Superlative (for comparing more than two things): cleanest, most beautiful, least offensive

Adjective Clauses See **Dependent Clauses.**

Adverbs Modify verbs, verb forms, adjectives, and other adverbs. (See section 15.) Descriptive adverbs (for example, *fast, graceful, awkward*) have three forms:

Positive: fast, graceful, awkward

Comparative (for comparing two things): faster, more graceful, less awkward

Superlative (for comparing more than two things): fastest, most graceful, least awkward

Adverb Clauses See **Dependent Clauses.**

Agreement The use of the corresponding form for related words in order to have them agree in number, person, or gender. (See sections 13a and 14b.)

> John runs. (Both subject and verb are singular.)

> It is necessary to flush the **pipes** regularly so that **they** don't freeze.

> (Both subjects, *it* and *they,* are in third person; *they* agrees in number with the antecedent, *pipes.*)

Antecedents Words or groups of words to which pronouns refer.

> When the **bell** was rung, **it** sounded very loudly.

> (*Bell* is the antecedent of it.)

Antonyms Words with opposite meanings.

Word	Antonym
hot	cold
fast	slow
noisy	quiet

Appositives Nonessential phrases and clauses that follow nouns and identify or explain them. (See section 19c.)

> My uncle, **who lives in Wyoming,** is taking windsurfing
>
> (appositive)
>
> lessons in Florida.

Articles See **noun determiners** and section 32.

Auxiliary Verbs Verbs used with main verbs in verb phrases.

should be going   **has** taken

(auxiliary verb)   (auxiliary verb)

Cardinal Numbers See **Noun Determiners.**

Case The form or position of a noun or pronoun that shows its use or relationship to other words in a sentence. The three cases in English are (1) subject (or subjective or nominative), (2) object (or objective), and (3) possessive (or genitive). (See section 14a.)

Clauses Groups of related words that contain both subjects and predicates and function either as sentences or as parts of sentences. Clauses are either independent (or main) or dependent (or subordinate). (See section 11.)

Collective Nouns Nouns that refer to groups of people or things, such as a *committee, team,* or *jury.* When the group includes a number of members acting as a unit and is the subject of the sentence, the verb is also singular. (See section 13a.)

The **jury** has made a decision.

Comma Splices Punctuation errors in which two or more independent clauses in compound sentences are separated only by commas and no coordinating conjunctions. (See section 12.)

but (or);

Jessie said he could not help, ∧

that was typical of his responses to requests.

Common Nouns Nouns that refer to general rather than specific categories of people, places, and things and are not capitalized. (See section 24a.)

basket, person, history, tractor

Comparative The form of adjectives and adverbs used when two things are being compared. (See section 15.)

higher, more intelligent, less friendly

Complement When linking verbs link subjects to adjectives or nouns, the adjectives or nouns are complements.

Phyllis was **tired.**

(complement)

She became a **musician.**

(complement)

Complex Sentences Sentences with at least one independent clause and at least one dependent clause arranged in any order.

Compound Nouns Words such as *swimming pool, dropout, roommate,* and *stepmother,* in which more than one word is needed.

Compound Sentences   Sentences with two or more independent clauses and no dependent clauses. (See section 12.)

Compound-Complex Sentences   Sentences with at least two independent clauses and at least one dependent clause arranged in any order.

Conjunctions   Words that connect other words, phrases, and clauses in sentences. *Coordinating conjunctions* connect independent clauses; *subordinating conjunctions* connect dependent or subordinating clauses with independent or main clauses.

Coordinating   and, but, for, or, nor, so, yet
Conjunctions: until, while

Some Subordinating Conjunctions: after, although, because, if, since

Conjunctive Adverbs   Words that begin or join independent clauses. (See section 19a.)

consequently, however, therefore, thus, moreover

Connotation   The attitudes and emotional overtones beyond the direct definition of a word.

The words *plump* and *fat* both mean *fleshy,* but *plump* has a more positive connotation than fat.

Consistency   Maintaining the same voice with pronouns, the same tense with verbs, and the same tone, voice, or mode of discourse. (See section 17.)

Coordinating Conjunctions   See **Conjunctions.**

Coordination   Of equal importance. Two independent clauses in the same sentence are coordinate because they have equal importance and the same emphasis.

Correlative Conjunctions   Words that work in pairs and give emphasis.

both . . . and   neither . . . nor   either . . . or

not . . . but also

Dangling Modifiers   Phrases or clauses in which the doer of the action is not clearly indicated. (See section 16a.)

Tim thought

Missing an opportunity to study, $_\wedge$

the exam seemed especially difficult.

Declarative Mood   See **Mood.**

Demonstrative Pronouns   Pronouns that refer to things. (See **Noun Determiners.**)

this, that, these, those

Denotation   The explicit dictionary definition of a word, as opposed to the connotation of a word. (See **Connotation.**)

Dependent Clauses (Subordinate Clauses)   Clauses that cannot stand alone as complete sentences. (See section

11.) There are two kinds of dependent clauses: adverb clauses and adjective clauses.

Adverb clauses: Begin with subordinating conjunctions such as *after, if, because, while, when.*

Adjective clauses: Tell more about nouns or pronouns in sentences and begin with words such as *who, which, that, whose, whom.*

Determiner See **Noun Determiner.**

Diagrams See **Sentence Diagrams.**

Direct Discourse See **Mode of Discourse.**

Direct/Indirect Quotations Direct quotations are the exact words said by someone or the exact words in print that are being copied. Indirect quotations are not the exact words but the rephrasing or summarizing of someone else's words. (See section 22a.)

Direct Objects Nouns or pronouns that follow a transitive verb and complete the meaning or receive the action of the verb. The direct object answers the question *what?* or *whom?*

Ellipsis A series of three dots to indicate that words or parts of sentences are being omitted from material being quoted. (See section 23.)

Essential and Nonessential Clauses and Phrases
Essential (also called restrictive) clauses and phrases appear after nouns and are necessary or essential to complete the meaning of the sentence. *Nonessential* (also called nonrestrictive) clauses and phrases appear after nouns and add extra information, but that information can be removed from the sentence without altering the meaning. (See section 19c.)

> Apples **that are green** are not sweet.
>
> *(essential clause)*
>
> Golden Delicious apples, **which are yellow,** are sweet.
>
> *(nonessential clause)*

Excessive Coordination Occurs when too many equal clauses are strung together with coordinators into one sentence.

Excessive Subordination Occurs when too many subordinate clauses are strung together in a complex sentence.

Faulty Coordination Occurs when two clauses that are either unequal in importance or that have little or no connection to each other are combined in one sentence and written as independent clauses.

Faulty Parallelism See **Parallel Construction.**

Faulty Predication Occurs when a predicate does not appropriately fit the subject. This happens most often after forms of the to be verb. (See section 6.)

He

~~The reason he~~ ꓥ was late ~~was~~

because he had to study.

Fragments Groups of words punctuated as sentences that either do not have both a subject and a complete verb or that are dependent clauses. (See section 11.)

Whenever we wanted to pick fresh fruit while we were

, we would head for the orchard with buckets

staying on my grandmother's farm ꓥ.

Fused Sentences Punctuation errors (also called *run-ons*) in which there is no punctuation between independent clauses in the sentence. (See section 12.)

;

Jennifer never learned how to ask politely ꓥ

she just took what she wanted.

Gerunds Verbal forms ending in -ing that function as nouns. (See **Phrases** and **Verbals**.)

Arnon enjoys **cooking.**

(gerund)

Jogging is another of his pastimes.

(gerund)

Homonyms Words that sound alike but are spelled differently and have different meanings. (See section 28b.)

hear/here   passed/past   buy/by

Idioms Expressions meaning something beyond the simple definition or literal translation into another language. For example, Idioms such as "short and sweet" or "wearing his heart on his sleeve" are expressions in English that cannot be translated literally into another language. (See section 35.)

Imperative Mood See **Mood.**

Indefinite Pronouns Pronouns that make indefinite reference to nouns.

anyone, everyone, nobody, something

Independent Clauses Clauses that can stand alone as complete sentences because they do not depend on other clauses to complete their meanings. (See section 11.)

Indirect Discourse See **Mode of Discourse.**

Indirect Objects Words that follow transitive verbs and come before direct objects. They indicate the one to whom or for whom something is given, said, or done and answer the questions to what? or to whom? Indirect objects can always be paraphrased by a prepositional phrase beginning with to or for.

Alice gave **me** some money.

(indirect object)

Paraphrase: Alice gave some money to me.

Infinitives Phrases made up of the present form of the verb preceded by to. Infinitives can have subjects, objects, complements, or modifiers. (See section 16c.)

Everyone wanted to **swim** in the new pool.

(infinitive)

Intensifiers Modifying words used for emphasis.

She **most certainly** did fix that car!

(intensifiers)

Interjections Words used as exclamations.

Oh, I don't think I want to know about that.

(interjection)

Interrogative Pronouns Pronouns used in questions.

who, whose, whom, which, that

Irregular Verbs Verbs in which the past tense forms and/or the past participles are not formed by adding -ed or -d. (See section 13b.)

do, did, done   begin, began, begun

Jargon Words and phrases that are either the specialized language of various fields or, in a negative sense, unnecessarily technical or inflated terms. (See section 5.)

Intransitive Verbs See **Verbs.**

Linking Verbs Verbs linking the subject to the subject complement. The most common linking verbs are *appear, seem, become, feel, look, taste, sound, and be.*

I **feel** sleepy. He **became** the president.

(linking verb)   (linking verb)

Misplaced Modifiers Modifiers not placed next to or close to the word(s) being modified. (See section 16a.)

on television

We saw an advertisement₍ₐ₎ for an excellent new stereo system with dual headphones ~~on television.~~

Modal Verbs Helping verbs such as *shall, should, will, would, can, could, may, might, must, ought to,* and *used to* that express an attitude such as interest, possibility, or obligation. (See section 30b.)

Mode of Discourse   Direct discourse repeats the exact words that someone says, and indirect discourse reports the words but changes some of the words.

Everett said, **"I want to become a physicist."**

(direct discourse)

Everett said **that he wants to become a physicist.**

(indirect discourse)

Modifiers   Words or groups of words that describe or limit other words, phrases, and clauses. The most common modifiers are adjectives and adverbs. (See section 16.)

Mood   Verbs indicate whether a sentence expresses a fact (the declarative or indicative mood); expresses some doubt or something contrary to fact or states a recommendation (the subjunctive mood); or issues a command (the imperative mood).

Nonessential Clauses and Phrases   See **Essential and Nonessential Clauses and Phrases.**

Nonrestrictive Clauses and Phrases   See **Essential and Nonessential Clauses and Phrases.**

Nouns   Words that name people, places, things, and ideas and have plural or possessive endings. Nouns function as subjects, direct objects, predicate nominatives, objects of prepositions, and indirect objects.

Noun Clauses   Subordinate clauses used as nouns.

What I see here is adequate.

(noun clause)

Noun Determiners   Words that signal a noun is about to follow. They stand next to their nouns or can be separated by adjectives. Some noun determiners can also function as nouns. There are five types of noun determiners:

1. Articles: definite: the; indefinite: a, an
2. Demonstratives: this, that, these, those
3. Possessives: *my, our, your, his, her, its, their*
4. Cardinal numbers: *one, two, three,* and so on
5. Miscellaneous: *all, another, each, every, much,* and others

Noun Phrases   See **Phrases.**

Number   The quantity expressed by a noun or pronoun, either singular (one) or plural (more than one).

Objects   See **Direct Objects** and **Object Complements.**

Object Complements   The adjectives in predicates modifying the object of the verb (not the subject).

The enlargement makes the picture **clear.**

(object complement)

Object of the Preposition Noun following the preposition. The preposition, its object, and any modifiers make up the prepositional phrase.

For **Daniel**

(object of the preposition for)

She knocked twice **on the big wooden door.**

(prepositional phrase)

Objective Case of Pronouns The case needed when the pronoun is the direct or indirect object of the verb or the object of a preposition.

Singular	Plural
First person: me	First person: us
Second person: you	Second person: you
Third person: him, her, it	Third person: them

Parallel Construction When two or more items are listed or compared, they must be in the same grammatical form as equal elements. When items are not in the same grammatical form, they lack parallel structure (often called *faulty parallelism*). (See section 8.)

She was sure that **being an apprentice in a photographer's studio** would be more useful than **being a student in photography classes.**

(The phrases in bold type are parallel because they have the same grammatical form.)

Parenthetical Elements Nonessential words, phrases, and clauses set off by commas, dashes, or parentheses.

Participles Verb forms that may be part of the complete verb or function as adjectives or adverbs. The present participle ends in *-ing,* and the past participle usually ends in *-ed, -d, -n, or -t.* (See **Phrases.**)

Present participles: running, sleeping, digging

She is **running** for mayor in this campaign.

(present participle)

Past participles: walked, deleted, chosen

The **elected** candidate will take office in January.

(past participle)

Parts of Speech The eight classes into which words are grouped according to their function, place, meaning, and use in a sentence: nouns, pronouns, verbs, adjectives, adverbs, prepositions, conjunctions, and interjections.

Passive Voice See **Voice.**

Past Participle See **Participles.**

Perfect Progressive Tense See **Verb Tenses.**

Perfect Tenses See **Verb Tenses.**

Person There are three "persons" in English.

First person: the person(s) speaking
I or we
Second person: the person(s) spoken to
you
Third person: the person(s) spoken about
he, she, it, they, anyone, etc.

Personal Pronouns Refer to people or things.

	Subject	Object	Possessive
Singular			
First person	I	me	my, mine
Second person	you	you	your, yours
Third person	he, she, it	him, her, it	his, her, hers, its

	Subject	Object	Possessive
Plural			
First person	we	us	our, ours
Second person	you	you	your, yours
Third person	they	them	their, theirs

Phrases Groups of related words without subjects and predicates.
Verb phrases function as verbs.

She **has been eating** too much sugar.

(verb phrase)

Noun phrases function as nouns.

A major winter storm hit **the eastern coast of Maine.**

(noun phrase)   (noun phrase)

Prepositional phrases usually function as modifiers.

That book **of hers** is overdue at the library.

(prepositional phrase)

Participial phrases, gerund phrases, infinitive phrases, appositive phrases, and absolute phrases function as adjectives, adverbs, or nouns.

Participial Phrase: I saw people **staring at my peculiar-looking haircut.**

Gerund Phrase: Making copies of videotapes can be illegal.

Infinitive Phrase: He likes **to give expensive presents.**

Appositive Phrase: You ought to see Dr. Elman, a **dermatologist.**

Absolute Phrase: The test done, he sighed with relief.

Possessive Pronouns See **Personal Pronouns, Noun Determiners,** and section 14a.

Predicate Adjectives See **Subject Complements.**

Predicate Nominatives See **Subject Complements.**

Predication Words or groups of words that express action or state of beginning in a sentence and consist of one or more verbs, plus any complements or modifiers.

Prefixes Word parts added to the beginning of words.

Prefix	Word
bio- (life)	biography
mis- (wrong, bad)	misspell

Prepositions Link and relate their objects (usually nouns or pronouns) to some other word or words in a sentence. Prepositions usually precede their objects but may follow the objects and appear at the end of the sentence.

The waiter gave the check **to my date** by mistake.
(prepositional phrase)

I wonder **what** she is asking **for.**
(object of the preposition) (preposition)

Prepositional Phrases See **Phrases.**

Progressive Tenses See **Verb Tenses.**

Pronouns Words that substitute for nouns. (See section 14.) Pronouns should refer to previously stated nouns, called antecedents.

When **Josh** came in, **he** brought some firewood.
(antecedent) (pronoun)

Forms of pronouns: personal, possessive, reflexive, interrogative, demonstrative, indefinite, and relative.

Pronoun Case Refers to the form of the pronoun that is needed in a sentence. See **Subject, Object,** and **Possessive Cases** and section 14a.

Proper Nouns Refer to specific people, places, and things. Proper nouns are always capitalized. (See section 24a.)

Copenhagen Honda House of Representatives Spanish

Reflexive Pronouns Pronouns that show someone or something in the sentence is acting for itself or on itself. Because a reflexive pronoun must refer to a word in a sentence, it is not the subject or direct object. If used to show emphasis, reflexive pronouns are called *intensive pronouns.* (See section 14a.)

Singular	Plural
First person: myself	First person: ourselves
Second person: yourself	Second person: yourselves
Third person: himself, herself, itself	Third person: themselves

She returned the book **herself** rather than giving it to

(reflexive pronoun)

her roommate to bring back.

Relative Pronouns   Pronouns that show the relationship of a dependent clause to a noun in the sentence. Relative pronouns substitute for nouns already mentioned in sentences and introduce adjective or noun clauses.

Relative pronouns: that, which, who, whom, whose

This was the movie **that** won the Academy Award.

Restrictive Clauses and Phrases   See **Essential and Nonessential Clauses and Phrases.**

Run-on Sentences   See **fused sentences** and section 12.

Sentences   Groups of words that have at least one independent clause (a complete unit of thought with a subject and predicate). Sentences can be classified by their structure as simple, compound, complex, and compound-complex.

Simple:	one independent clause
Compound:	two or more independent clauses
Complex:	one or more independent clauses and one or more dependent clauses
Compound-complex:	two or more independent clauses and one or more dependent clauses

Sentences can also be classified by their function as declarative, interrogative, imperative, and exclamatory.

Declarative:	makes a statement
Interrogative:	asks a question
Imperative:	issues a command
Exclamatory:	makes an exclamation

Sentence Diagrams   A method of showing relationships within a **sentence.**

Marnie's **cousin,** who has no taste in food, **ordered** a **hamburger** with coleslaw at the Chinese restaurant.

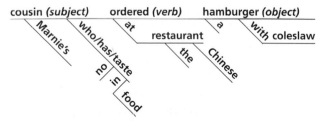

Sentence Fragment   See **Fragment.**

Simple Sentence   See **Sentence.**

Simple Tenses   See **Verb Tenses.**

Split Infinitives   Phrases in which modifiers are inserted between *to* and the verb. Some people object to split infinitives, but others consider them grammatically acceptable.

to quickly turn   to easily reach   to forcefully enter

Subject The word or words in a sentence that act or are acted upon by the verb or are linked by the verb to another word or words in the sentence. The *simple subject* includes only the noun or other main word or words, and the *complete subject* includes all the modifiers with the subject.

Harvey objected to his roommate's alarm going off at 9 A.M.

(Harvey is the subject.)

Every single one of the people in the room heard her giggle.

(The simple subject is one; the complete subject is the whole phrase.)

Subject Complement The noun or adjective in the predicate (predicate noun or adjective) that refers to the same entity as the subject in sentences with linking verbs, such as is/are, feel, look, smell, sound, taste, and seem.

She feels **happy.**

(subject complement)

He is a **pharmacist.**

(subject complement)

Subject Case of Pronouns See **Personal Pronouns** and section 14.

Subjunctive Mood See **Mood.**

Subordinating Conjunctions Words such as *although, if, until,* and *when,* that join two clauses and subordinate one to the other.

She is late. She overslept.

She is late **because** she overslept.

Subordination The act of placing one clause in a subordinate or dependent relationship to another in a sentence because it is less important and is dependent for its meaning on the other clause.

Suffix Word part added to the end of a word.

Suffix	Word
-ful	careful
-less	nameless

Superlative Forms of Adjectives and Adverbs See **Adjectives and Adverbs** and section 15.

Synonyms   Words with similar meanings.

Word	Synonym
damp	moist
pretty	attractive

Tense   See **Verb Tense.**

Tone   The attitude or level of formality reflected in the word choices in a piece of writing. (See section 5.)

Transitions   Words in sentences that show relationships between sentences and paragraphs. (See section 9.)

Transitive Verbs   See **Verbs.**

Verbals   Words that are derived from verbs but do not act as verbs in sentences. Three types of verbals are infinitives, participles, and gerunds.

Infinitives   to **verb**

to wind   to say

Participles: Words used as modifiers or with helping verbs. The present participle ends in *-ing,* and many past participles end in *-ed.*

The dog is **panting.**

(present participle)

He bought only **used** clothing.

(past participle)

Gerunds: Present participles used as nouns.

Smiling was not a natural act for her.

(gerund)

Verbs   Words or groups of words (verb phrases) in predicates that express action, show a state of being, or act as a link between the subject and the rest of the predicate. Verbs change form to show time (tense), mood, and voice and are classified as transitive, intransitive, and linking verbs. (See section 30.)

Transitive verbs: Require objects to complete the predicate.

He **cut** the cardboard **box** with his knife.

(transitive verb)   (object)

Intransitive verbs: Do not require objects.

My ancient cat often **lies** on the porch.

(intransitive verb)

Linking verbs: Link the subject to the following noun or adjective.

The trees **are** bare.

(linking verb)

Verb Conjugations   The forms of verbs in various tenses. (See section 30a.)

Regular:

Present
Simple present:

I walk	we walk
you walk	you walk
he, she, it walks	they walk

Present progressive:

I am walking	we are walking
you are walking	you are walking
he, she, it is walking	they are walking

Present perfect:

I have walked	we have walked
you have walked	you have walked
he, she, it has walked	they have walked

Present perfect progressive:

I have been walking	we have been walking
you have been walking	you have been walking
he, she, it has been walking	they have been walking

Past
Simple past:

I walked	we walked
you walked	you walked
he, she, it walked	they walked

Past progressive:

I was walking	we were walking
you were walking	you were walking
he, she, it was walking	they were walking

Past perfect:

I had walked	we had walked
you had walked	you had walked
he, she, it had walked	they had walked

Past perfect progressive:

I had been walking	we had been walking
you had been walking	you had been walking
he, she, it had been walking	they had been walking

Future
Simple future:

I shall walk	we shall walk
you will walk	you will walk
he, she, it will walk	they will walk

Future progressive:

I shall be walking	we shall be walking
you will be walking	you will be walking
he, she, it will be walking	they will be walking

Future perfect:

I shall have walked	we shall have walked
you will have walked	you will have walked
he, she, it will have walked	they will have walked

Future perfect progressive:

I shall have been walking	we shall have been walking
you will have been walking	you will have been walking
he, she, it will have been walking	they will have been walking

Irregular:

Present

Simple present:

I go	we go
you go	you go
he, she, it goes	they go

Present progressive:

I am going	we are going
you are going	you are going
he, she, it is going	they are going

Present perfect:

I have gone	we have gone
you have gone	you have gone
he, she, it has gone	they have gone

Present perfect progressive:

I have been going	we have been going
you have been going	you have been going
he, she, it has been going	they have been going

Past

Simple past:

I went	we went
you went	you went
he, she, it went	they went

Past progressive:

I was going	we were going
you were going	you were going
he, she, it was going	they were going

Past perfect:

I had gone	we had gone
you had gone	you had gone
he, she, it had gone	they had gone

Past perfect progressive:

I had been going	we had been going
you had been going	you had been going
he, she, it had been going	they had been going

Future

Simple:

I shall go	we shall go
you will go	you will go
he, she, it will go	they will go

Future progressive:

I shall be going	we shall be going
you will be going	you will be going
he, she, it will be going	they will be going

Future perfect:

I shall have gone	we shall have gone
you will have gone	you will have gone
he, she, it will have gone	they will have gone

Future perfect progressive:

I shall have been going	we shall have been going
you will have been going	you will have been going
he, she, it will have been going	they will have been going

Verb Phrases   See **Verbs.**

Verb Tenses   The times indicated by the verb forms in the past, present, or future. (For the verb forms, see **verb conjugations** and section 30a.)

Present

Simple present:

Describes actions or situations that exist now and are habitually or generally true.

I **walk** to class every afternoon.

Present progressive:

Indicates activity in progress, something not finished, or something continuing.

He **is studying** Swedish.

Present perfect:

Describes single or repeated actions that began in the past and lead up to and include the present.

She **has lived** in Alaska for two years.

Present perfect progressive:

Indicates action that began in the past, continues to the present, and may continue into the future.

They **have been building** that garage for six months.

Past

Simple past:

Describes completed actions or conditions in the past.

They **ate** breakfast in the cafeteria.

Past progressive:

Indicates past action that took place over a period of time.

He **was swimming** when the storm began.

Past perfect:

Indicates an action or event was completed before another event in the past.

No one **had heard** about the crisis when the newscast began.

Past perfect progressive:

Indicates an ongoing condition in the past that has ended.

I **had been planning** my trip to Mexico when I heard about the earthquake.

Future

Simple future:

Indicates actions or events in the future.

The store **will open** at 9 A.M.

Future progressive:

Indicates future action that will continue for some time.

I **will be working** on that project next week.

Future perfect:

Indicates action that will be completed by or before a specified time in the future.

Next summer, they **will have been** here for twenty years.

Future perfect progressive:

Indicates ongoing actions or conditions until a specific time in the future.

By tomorrow, **I will have been waiting** for the delivery for one month.

Voice   Verbs are either in the *active* or *passive* voice. In the active voice, the subject performs the action of the verb. In the passive, the subject receives the action. (See section 7.)

The dog **bit** the boy.
        ↑
      (active verb)

The boy **was bitten** by the dog.
            ↑
        (passive verb)

Index

a, an, 104
Abbreviations, 89–91
  dates, 90
  Latin expressions/
    documentation terms, 91
  measurements, 90
  numbers, 90
  organizations/other entities, 91
  places, 89–90
  titles, 89
Absolute adjectives/adverbs, 52
Academic Information Index, 124
accept, except, 96
Active verbs, 19–20
Addresses, 65, 88
Adjective
  absolute, 52
  comma, 64–65
  comparisons/superlatives,
    51–52
  functions, 50
Adverb
  absolute, 52
  comparisons/superlatives,
    51–52
  functions, 50
affect, effect, 96
Agreement
  pronoun-antecedent, 47–48
  subject-verb, 33–37
AllSearchEngines.com, 122
Ambiguous pronoun reference,
    48–49
American Psychological
    Association. *See* APA style
Antecedents, 47–48
APA references, 190–202
  books, 192–195
  cassette recording, 199
  conference proceedings, 198
  dissertation abstract, 198
  electronic resources, 195–197.
    See also Citing electronic
    resources (APA)
  film/videotape/artwork, 198–199
  government document, 198
  information service, 198
  interview, 198
  recording, 199
  sample pages, 199–202
  TOC, 191–192
  TV broadcast/series, 199
  unpublished paper presented
    at meeting, 199
APA style, 185–202
  footnotes, 190
  in-text citations, 186–190
  MLA, compared, 185
  reference book, 185
  references list, 190–202. *See
    also* APA references
Apostrophe, 67–69, 95
Articles, 104–105
Auxiliary verbs, 102

bad, badly, well, good, 50–51
Bibliographic utilities, 115
Bibliography. *See*
    Documentation

Bilingual speakers. *See*
    Multilingual speakers (ESL)
Books in Print, 114
Books online, 122
Brackets, 78
Buried subject, 14

Capitalization, 83–86
  lists, 85–86
  proper nouns *vs.* common
    nouns, 83–85
  quotations, 85
  sentences, 85
Chicago Manual of Style, 203–212
Choppy sentences, 16
Citing electronic sources
    (APA), 195–197
  abstract, 196
  article in Internet-only
    journal, 196
  CD-ROM, 197
  chapter/section in Internet
    document, 196
  computer program/software, 197
  electronic database, 197
  e-mail, 197
  government report, 197
  journal article, 195–196
  message posted to electronic
    mailing list, 197
  message posted to
    newsgroup, 197
  newspaper article, 196
  stand-alone document, 196
Citing electronic sources
    (MLA), 167–178
  advertisement, 178
  article in online periodical,
    174–175
  cartoon, 177
  CD-ROMS/portable
    databases, 167–168
  e-mail, 178
  film/film clip, 177
  home page (course/academic
    dept), 172
  Internet/online databases, 168
  interview, 177
  letter to the editor, 175
  online books, 173–174
  online posting, 178
  online subscription service,
    175–176
  painting/sculpture/
    photograph, 177
  personal home page, 172–173
  scholarly journal, 174
  sound recording/clip, 177
  synchronous communication,
    178
  TV/radio, 177
Citing sources. *See*
    Documentation
Clarity, 12–14
Collective noun, 35, 48
Collier's Encyclopedia, 114
Colon, 75
*Columbia Guide to Online Style,
    The* (Walker/Taylor), 217

Columbia Online Style (COS), 217–225
Comma, 62–66
  addresses, 65
  adjectives, 64–65
  compound sentences, 33
  dates, 65
  geographical names, 66
  hints, 64
  independent clauses, 62–63
  interrupting words/phrases, 65
  introductory word groups, 63
  nonessential items, 63
  numbers, 66
  quotations, 66
  series/lists, 63–64
  unnecessary usage, 66
Comma splice, 32–33
Common noun, 83, 103
Comparatives, 51–52
Compound sentence, 32, 33, 62
Compound subjects, 34–35
Compound words, 73
Computerized bibliographic utilities, 115
Computers, 7, 8
Conciseness, 14–15, 99
Conclusion, 5–6
Contractions, 67
COS, 217–225
Council of Science Editors (CSE), 212–217
Count noun, 103
CSE, 212–217

Dangling modifiers, 18, 53
Dash, 77
Dates
  abbreviation, 90
  comma, 65
  when year omitted, 88
Decimals, 88
Documentation, 149–227
  APA, 185–202. See also APA style
  Chicago Manual of Style, 203–212
  Columbia Online Style (COS), 217–225
  Council of Science Editors (CSE), 212–217
  electronic source (Chicago), 209–211
  electronic sources (APA), 195–197
  electronic sources (MLA), 167–178. See also Citing electronic sources (MLA)
  MLA, 152–184. See also MLA style
  reference list, 190–202. See also APA references
  style manuals, 225–227. See also Style manuals
  Works Cited, 158–181. See also Works Cited
Double negative, 12

either, or subjects, 35
Electronic databases, 115

Electronic sources
  APA, 195–197
  Chicago Manual of Style, 209–211
  COS, 221–225
  MLA, 167–168. See also Citing electronic sources (MLA)
Electronic sources (MLA), 167–178. See also Citing electronic sources (MLA)
Ellipsis, 78–79
End punctuation, 76–77
English as a second language. See Multilingual speakers (ESL)
ESL. See Multilingual speakers (ESL)
Essay. See Student paper
Essential/nonessential clauses, 64
Evasive negative, 12
everyone ... his, 25
Exclamation mark, 77

FAN BOYS, 62
Fillers, 14
First person, 55
FirstSearch, 115
Footnotes
  APA, 190
  MLA, 157–158
Fractions, 73
Fused sentence, 23, 32–33
Future perfect progressive tense, 102
Future perfect tense, 101
Future progressive tense, 101
Future tense, 101

Gender neutral language, 24–25, 48
Generic noun, 48
Geographical names, 66, 89–90
good, bad, badly, well, 50–51
Grammar checker, 7

Harvard Guide to American History, 114
hear, here, 96
Helping verbs, 102
Higher order concerns (HOCs), 3–6
Hints
  apostrophes, 68, 95
  capitalization, 83
  commas, 64
  comparisons, 51
  compound sentences, commas, 33
  ESL, 104, 114, 143
  everyone ... his, 25
  fragments, 31
  LOCs, 6
  modifiers, 54
  negative words, 12
  noncount nouns, 104
  parallel structure, 22
  plagiarism, 143
  pronouns, 44
  subject-verb agreement, 34
  use verbs instead of nouns, 13

Hints—*continued*
  verb endings, 42
  we, us, 46
  who, whom, 46
  words that start sentences, 23
Homonyms, 96
Hyphen, 73–74

Identification numbers, 88
Idioms, 108
Imperative mood, 42
Indefinite pronouns, 47–48
Independent clause, 30, 62
Indicative mood, 42
Internet, 115–117. *See also* Web
    resources
  current news, 116
  evaluating sources, 134–137
  government sources, 116
  library catalogs online, 116
  non-profit public interest
    groups, 116
  older books, 117
  search engine options,
    119–120
  search engine strategies,
    117–119
In-text citation
  APA, 186–190
  COS, 218
  CSE, 213
  MLA, 153–157
Introduction, 5
Irregular forms of comparison, 52
Irregular verbs, 38–40
Italics, 86–87
its, it's, 96

Jargon, 17–18
Journals, 122

Later order concerns (LOCs), 6
lay, lie, 41
Libraries online, 126
Library catalogs online, 116
Library of Congress, 115
*Library of Congress Subject
   Headings,* 115
Library sources, 114–115
lie, lay, 41
Linking verbs, 36, 50
Lists, 63–64, 85–86. *See also*
   Series
Listservs, 118, 122
LOCs, 6

Magazines, 123
*Manual for Writers of Term
   Papers, Theses, and
   Dissertations, A,* 203
Mechanics, 81–96
  abbreviations, 89–91. *See also*
    Abbreviations
  capitalization, 83–86
  italics, 86–87
  numbers, 87–88
  spelling, 92–96. *See also*
    Spelling
Mismatched
  subjects/predicates, 19
Misplaced modifiers, 54
Mixed constructions, 18–19

*MLA Handbook for Writers of
   Research,* 152
MLA style, 152–184
  APA, compared, 185
  endnotes, 157
  footnotes, 158
  in-text citations, 153–157
  reference book, 152
  sample pages, 182–184
  Works Cited, 158–181. *See also*
    Works Cited
Modern Language Association.
   See MLA style
Modifiers, 18, 53–55
Mood, 42–43
Multilingual speakers (ESL),
   97–108
  articles, 104–105
  count/noncount nouns,
    103–104
  helping verbs, 102
  hints, 104, 114, 143
  idioms, 108
  omitted words, 106–107
  prepositions, 105–106
  repeated words, 107
  style, 99–100
  two-word (phrasal) verbs, 102
  verb tenses, 100–102
  verbs with *ing, to* + verb
    form, 102–103

Negative statements, 12
Negative words, 12
News services, 123
Newsbank CD News, 115
Newsgroups, 118, 122
Newspapers, 123
Nexis/Lexis, 115
Noncount nouns, 104
Nonessential/essential clauses,
   64
Nonsexist language, 24–25, 48
Note cards, 129
Notetaking, 129
Noun
  collective, 35, 48
  common, 83, 103
  count/noncount, 103–104
  generic, 48
  proper, 83, 103
Numbers, 87–88
  abbreviation, 90
  comma, 66
  hyphen, 73

Object case, 43
Omitted words, 106–107
Omitted words/ellipsis, 78–79
*Oxford Companion to English
   Literature,* 114

Paper. *See* Student paper
Paragraph length, 5
Parallelism, 20–22
Paraphrase, 139–140
Parentheses, 78
Passive verb, 19–20
Past participle, 37
Past perfect progressive tense,
   101
Past perfect tense, 101

Past progressive tense, 101
Past tense, 101
Percentages, 88
Perfect progressive tense, 41
Perfect tense, 100–101
Period, 76
Periodicals, 122
Person, 55
Phrasal verbs, 102
Plurals, 68, 95
Pointers. See Hints
Possessive case, 43
Possessives, 67
Prepositions, 105–106
Present perfect progressive
    tense, 101
Present perfect tense, 101
Present progressive tense,
    100–101
Present tense, 100–101
Pretentiousness, 17–18
Primary sources, 113
Progressive tense, 41, 100–101
Pronoun
    antecedents, 47–48
    case, 43–47
    hints, 44
    reference, 48–49
    transitions, 22
Pronoun-antecedent
    agreement, 47–48
Pronoun case, 43–47
Pronoun reference, 48–49
Proofreading, 7
Proper noun, 83, 103
*Publication Manual of the
    American Psychological
    Association,* 185
Punctuation, 57–79
    apostrophe, 67–69
    brackets, 78
    colon, 75
    comma, 62–66. See also Comma
    dash, 77
    ellipsis, 78–79
    exclamation mark, 77
    hyphen, 73–74
    parentheses, 78
    period, 76
    question mark, 76–77
    quotation marks, 70–73
    semicolon, 69–70
    sentence punctuation
        patterns, 61–62
    slash, 77–78

Question mark, 76–77
quiet, quite, quit, 96
Quotation
    capitalization, 85
    colon, 75
    comma, 66
    research, 139, 141–142
Quotation marks, 70–73, 75
raise, rise, 41
*Reader's Guide to Periodical
    Literature,* 114

Regular forms of comparison, 52
Regular verbs, 37
Repeated words, 107
Repetition, 14, 22

Research, 109–144
    community sources, 117
    evaluating bibliographic
        citations, 131–133
    evaluating content, 133–137
    evaluating sources, 129–137
    integrating sources, 137–142
    Internet sources, 115–117. *See
        also* Internet, Web
        resources
    interviews/surveys, 117
    journals (various disciplines),
        126–128
    library sources, 114–115
    paraphrases, 139–140
    plagiarism, 142–144
    quotations, 139, 141–142
    signal words, 140–142
    sources of information, 113–117
    summaries, 139
    taking notes, 129
    topic selection, 112–113
rise, raise, 41
Run-on sentence, 32

*Scientific Style and Format: The
    CBE Manual for Authors,
    Editors, and Publishers,* 212
Search engine options, 119–120
Search engine strategies,
    117–119
Search engines, 122
Second person, 55
Secondary sources, 113
Semicolon, 69–70
Sentence
    compound, 32, 33
    fused (run-on), 32–33
Sentence choices, 9–25
    active/passive verbs, 19–20
    clarity, 12–14
    conciseness, 14–15
    mixed constructions, 18–19
    nonsexist language, 24–25
    parallelism, 20–22
    transitions, 22–23
    variety, 16
    voice, 17–18
Sentence fragment, 30–31
Sentence grammar, 26–56
    adjectives/adverbs, 50–52
    comma splice, 32–33
    fragments, 30–31
    fused sentence, 32–33
    modifiers, 53–55
    pronoun, 43–49
    shifts, 55–56
    split infinitives, 54–55
    subject-verb agreement,
        33–37
    verb, 37–43. *See also* Verb
Sentence order, 16
Sentence punctuation patterns,
    61–62
Series
    comma, 63–64
    numbers, 88
    semicolon, 70
set, sit, 41
Sexist language, 24–25, 48
Shifts, 55–56
Signal words, 140–142

Simple future tense, 101
Simple past tense, 101
Simple present tense, 100–101
Simple tense, 41
sit, set, 41
Slang, 17
Slash, 77–78
Sound-alike words
    (homonyms), 96
Spell checker, 8, 92–93
Spelling, 92–96
    apostrophe, 95
    doubling consonants, 94
    final silent *e,* 94
    ie, ei, 93–94
    plurals, 95
    sound-alike words
        (homonyms), 96
    spell checker, 92–93
Split infinitives, 54–55
Sponsored links, 117–118
*Statistical Abstracts of the
    United States,* 115
Statistics, 88
Student paper
    document design, 144–148
    documentation, 149–227. *See
        also* Documentation
    Internet (*See* Internet, Web
        resources)
    paper presentation, 144–146
    research, 109–144. *See also*
        Research
    style manuals, 225–227. *See
        also* Style manuals
    visual elements, 147–148
    writing, 1–8. *See also* Writing
Style manuals, 225–227
    anthropology, 225
    astronomy (physics), 226
    biology, 225
    chemistry, 226
    education, 226
    English, 226
    history, 226
    journalism, 226
    mathematics, 226
    medicine, 226
    music, 226
    philosophy, 226
    physics, 226
    political sciences, 227
    psychology, 227
Subject
    buried, 14
    compound, 34–35
    either, or, 35
    indefinites, 35
    omitted, 107
    predicate, and, 19
Subject case, 43
Subject complement, 50
Subject-verb agreement, 33–37
Subjunctive mood, 42
Summaries, 139
Superlatives, 51–52
Synonyms, 22

Taking notes, 129
Term paper. *See* Student paper
than, then, 96

that, who, which, 36
the, 104–105
there is, there are, 20, 36
Thesis statement, 3–4, 113
Third person, 55
Tight organization, 99
Time of day, 88
Tips. *See* Hints
Titles
    abbreviations, 89
    italics, 86
    quotation marks, 72
to, too, 96
Tone, 56
Transitions, 5, 22–23
Two-word (phrasal) verbs, 102
Two-word units, 73

Unclear negative, 12
Underlining, 86–87
Unnecessary words, 14
us, we, 46
Usenet newsgroups, 118, 122

Vague pronoun reference, 49
Verb, 27–33
    active, 19–20
    helping, 102
    irregular, 38–40
    mood, 42–43
    omitted, 107
    passive, 19–20
    phrasal, 102
    regular, 37
    tense (*See* Verb tense)
    voice, 42
Verb endings, 42
Verb instead of noun, 13
Verb mood, 42–43
Verb tense
    ESL, 100–102
    shifts, 55–56
    tenses, listed, 41, 100–102
Verb voice, 42
Voice, 17–18

we, us, 46
Web resources, 121–126. *See
        also* Internet
    African American history and
        study, 124
    books online, 122
    business, 124
    education, 124
    evaluation, 136–137
    fields of study, 124–126
    general subject directories, 122
    government, 126
    humanities, 124–125
    journals/periodicals, 122
    libraries online, 126
    listservs/newsgroups, 122
    natural sciences, 125–126
    newspapers/magazines/news
        services, 122
    scholarly electronic
        conferences, 123
    scholarly societies, 123
    search engines, 122
    universities, 123
    writing, 121–122

well, bad, badly, good, 50–51
were, we're, where, 96
who, which, that, 36
who, whom, 45, 46
who's, whose, 96
Words that start sentences, 23
Working bibliography, 129
Works Cited, 158–181
  abstract of dissertation, 181
  advertisement, 181
  articles in periodicals, 166–167
  books, 162–165
  cartoon, 181
  computer software, 178
  electronic sources, 167–178.
    See also Citing electronic
    sources (MLA)
  film/video recording, 179
  index to examples, 159–162
  lecture/speech/address, 181
  letter/memo, 180
  live performance of play,
    179–100
  map/chart, 180
  musical composition, 180
  pamphlet, 181
  personal interview, 180

  published dissertation, 181
  published interview, 180
  radio/TV interview, 180
  record/tape cassette/CV, 179
  TV/radio program, 178–179
  unpublished dissertation, 181
  work of art, 180
Writing, 1–8
  audience, 3
  computers, 7, 8
  conclusion, 5–6
  development, 5
  HOCs, 3–6
  introduction, 5
  LOCs, 6
  organization, 4–5
  paragraph length, 5
  proofreading, 7
  purpose, 3
  strategies, 6–8
  thesis statement, 3–4
  transitions, 5
Writing guides, 121

you, it, they, 49
your, you're, 96

Correction Symbols

Symbol	Problem	Section
abbr	abbreviation error	27
ad	adjective / adverb error	15
agr	agreement error	13a, 14c
art	article	32
cap(s)	capitalization error	24
ca	case	14a
cs	comma splice	12
dm	dangling modifier	16a
frag	fragment	11
fs	fused/run-on sentence	12
hyph	hyphen	23a
ital	italics	25
lc	lowercase	24
mix(ed)	mixed construction	6
mm	misplaced modifier	16b
num	number use error	26
om	omitted word	34a
//	parallelism error	8
p	punctuation error	18–23
pl	plural needed	31
ref	reference error	14c
shft	shift error	17
sp	spelling error	28
t	verb-tense error	30a
trans	transition needed	9
usage	usage error	Glossary of Usage
v	verb error	13, 30
var	variety needed	4
w	wordy	3
wc	word choice / wrong word	5, 7, 10
x	obvious error	
^	insert	
∩/tr	transpose	
ℓ/	delete	

User's Guide

Your question   SECTION

WRITING
- What should I look for when I revise?   1a
- What goes into introductions and conclusions?   1a
- How useful is a spell checker?   1c, 28

SENTENCE CHOICES
- Are phrases like "It is a fact that . . ." OK to use?   2e
- How can I make my writing less choppy?   4, 9
- What is passive voice?   7
- Can I start sentences with "And" or "But"?   9

SENTENCE GRAMMAR
- What is wrong with the following?
  –I'm a vegetarian. Because I don't want to eat animals.   11
- Which is correct? – Between you and (I/me) . . .   14a
- Are these phrases correct? –"real bad" –"talk loud"   15
- Can I write the following? – She is so happy.   15

PUNCTUATION
- How are sentences punctuated?   18
- Am I using too many commas?   19i
- How do I punctuate – dates and addresses?   19g
  –quotations   19h, 22a, 22d
- What's the difference between "its" and "it's"?   20b
- Are these apostrophes correct? –his' car   14a, 20d
  –the melon's are ripe   20d
- How do I show left-out words in a quotation?   23h
- Which is correct?
  –well-known speaker / well known speaker   23a

MECHANICS
- Which is correct?

–spring semester	(or)	Spring semester	24a
–"The Simpsons"	(or)	<u>The Simpsons</u>	25a
–April 1	(or)	April first	26
–6 million	(or)	6,000,000	26, 27c
–The data is . . .	(or)	The data are . . .	28a

- What does "e.g." mean, and how do I use it?   27g
- Do I write "your" or "you're" and "whose" or "who's"?   28b

MULTILINGUAL (ESL)
- How is academic writing in American English different
  from academic writing in my country?   29
- What are the meanings of English verb tenses?   30a
- Which is correct?
  –She enjoys (to drink / drinking) coffee.   30d
  –two furnitures (or) some furniture   31
- When do I use "the," "a," and "an"?   32
- Do I write "in Tuesday" or "on Tuesday"?   33